I0819076

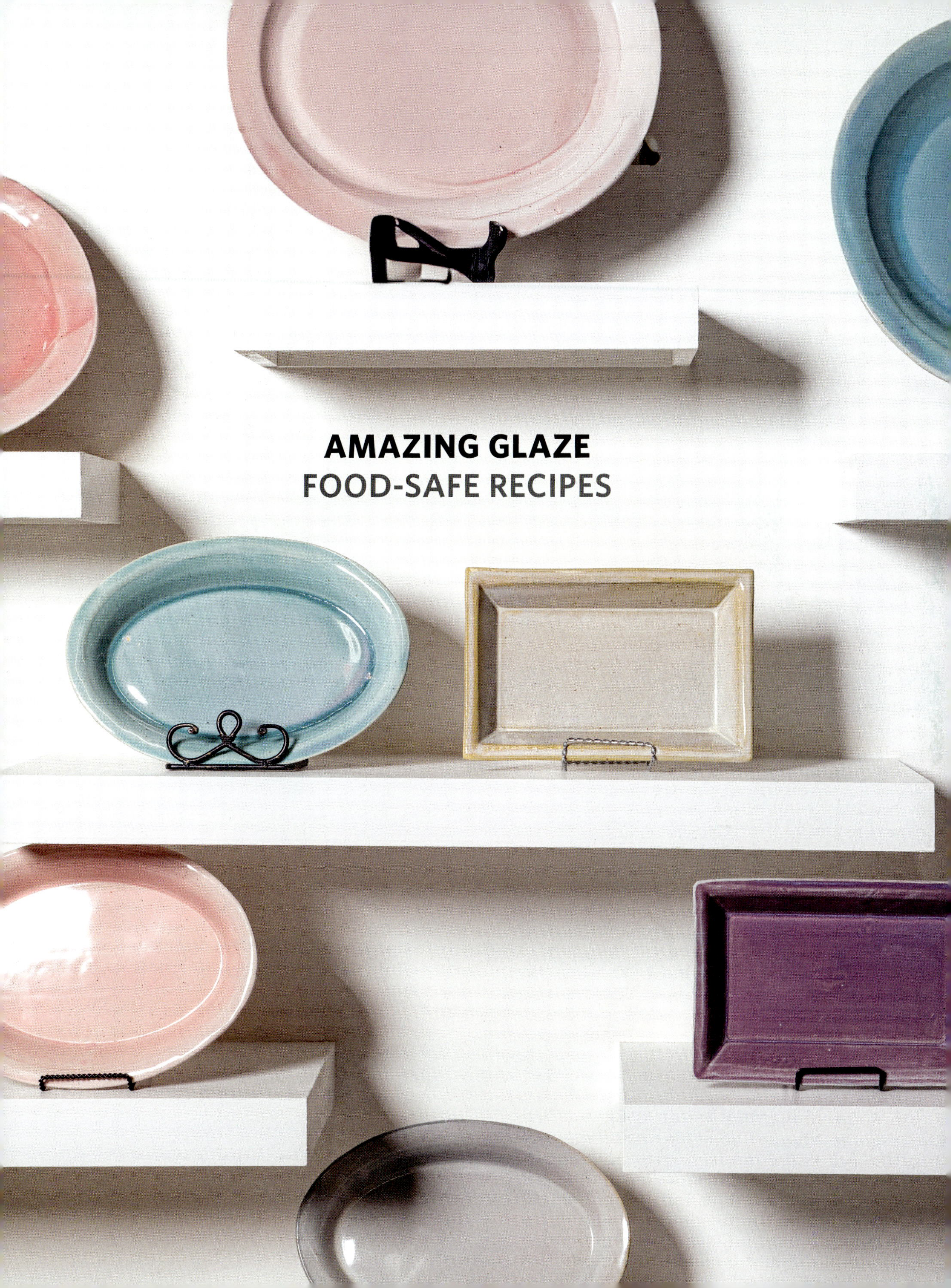

AMAZING GLAZE
FOOD-SAFE RECIPES

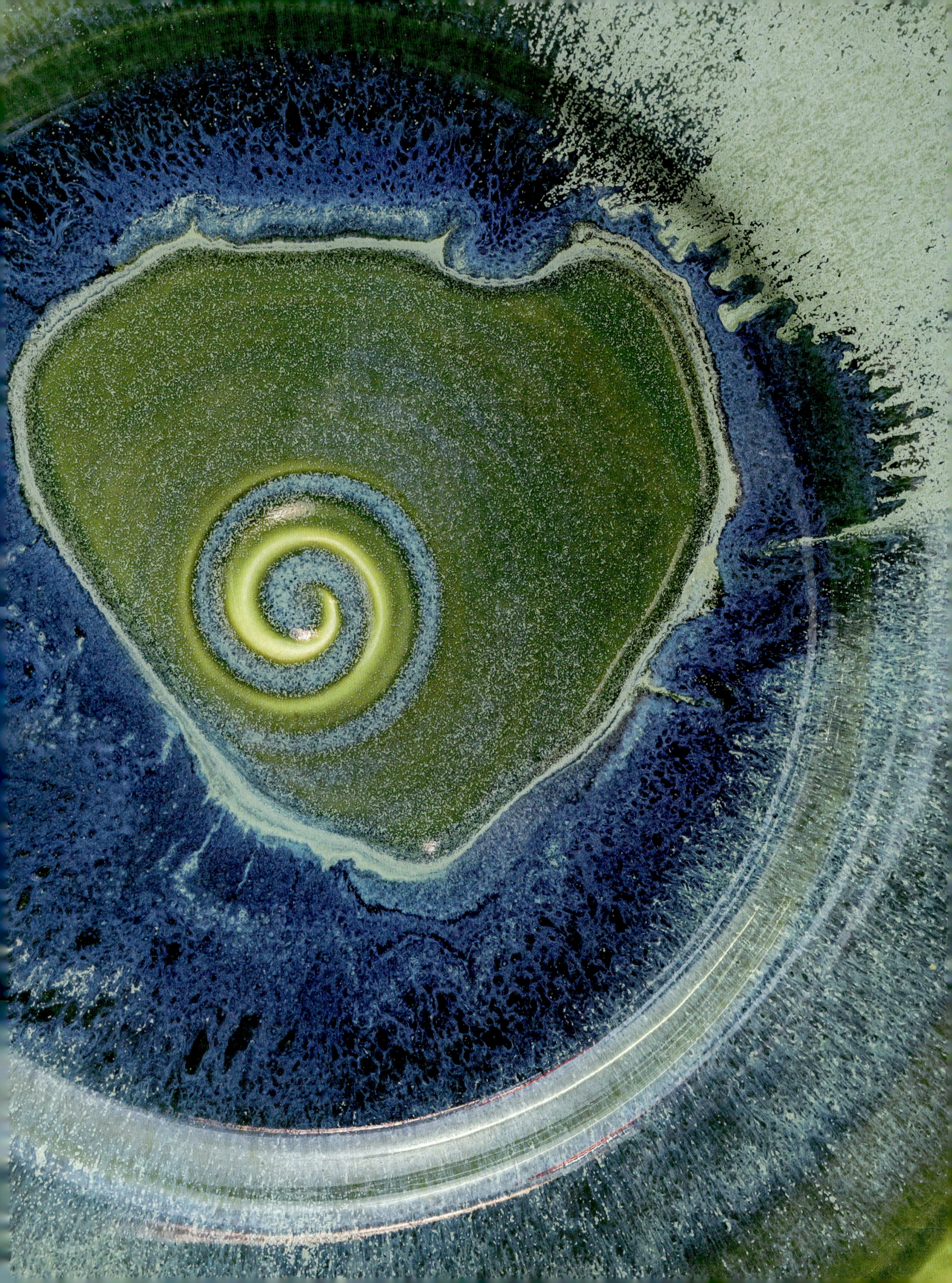

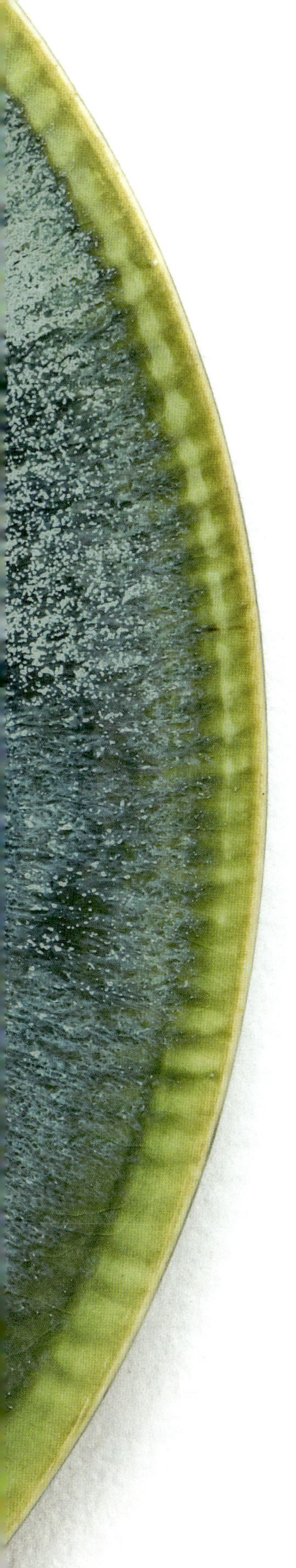

AMAZING GLAZE

FOOD-SAFE RECIPES

Innovative, Lab-Tested Techniques and Recipes

GABRIEL KLINE and
BILL COLLINS, PhD

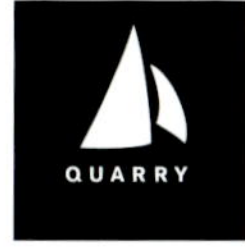

Quarto.com

First Published in 2025 by Quarry Books, an imprint of The Quarto Group,
100 Cummings Center, Suite 265-D, Beverly, MA 01915, USA.
T (978) 282-9590   F (978) 283-2742

EEA Representation, WTS Tax d.o.o.,
Žanova ulica 3, 4000 Kranj, Slovenia.
www.wts-tax.si

10 9 8 7 6 5 4 3 2 1

ISBN: 978-0-7603-9228-7

Digital edition published in 2025
eISBN: 978-0-7603-9229-4

Library of Congress Cataloging-in-Publication Data available

Design and Page Layout: Laura Shaw Design
Photography: Tim Robison Creative except Alex Thullen on pages 23 (bottom right), 39 (top left), 57 (bottom right), 115 (top right), 116, 135 (all), 136, 137 (both), 138 (left), 140; Anja Bartels on pages 5, 24, 153; Ann Ruel on pages 22 (top right), 38 (bottom left), 57 (top right), 114 (top left); Bill Collins on page 151; Channa Alterman on page 57 (top left); Cole Davis on pages 29 (all), 52 (all), 119 (both), 120 (all), 152; Eva Hart on page 39 (bottom); Glazy.org on page 146; Jason Rojas on page 57 (bottom left); Jennifer Rosseter on pages 22 (bottom), 23 (top left), 39 (top right), 58, 99, 115 (top left, bottom), 138 (bottom right); Joe Thompson on pages 22 (top left), 110, 111 (both), 112 (both), 113; John Britt on pages 54 (both), 55 (both), 56; Lauren Breitling on page 38 (bottom right); Lex Dodson on page 134; Linda Bloomfield on pages 36, 37 (all); Maddison Graybill on page 83; Marian Draper on page 23 (bottom left); Matt Katz on page 20 (top); Micah Thanhauser on page 139 (bottom left); Rose and Matt Katz on pages 20 (bottom), 21 (left, middle), 51; Silvia Ferrari-Palmer on page 53; Trish Cutler on pages 38 (top left), 139 (bottom right); and Tyler Anderson on page 38 (top right)
Cover: Tim Robinson Creative (front), Tim Barnwell (back, top), Jennifer Rosseter (back, middle), and Marian Draper (back, bottom)

Printed in Guangdong, China TT 062025

(opposite) **Stoneware Vase. Gabriel Kline**
(page 6) **Purple Charger. Gabriel Kline.** Fancy Pants Purple (page 75) looks wonderful over porcelain.

FOR STELLA, MAGGIE, AND TJ

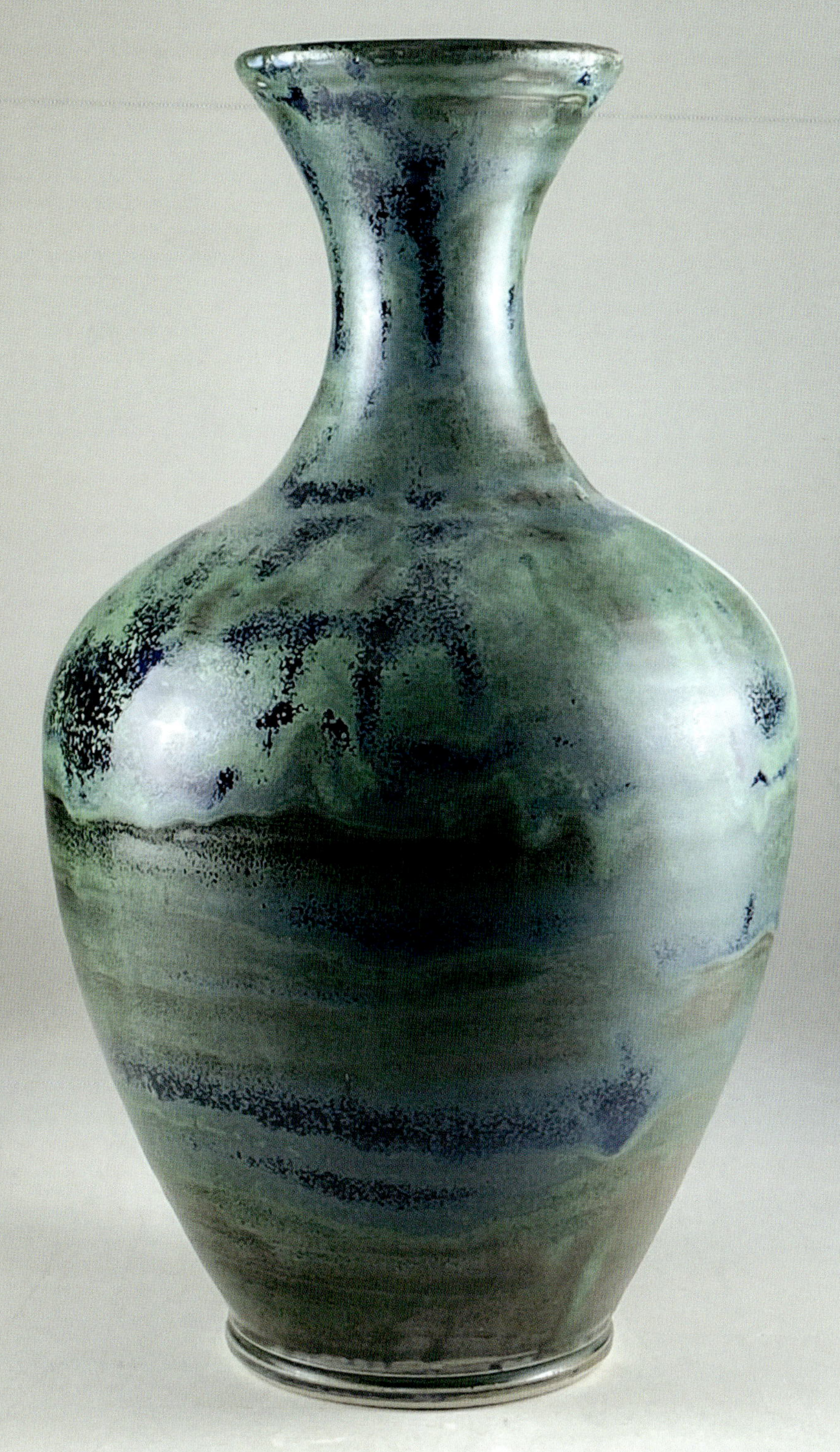

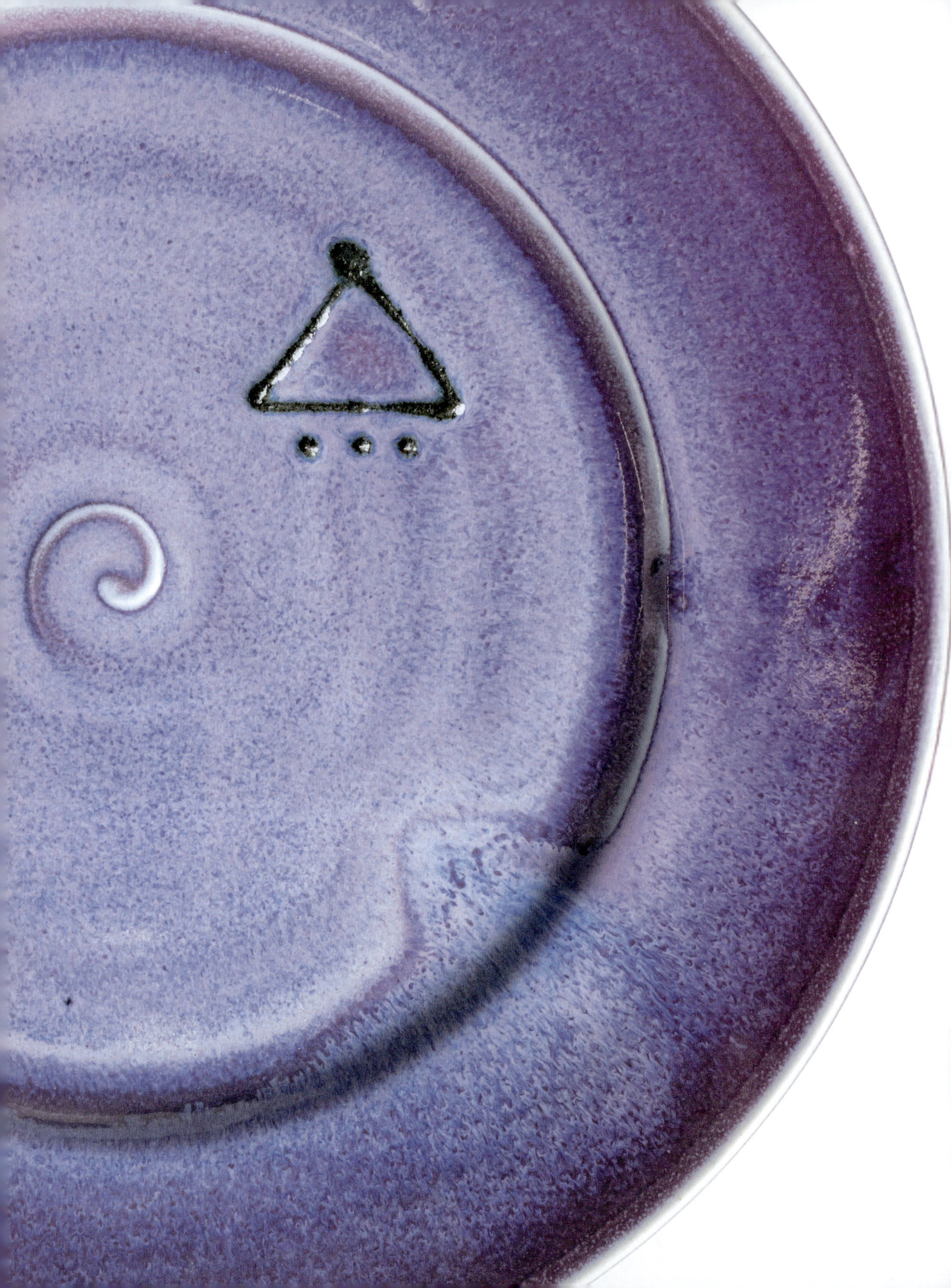

CONTENTS

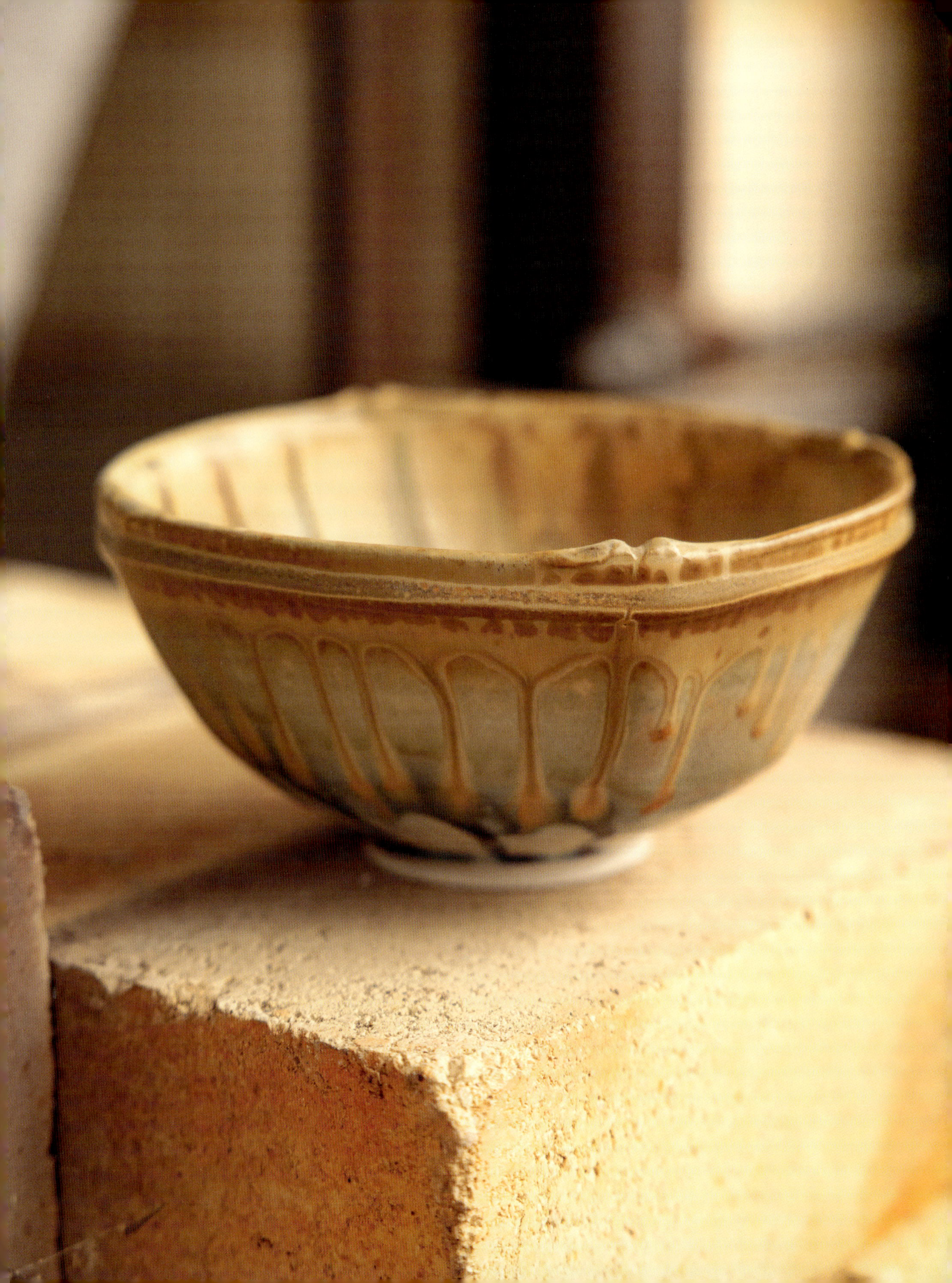

INTRODUCTION

DO YOU LOVE serving guests using handmade pottery? Or, like us, does your morning coffee mean everything to you . . . so you crafted the perfect mug? As potters, we derive great satisfaction from engineering the seamless interaction of food and bowl, of tea and cup. But being a functional potter comes with the responsibility that the pots we create are safe to use. This includes ensuring that the food bearing surface of our work is covered with a safe, stable glaze. Yet there is so much confusion about what makes a glaze "food safe." There are a number of layperson tests to determine the durability of a glaze. Perhaps you've tried some of these, like leaving a lemon on your work overnight to see if the glaze changes color or trying to scratch the surface of your glaze with cutlery to see if it scores. While these tests can indicate some kinds of faults, they can miss many others. The laboratory tests and equipment needed to thoroughly analyze a glaze's safety cost hundreds of thousands of dollars and are generally unavailable to the studio potter . . . until now!

One of the great functions of art is to give its creator peace of mind. *Amazing Glaze Food-Safe Recipes* is a collaboration between potters and chemists, designed to demystify what makes a glaze food safe and to provide proven, lab tested glaze recipes for you to use. Our goal is to give you the knowledge you need to make informed decisions, dispel common fears, and bolster your confidence in the glaze kitchen. First, we'll come to a standard definition of food safety for ceramics. Then, we'll show you the equipment we use to test our glazes and how we analyze the results in the lab. We'll offer over 100 recipes and combinations that meet the highest standards of food safety so you can begin glazing knowing that you are providing a quality product that is safe to use for years to come. Finally, we'll leave you with a set of guidelines and resources you can use in any studio. Ready? Let's start the show!

THE ART OF SCIENCE

In this series of interviews, we pose a series of questions to six ceramic artists with strong backgrounds in science. The artists we interviewed:

- Rose and Matt Katz (pages 20–21)
- Linda Bloomfield (pages 36–37)
- John Britt (pages 53–56)
- Joe Thompson (pages 110–113)
- Alex Thullen (pages 134–137)

Ash-Glazed Bowl. Tisha Cook.

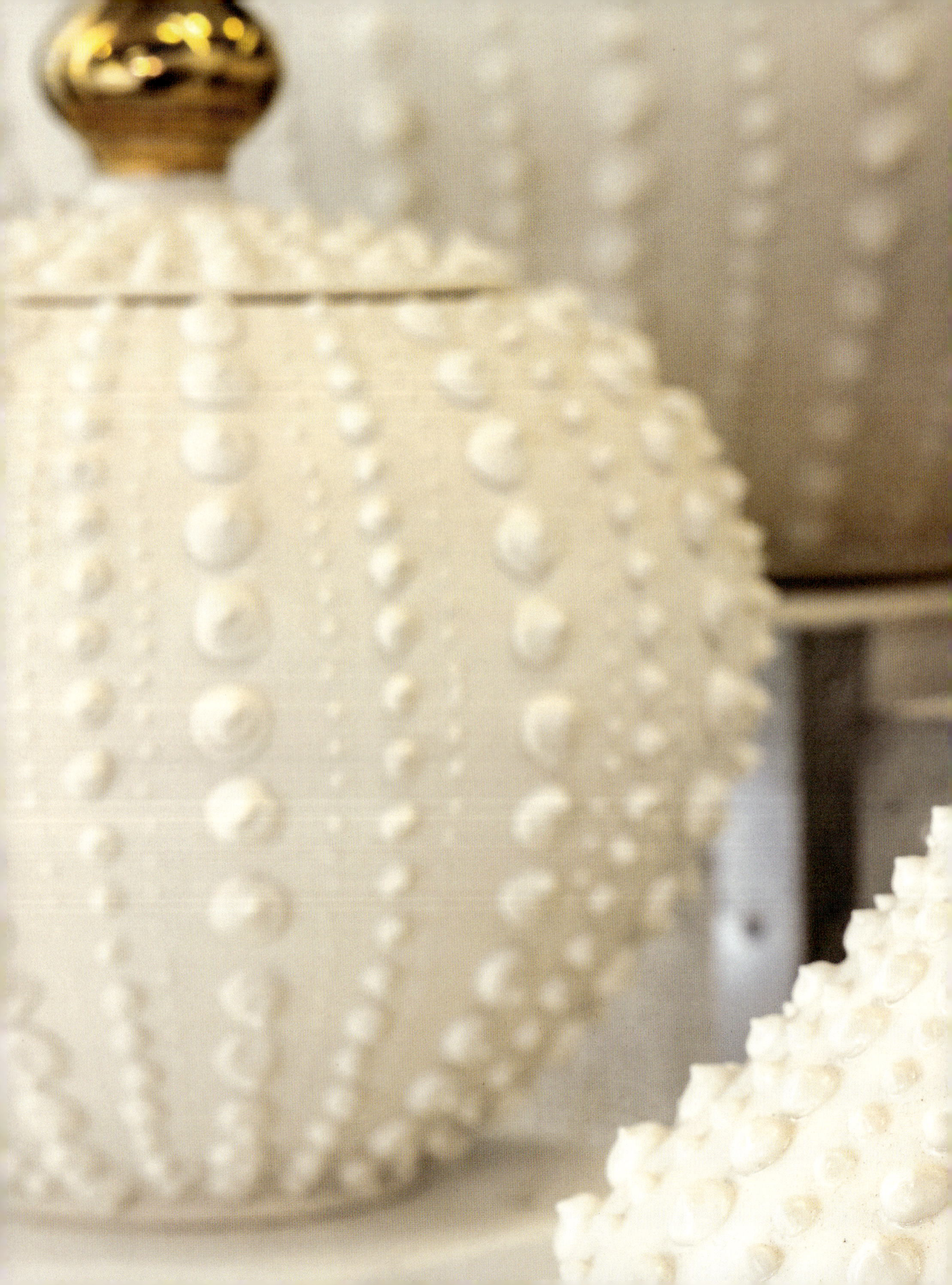

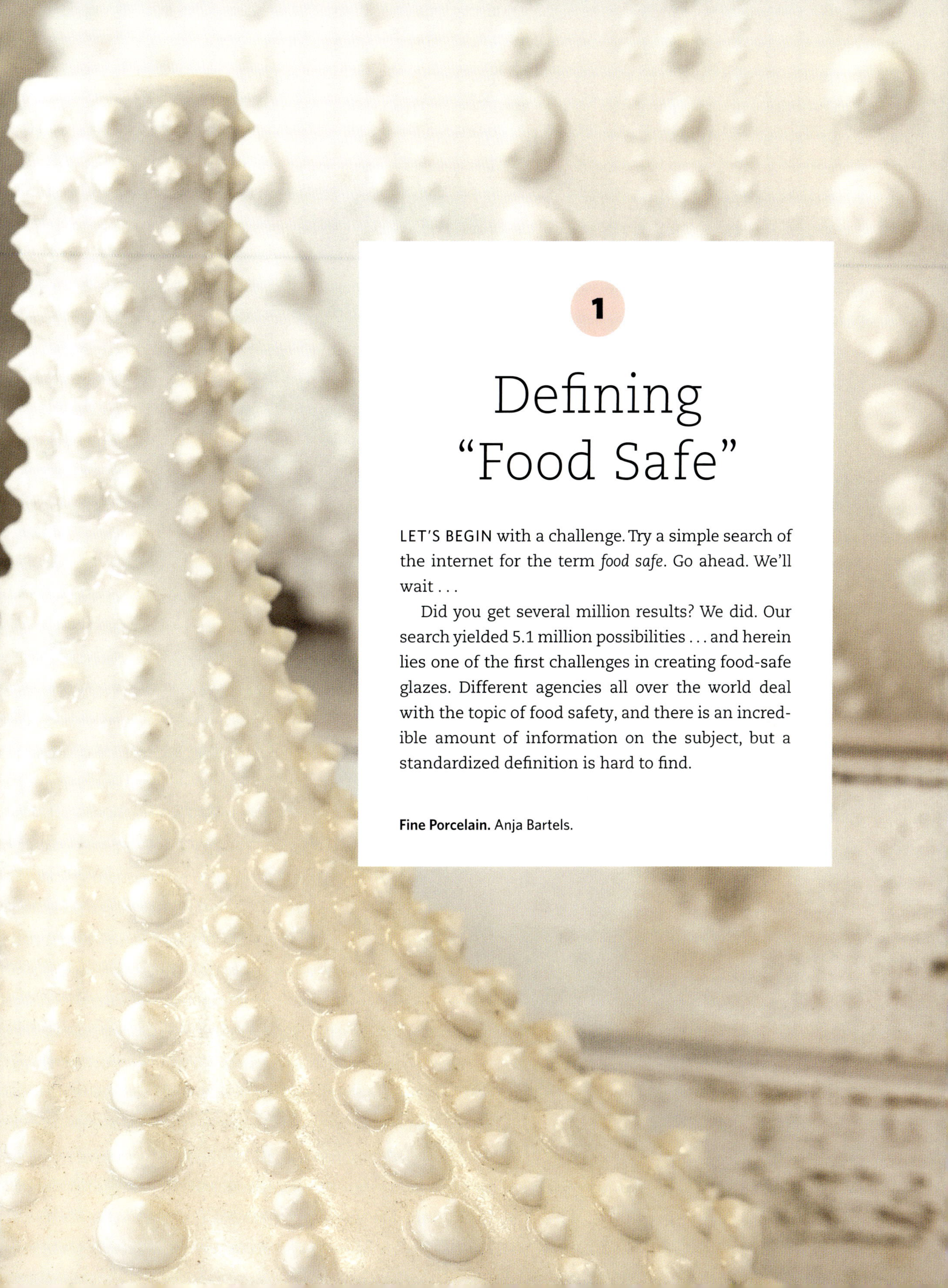

1

Defining "Food Safe"

LET'S BEGIN with a challenge. Try a simple search of the internet for the term *food safe*. Go ahead. We'll wait . . .

Did you get several million results? We did. Our search yielded 5.1 million possibilities . . . and herein lies one of the first challenges in creating food-safe glazes. Different agencies all over the world deal with the topic of food safety, and there is an incredible amount of information on the subject, but a standardized definition is hard to find.

Fine Porcelain. Anja Bartels.

A TERM WITHOUT LEGAL DEFINITION

This makes for a great starting point! What is food safe? And what makes for a food-safe glaze? In order to come up with a definition of what it means for pottery to be "food safe," let us start by defining what constitutes "safe food." **We might even say that is the goal of this book—to ensure that the pottery we produce does not compromise the safety of the foods we eat.** We define safe food (and drink) as not being contaminated with dangerous levels of potentially harmful bacteria, parasites, viruses, chemicals, and/or radionuclides. By extension, we might say that a pottery glaze is "food safe" if it cannot contaminate food or drink with dangerous levels of any of the agents listed above.

CURRENT RULES AND REGULATIONS FOR CERAMICS

In the United States, where this book is being written, the regulation of ceramicware falls under the jurisdiction of the U.S. Food and Drug Administration (FDA). The FDA is responsible for ensuring the safety of food and food-contact materials, including ceramic and glassware that may come in contact with food.

The FDA (2002 Food Code 4-1001.11) has established regulations and standards for these items, though in some cases the terminology is very general.

> "A. Materials that are used in the construction of utensils and food-contact surfaces of equipment may not allow the migration of deleterious substances or impart colors, odors, or tastes to food and under normal use conditions must be: 1. Safe; 2. Durable, corrosion-resistant, and nonabsorbent; 3. Sufficient in weight and thickness to withstand repeated warewashing; 4. Finished to have a smooth, easily cleanable surface; and 5. Resistant to pitting, chipping, crazing, scratching, scoring, distortion, and decomposition."

Deleterious is a great word! (It means causing harm or damage. We had to look it up . . .) These parameters, while general, have implications for the clay, glaze, and firing techniques used to create the work. Over the course of this book, we will be addressing each of these in turn.

The FDA is extremely specific, however, with regard to the presence of two glaze ingredients that can potentially leach into food or drink: lead and cadmium.

This makes sense because the ceramic community had a long history of using these materials. Lead yields really wonderful, smooth glazes at low-fire temperatures. Cadmium produces vibrant reds and oranges. But when the government realized the health effects on both factory workers and consumers, it had to intervene.

Regarding lead, the FDA Compliance Policy Guide (CPG 545.400) website comments:

> "Some ceramic foodwares have been found to leach significant quantities of lead from potential food contact surfaces. The metal is extractable by foods and can cause a wide variety of adverse health effects including the traditional effects of chronic lead poisoning under continued food use."

And similarly with regard to cadmium (CPG 545.450):

> "Imported and domestic ceramic ware has been found to have significant quantities of extractable cadmium. The metal is extractable by acid foods and could cause chronic cadmium poisoning under continued food use."

However, the FDA standard is that lead and cadmium are the only materials that need to be tested . . . but we think this lags behind what policies from other health agencies throughout the world suggest, including other governmental organizations within the United States. So,

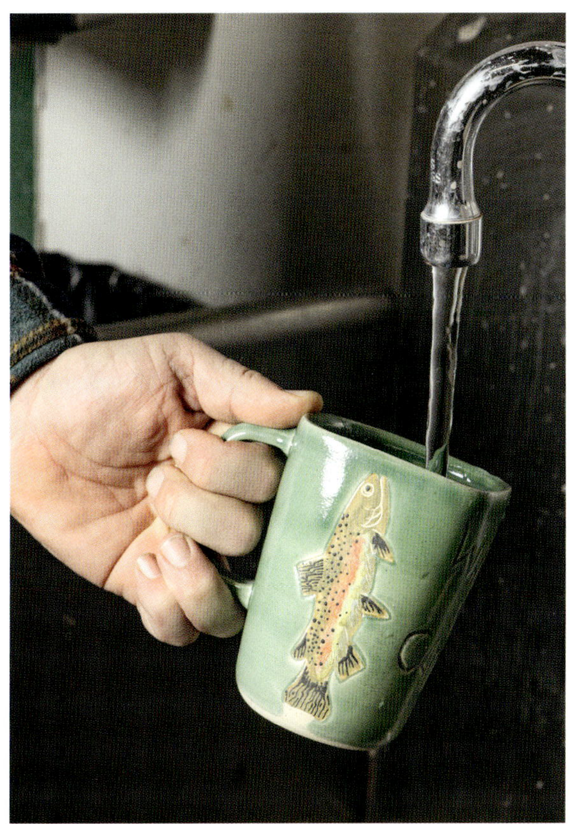

We think the same safety standards should apply to the water and the mug. Trout mug by Brooke Kinkade.

our goal in this book is to create a standard that more accurately reflects the guidelines set out by these agencies, using the strictest among them to create the most up-to-date reflection of safety standards in the world.

Let's think of things this way: If you go to your tap and pour water into your mug, the Environmental Protection Agency (EPA) regulates the amount of barium, copper, chromium, and other materials in the water but the FDA currently does NOT regulate the amount that could potentially leach out of the mug into the water. For this reason, **we think it makes sense to use drinking water standards as a baseline and apply the same standards to our pottery**. This means that some of the glazes we've previously labeled as food safe and have been using for years may fail our tests. But we do not believe this should be cause for anxiety about pieces we have already created. In fact, we see this as an opportunity to dispel some of the fear surrounding the leaching of materials.

Here is an interesting fact to consider: Many of the chemicals that we are testing for are foundational to human health and are provided by vegetables, grains, legumes, meats, and other supplements. If you look on the back of a bottle of multivitamins, you might think you were looking at a glaze recipe. Copper, iron, chromium, zinc, and manganese, which we test for, are also critically important micronutrients. Other ingredients we consider nontoxic, such as calcium, sodium, potassium, and magnesium, are both ceramic fluxes in glazes and necessary in the human body for bone and muscle health, proper neuron functioning, energy production, and blood pressure regulation.

For example, calcium carbonate is a common antacid. Ever take Tums after a feast? Then you've eaten calcium carbonate, also known as whiting or chalk. Potassium carbonate is used as a leavening agent in bread. By extension, you could probably try making a Lemon Lime Gatorade Glaze or even a Centrum Silver Celadon . . . the amount of ceramic ingredients is small in these products, but measurable, and every molecule informs the final product.

As we shall see in the following section on drinking water standards, the recommended allowable standards for consumption provided by governmental organizations are generally ten times below the lowest known level of toxicity in humans. That means if a favorite glaze just fails our incredibly stringent tests*, in many cases it will still be eight to ten times below the point of toxicity and theoretically you would not be doing any damage to yourself by drinking out of this mug.

There are, however, some glazes that failed our tests in a more concerning manner. We want to stress that these were INCREDIBLY rare. Out of the hundreds of tests we performed in our research, less than 5 percent of the glazes we tested failed to the point of any known toxicity. But although rare, we feel that necessitated the writing of this book. **We want to provide you with glazes that give you the greatest peace of mind.**

For that reason, we consider lab testing to be an incredibly useful tool in the name of the common good. Our goal is to reduce anxiety about the glazing process so you can enjoy it more. And while we could only test a fraction of extant glaze recipes, part of the purpose of the book is to give you the resources to be able to evaluate if testing is necessary at all. Many glazes are made up of ingredients that have no known toxicity, which would preclude any testing. For glazes that do need testing, we want to pass on the knowledge of where and how to get them tested (see appendix E for a list of labs). We hope that eventually lab-certified leaching tests could be added to glaze recipes on Glazy.org and would become a standard in glaze presentation. This would give ceramic artists a greater amount of information about a glaze's performance, including its relative degree of food safety with regard to leaching.

NOTE: *Spoiler alert—A favorite glaze, cone 6 Spearmint, just barely failed our test for copper. However, it passed when we lowered the amount of copper in the glaze to 3 percent. But, oh, the horror we experienced at first! Having glazed tons of pieces with Spearmint over the years, we were at first mortified. But then we calmed down. Because, we asked ourselves, is this mug toxic? No. It would have to leach approximately ten times more copper to reach what is considered toxic levels of copper. And have we done anything illegal in producing work with Spearmint? Also, no. Copper is used in all kinds of commercial ceramic products. So again, breathe easy. We wrote this book to give you peace of mind, not take it away.

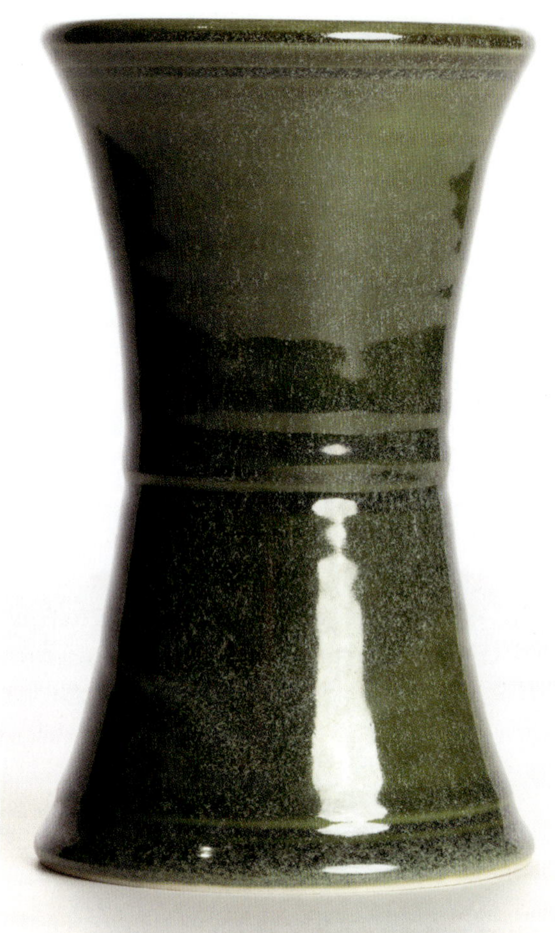

SPEARMINT (CONE 6)

INGREDIENTS	AMOUNTS
Wollastonite	28.00
EPK	28.00
Ferro Frit 3134	23.00
Silica	17.00
Nepheline Syenite	4.00
Total	**100.00**

Also Add:

Light Rutile	6.00
Copper Carbonate	3.00
Bentonite	2.00

NOTES:
Chemical Analysis:
3% Copper Carbonate: 1.22 ppm (max 1.3 ppm)
4% Copper Carbonate: 1.85 ppm (max 1.3 ppm)

DRINKING WATER STANDARDS

ENVIRONMENTAL PROTECTION AGENCY GUIDELINES

Beyond ceramicware, in the United States, the regulation of drinking water, including the establishment of standards for contaminants such as heavy metals, is primarily the responsibility of the U.S. Environmental Protection Agency (EPA). The specific regulations governing drinking water quality are outlined in the Safe Drinking Water Act, a federal law enacted to protect public health by regulating the nation's drinking water supply. The EPA establishes Maximum Contaminant Levels (MCLs).

Before we go any further, we should mention that we know this chapter is full of acronyms for the various organizations, measurements, and processes used to evaluate food safety! But don't worry, there'll be no test, and you really don't need to know what the letters stand for to understand the concepts. What is important here is that we know that there are organizations that exist for the sole purpose of protecting the health of humanity and the larger environment and that it is important for those organizations to share a common way of testing for and expressing safe levels of consumption. For this, you guessed it! We'll look to another acronymed organization.

ASTM International (formerly known as the American Society for Testing and Materials) is a globally recognized standards organization that develops and publishes technical standards for a wide range of materials, processes, and chemical analyses. ASTM standards are used by industries worldwide to ensure the quality, safety, and performance of various materials. We will use an ASTM method in this book to determine how much of certain elements leach out of ceramic glazes. As the ASTM method does, we will also use the unit *ppm* or "parts per million" as the unit standard to express the results of our tests. This allows anyone else in the world to compare their results to ours, and vice versa.

PARTS PER MILLION—HOW MUCH IS THAT, REALLY?

The unit *ppm* stands for "parts per million," and it is a unit of measurement used to express the concentration of one substance for every one million parts of the solution. This is expressed in mg/L. For example, if a solution contains 3 atoms of copper for every one million parts of the solution, the concentration is 3 ppm. This could also be expressed as 3 milligrams of copper for every 1 liter of solution. Other ways to think about how small these quantities are: 1 ppm would be one cup (235 ml) of water in an Olympic-size swimming pool, an inch (2.5 cm) in 16 miles (26 km), or a minute out of 1.9 years.

To begin to establish our standard for leaching, let's start by taking a look at a table of some of the materials that are tested in tap water by the EPA. Note the addition of the common ceramic ingredients copper, chromium, and barium to the cadmium and lead tested for by the FDA.

EPA TAP WATER CONTAMINANTS LIMITS

Contaminant	Maximum Contaminant Level ppm (mg/L)
Antimony	0.006
Arsenic	0.010
Barium	2
Beryllium	0.004
Cadmium	0.005
Chromium	0.1
Copper	1.3
Cyanide	0.2
Fluoride	4.0
Mercury	0.00
Nitrate	10
Nitrite	1
Selenium	0.05
Thallium	0.002

Already we can see how a stricter standard could be applied to ceramicware using the EPA standards. With the goal of creating a standard that would maximize peace of mind for the greatest number of people, we took it one step further and did a survey of drinking water standards from three more agencies in the United States and abroad: The World Health Organization, the Centers for Disease Control, and the European Union Drinking Water Directive. We then compiled a list of the strictest standards between them.

WORLD HEALTH ORGANIZATION GUIDELINES

The World Health Organization (WHO) provides guidelines for drinking water quality to support countries in establishing their own standards for the safety of drinking water. These guidelines are outlined in the *Guidelines for drinking-water quality* (GDWQ). In this document, the WHO provides maximum allowable concentrations for various heavy metals to identify potential hazards and establish appropriate control measures. The WHO also provides an assessment of limits for chemical contaminants in food. This document describes the standards and the way they determined the Maximum Contaminant Level standards. Importantly, the guidelines in both of these documents are not regulatory standards themselves; instead, they provide a scientific basis and best practices for the development of national or local drinking water regulations.

EUROPEAN DRINKING WATER DIRECTIVE GUIDELINES

Similar to the United States Safe Water Drinking Act, the European Union (EU) has adopted its own legislation. This Drinking Water Directive (DWD) sets out parameters and limits for heavy metals. Notably, there is fairly good consensus between US and European toxicologists on safety metrics for heavy metal consumption in water.

OUR STANDARD FOR THIS BOOK

As you can see from the chart below, the drinking water regulations/guidelines found between the EPA, WHO, CDC, and EU DWD line up closely. In some cases, there are also some small discrepancies in value. **We decided that, in all cases, we would use the lowest and most stringent value for our standard.** See the sidebar for two ingredients with special considerations: lithium and cobalt.

The following are the standards used in this book (see the sidebar on the next page for more information on the asterisked ingredients):

- **Copper:** 1.3 ppm (EPA)
- **Iron:** 0.2 ppm (EU DWD)
- **Lithium***: 0.06 ppm (EPA/USGS)
- **Manganese:** 0.05 ppm (EPA/EU DWD)
- **Zinc:** 0.5 ppm (EPA)
- **Nickel:** 0.02 ppm (EU DWD)
- **Barium:** 1 ppm (EU DWD)
- **Chromium:** 0.05 ppm (WHO/EU DWD)
- **Cadmium:** 0.003 ppm (WHO)
- **Cobalt***: 0.5 ppm (CDC)

	Copper	Iron	Lithium	Manganese	Zinc
WHO (2011)	2.0			0.1	
US EPA (2018)	1.3	0.3		0.05	0.5
European DWD (2021)	2.0	0.2		0.05	
USGS - EPA			0.06		
CDC					
This Book	1.3	0.2	0.06	0.05	0.5

THE CASE FOR TESTING LITHIUM AND COBALT

There are two ingredients, lithium and cobalt, that we are including in our list though they are not currently being tested for by the EPA, WHO, or EU. Lithium drinking water standards are currently being discussed and regulatory panels are determining if including lithium in the National Primary Drinking Water Regulations (NPDWR) is necessary. While this is being determined, the United States Geological Survey (USGS) in collaboration with the EPA calculated a nonregulatory Health-Based Screening Level (HBSL) for drinking water of 0.06 ppm.

Cobalt is not an ingredient included in any of our other organizations' literature. However, the Centers for Disease Control (CDC) has developed a profile for cobalt exposure. Minimal Risk Levels (MRLs) for oral exposure were derived based on a Lowest Observed Adverse Effect Level (LOAEL) found in various medical studies.

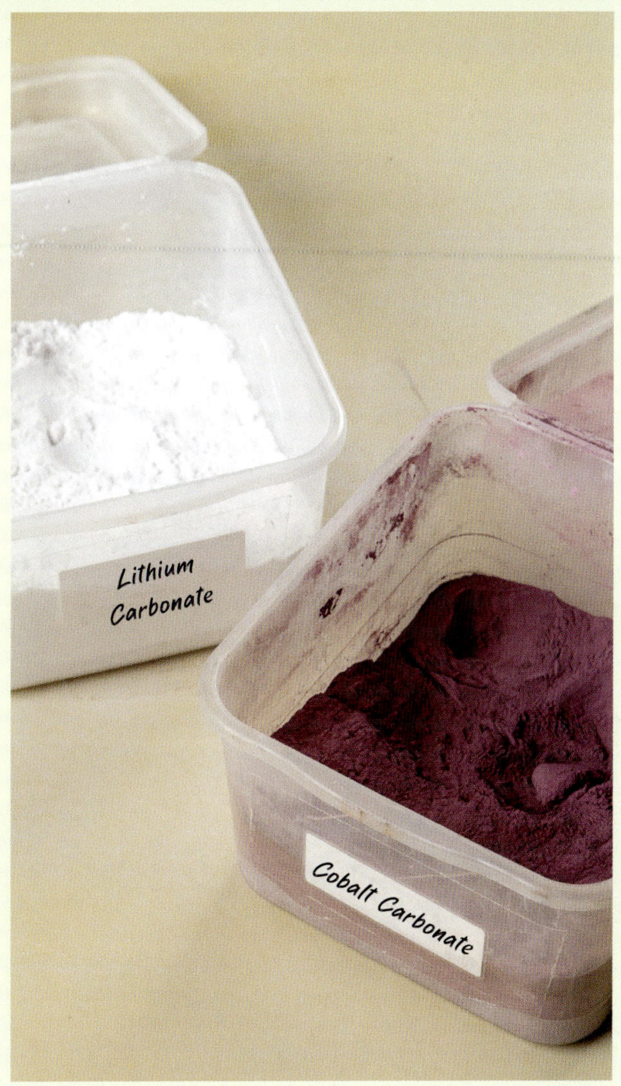

Lithium carbonate and cobalt carbonate in their pulverized forms.

Nickel	Barium	Chromium	Cadmium	Cobalt
0.07		0.05	0.003	
	2.0	0.1	0.005	
0.02	1.0	0.05	0.005	
				0.5
0.02	1.0	0.05	0.003	0.5

BEYOND LEACHING: OTHER CONSIDERATIONS

The primary consideration for this book will be the leaching of chemicals out of our glazes, but before we delve into our methods and test results, there are several other considerations to create food-safe pottery that we must be sure not to overlook. We are defining food-safe pottery as not being able to contaminate food or drink with dangerous levels of potentially harmful bacteria, parasites, viruses, chemicals, and/or radionuclides. We will use our ASTM–approved lab testing methods for chemicals leaching and check out the sidebar for an interesting read on radioactive pottery, which addresses radionuclides. That leaves the potentially harmful agents bacteria, parasites, and viruses (gross!). But thankfully the answers to creating pottery free from these offenders are simple: make pottery where the clay is vitrified (see sidebar) and the glazes are glossy and hard enough so they cannot be scratched. This ensures that bacteria and their friends do not have a place to live.

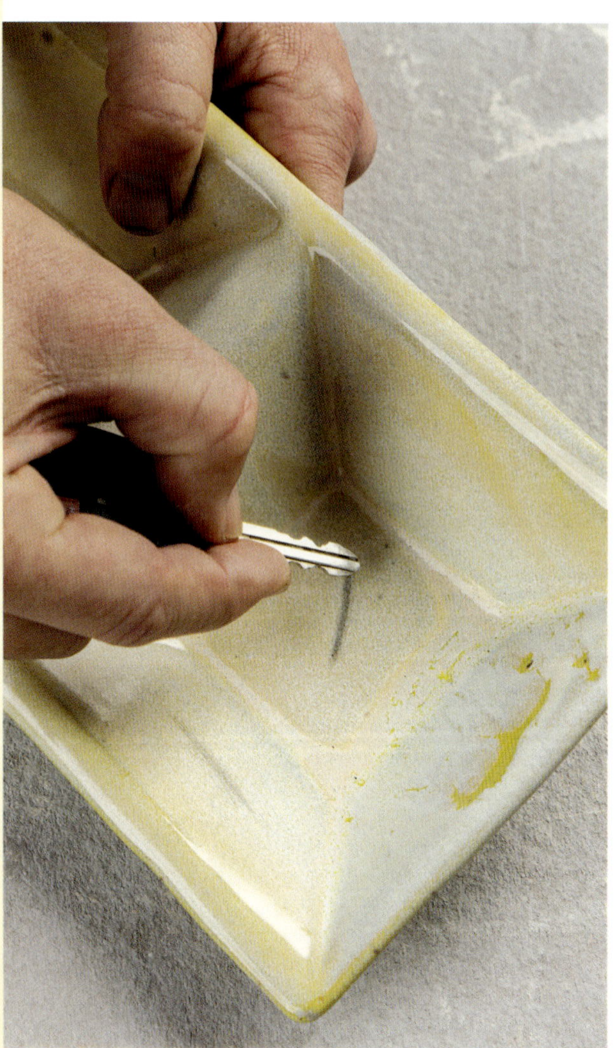

This matte combo failed our scratch test.

VITRIFICATION

Vitrification is the formation of glass in the clay and can be measured through the absorption rate of the clay, which should be available from your clay supplier. But if you mix your own or the information is unavailable, here is a standard test. This test requires a test tile fired to its desired cone. The International Organization for Standardization (ISO) method immerses the tile in boiling water for 2 hours and then keeps it in room temperature water for another 24 hours. The tile is wiped with a damp towel/sponge and then reweighed. (Wet weight - Dry weight)/Dry Weight = Absorption. You can then multiply this number by 100 to express in terms of a percentage.

All American/International standards agree that 0.5 percent or below is fully vitrified. Absorptions between 0.5 to 10 percent are described as semivitreous. Considering that the FDA indicates that dinnerware should be "nonabsorbent," we recommend 0.5 percent absorption or below in this book. We believe under 0.5 percent is best to avoid contamination with any of the unpleasant agents listed above.

RADIOACTIVE POTTERY?

In a memorable demonstration designed to illustrate the phenomenon of radioactivity to his students, Gabriel's high school physics teacher brought in a Geiger counter and two pieces of . . . pottery?!

As it turned out, Mr. Barrick explained, in the past, several manufacturers used uranium oxide to formulate their glazes and due to the uranium content (of up to 20 percent), they were able to create bright, bold yellows and reds. Uranium has fantastic color responses at ceramic temperatures. However, as Mr. B's Geiger counter demonstration showed, the plates themselves were releasing small amounts of radiation. Mr. B took a piece of red and a piece of yellow-glazed dinnerware that had been produced in the 1950s and held them up to the Geiger counter. The yellow plate registered several staticky clicks while the red plate made it crackle like a CB radio.

The release of radiation does not require the presence of an acid, as do the leach tests we will be performing. In other words, radiation is being released whether or not you have coffee in your mug. Thankfully, the use of uranium, like lead, has been all but abandoned in commercial ceramics production. Uranium oxide is not an ingredient that you can purchase from your local supplier. And for the purposes of our book, radionuclides are not an issue.

Once you have determined an appropriate clay body, then you can begin to look at the glaze, including the fit of the glaze on the clay body. Before measuring leaching, it's important to ensure that the glaze fits well, neither crazing nor crawling to ensure a "smooth easily cleanable surface." Both of these glaze fit issues can result in unsanitary conditions. Check out chapter 5 for some suggestions on how to address these problems.

Additionally, the glaze should be glossy and hard enough to resist scoring with silverware. We think you can perform this test in your own at home "lab." Simply take a piece of silverware and try to abrase the surface of the glaze. If you leave a mark you cannot remove by buffing with a cloth or a little Bar Keepers Friend, it suggests that you have created topography on the surface of the glaze, and that by extension, bacteria or viruses would be more difficult to remove.

If we have established that our clay is sufficiently vitrified at our firing temperature, and our glaze fits well and resists scoring, then we want to make sure that when food touches our art, that the art doesn't leach excessive amounts of metals back into our food. In order to do this, we will analyze our glazes using our state-of-the-art equipment in the chemistry lab for the final stamp of approval on our food-safe glazes.

Rose and Matt Katz

ceramicmaterialsworkshop.com Instagram @ceramicmaterialsworkshop

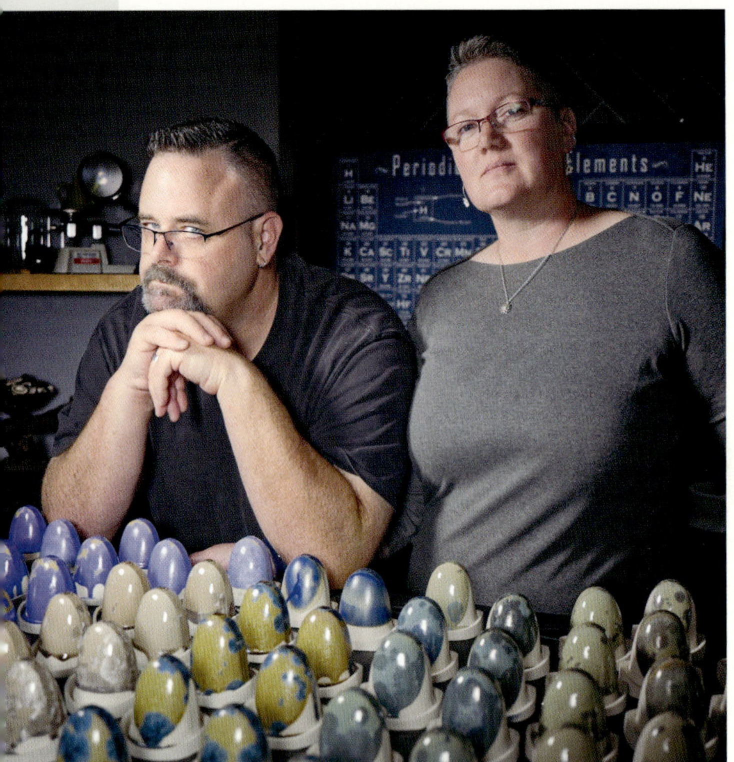

Rose and Matt Katz in their studio reviewing a battery of recent glaze tests.

"Ceramic Materials Workshop (CMW) was founded in 2016 by Rose and Matt Katz. Together they have over 40 years of combined ceramic material experience, both in the field and in the classroom. Their penchant to dive deeper and explore glaze and clay chemistry has allowed them to truly master all types of ceramic materials in a format that is easy for students of all levels to learn." —from the CMW website

These two! You can tell from the bio on their website, much less from the name of their podcast, *For Flux Sake*, that Rose and Matt Katz are not just scientists and artists, but court jesters of the highest order. But they say that those who take life seriously don't have to, and jesters are known for speaking truth to power, presenting that hard earned knowledge with levity and wit. In demystifying ceramic material science, Rose and Matt are pushing the field forward with their unique approach to teaching.

AMAZING GLAZE FOOD-SAFE RECIPES: *Why is it important for you to teach others glaze and clay body chemistry?*

ROSE AND MATT KATZ: We're skeptics. We always want to know *why* with most everything in life. We believe that everything has an answer. We just have to find the answer. And if it is not documented somewhere, we're going to go on the journey to find the answer.

That is why our students come to us.

Lots of people start in ceramics because working with clay looks fun (that's why we started). But as we progress in the medium, we want to improve and make objects that match the vision in our mind. But we often run headfirst into the wall that is the technical challenges of the material. Things don't work the way we want them to, and it can be daunting. In an ideal world, all studios and schools would make their students take a technical ceramics class. It would solve a lot of problems that may take makers years to overcome otherwise.

Ceramics is a technical artistic medium, unlike any other . . . In ceramics the last step is a traumatic technical evolution of the very object itself. The process matures and changes the object forever. And when it is done, it's the same . . . but it is also not the same.

The X-Files said, "The truth is out there." Sometimes the answer is a journey, and sometimes you find weird aliens along the way. But the search for truth is always a noble pursuit.

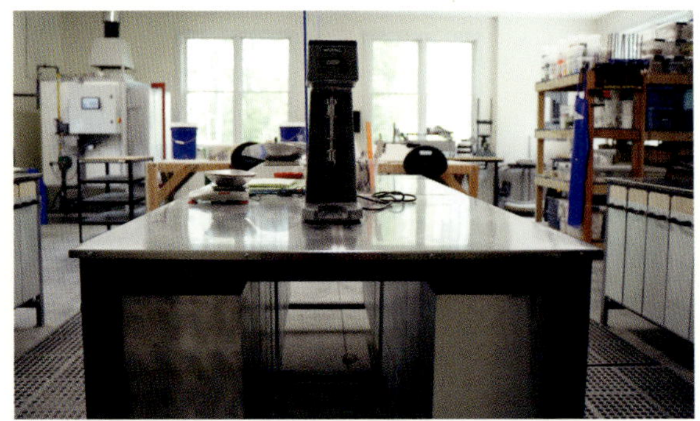

A clean and organized lab creates a space conducive to research.

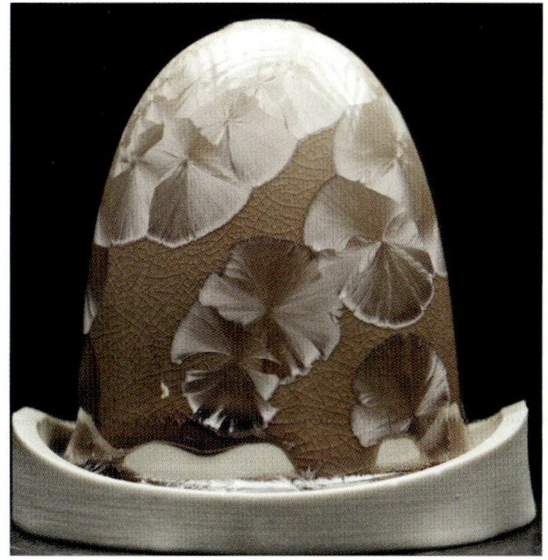

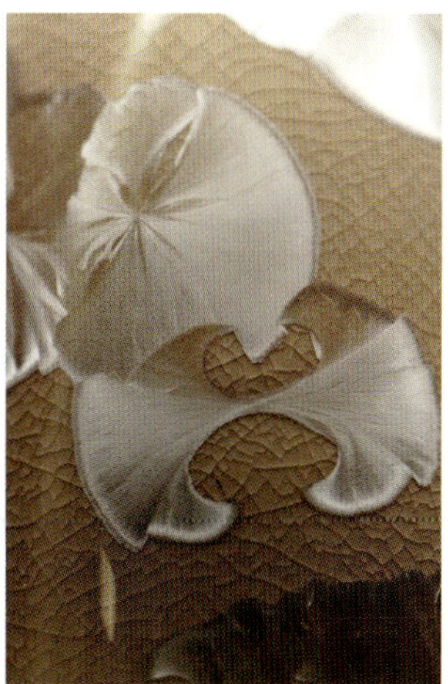

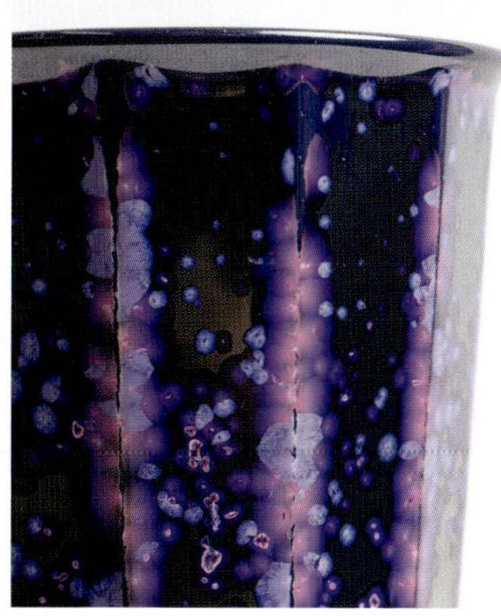

LEFT: Using an exacting firing schedule, Rose and Matt achieve excellent crystal growth in their glazes. **MIDDLE:** Detail, CMW crystalline glaze. **RIGHT:** TC Staton's innovative Cobalt Crystalline glaze.

AGFSR: *Glaze and clay body chemistry sits at the intersection of science and art. What are some of the challenges this creates? How do you overcome barriers when it comes to communicating scientific ideas to non-scientists?*

ROSE AND MATT: There is no way to learn this subject without confronting chemistry. What we have done is to teach in a way that boils the subjects down to exactly what students need to know at that moment and build up from there. Small steps. It also helps by contextualizing chemistry to the glaze results the students are interested in. And lots of dumb jokes; dumb jokes go a long way. An eye roll means they are paying attention.

AGFSR: *In what ways do you think that the ceramic education process (mentoring, apprenticeships, self-taught, university) could be improved?*

ROSE AND MATT: We would like to see teachers who embrace students where they are, and help that student evolve into who they are, not mold them into who the teacher thinks they should "be."

Education at a university is important, but we suspect that it was meeting all the people we now know as peers is the most important thing . . . Mentorship is probably the thing that helped us mature the most. Listening and learning from people that were actually doing their thing all day, every day. Seeing the good, and the bad, directly from the source.

The internet democratizes education, and that is amazing. But it is also a brutal filter, as you have to be self-motivated, and the concepts of community are different. We work very hard to create an online community at CMW, and we think that is a huge value to what we offer.

What we really think is missing in ceramics education is collaboration.

We believe that making ceramics is not done best as the pursuit of a single person. If you look at the history of ceramics, it was always the project of a collective. It takes a lot of people coming together to make pots well. Yet, we don't embrace making that process in education.

Discoveries are few and far between. In all our years, we've only ever invented one type of glaze that literally never existed before, The Cobalt Crystalline, which can be seen in the work of our student TC Staton (Cone Infinity). Everything else is just playing on a theme.

Many people expect there to be some magic wand because they are using commercial clay, commercial glazes, and a kiln from a reputable company.

This is a technical, chemical process. There is no easy way around that. They expect the glaze to look just like the picture on the jar, but without really understanding that commercial glazes are just the same as a handmade glaze. Commercial glazes are just put in a jar with some brushing agents added. The technical challenges are still there.

But what will bring the community progress is to educate yourself on how glazes and clays work. As that will push your success rate forward and refine your process to meet your vision.

GALLERY

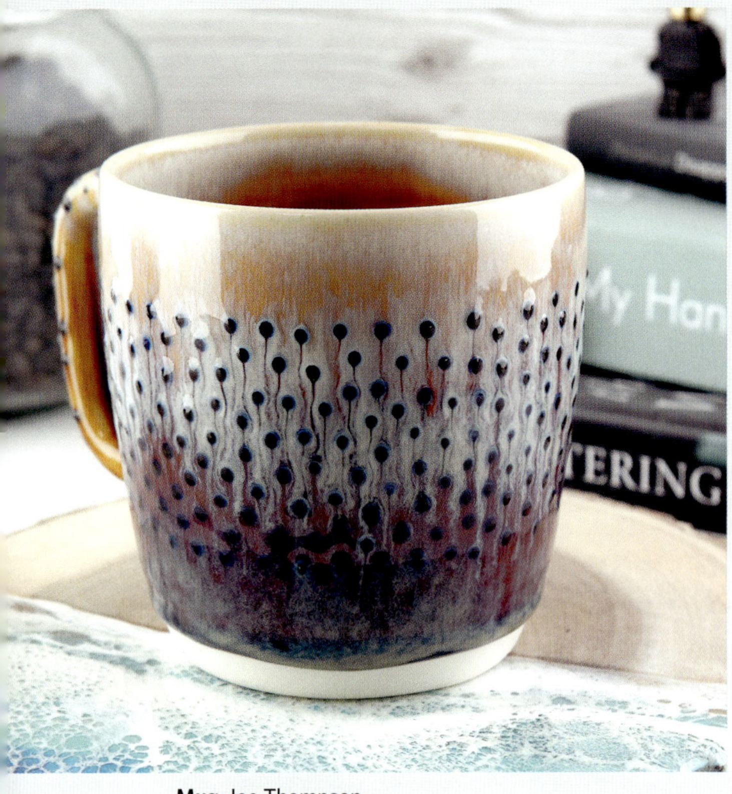

Mug. Joe Thompson.
Purple and peach cascade over black slip, creating satisfying glaze flows.

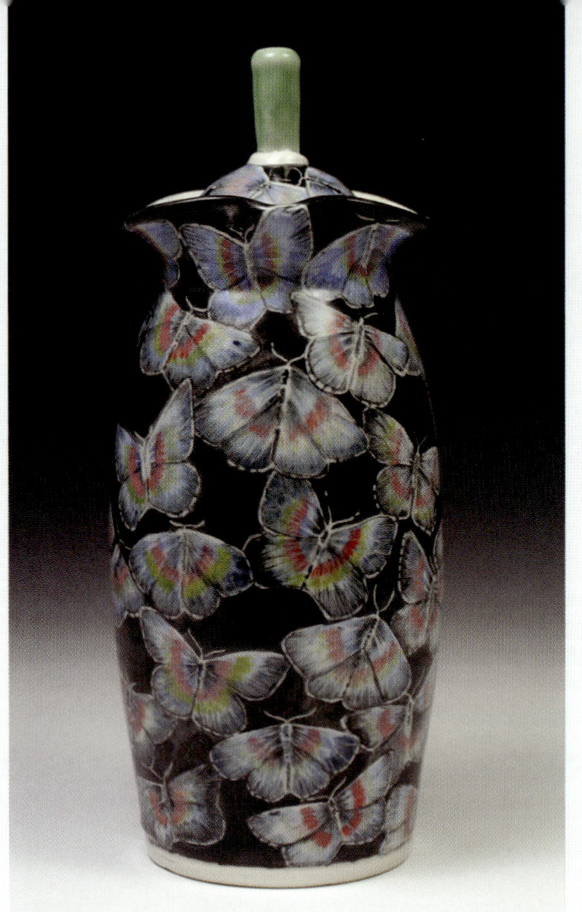

Covered Jar. Ann Ruel.
A flutter of butterflies decorates the exterior. Are there more inside?

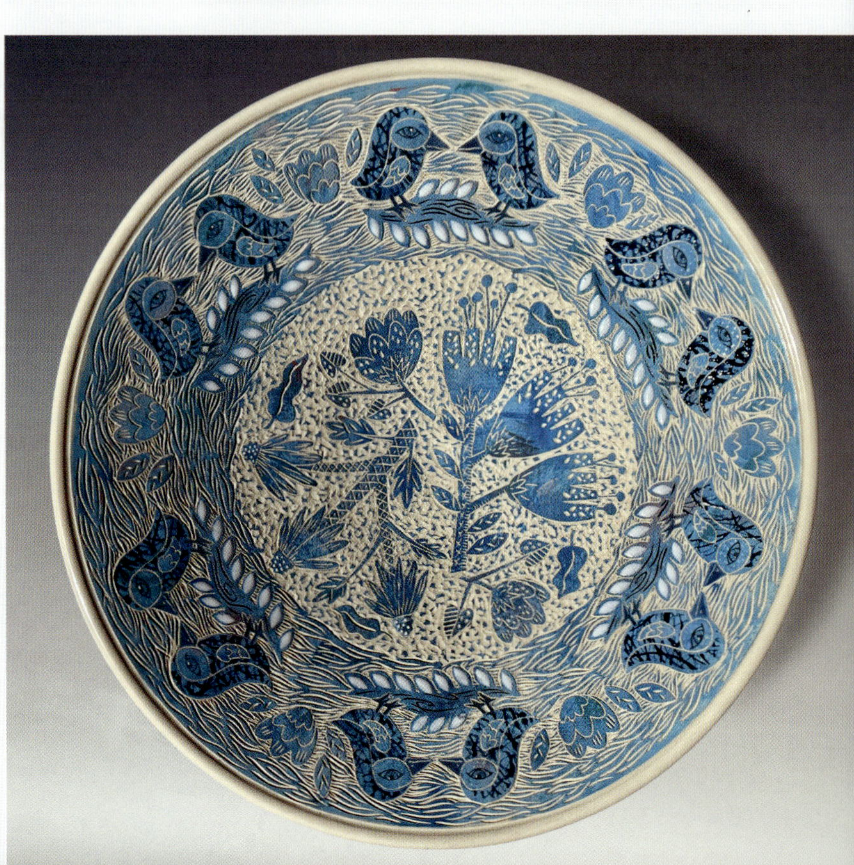

Blue and White Sgraffito Bowl, Bird Border. Jennifer Rosseter.
Incredible rhythm, pattern, and design give this piece impact.

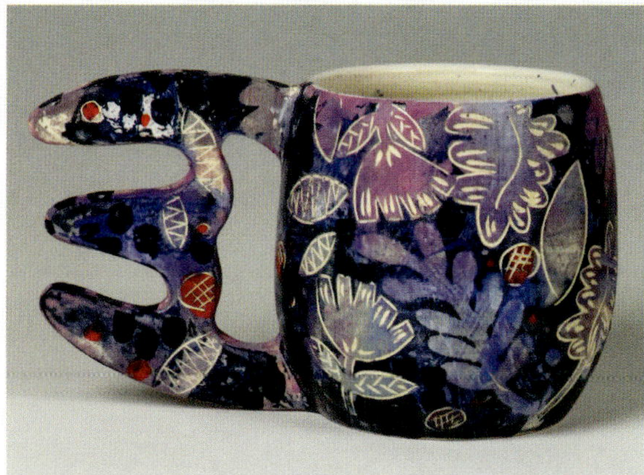

Purple Cup with Handle, Sgraffito. Jennifer Rosseter.
Complex and colorful on the outside. Calm and clean on the inside.

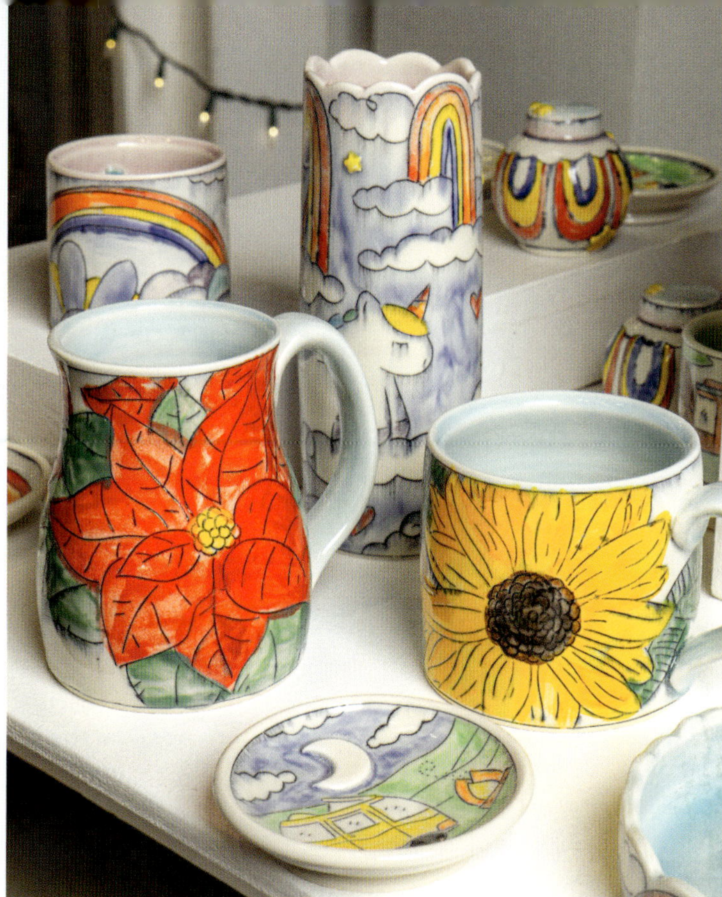

Grouping at Odyssey ClayWorks Gallery. Laurie Caffery Harris.
Taken together, Laurie's pots create a brightly colored rainbow. They are all lined with food-safe glazes.

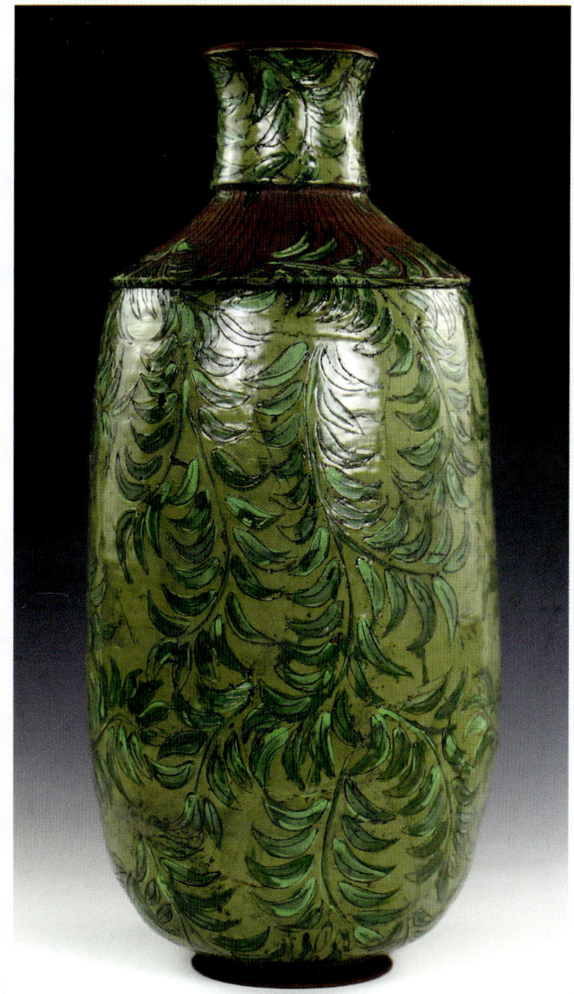

Large Vase. Marian Draper.
The exterior of this vase makes an excellent canvas for decoration. Leaving a little bit of the red clay exposed adds one more layer of visual interest. Clear glazed interior.

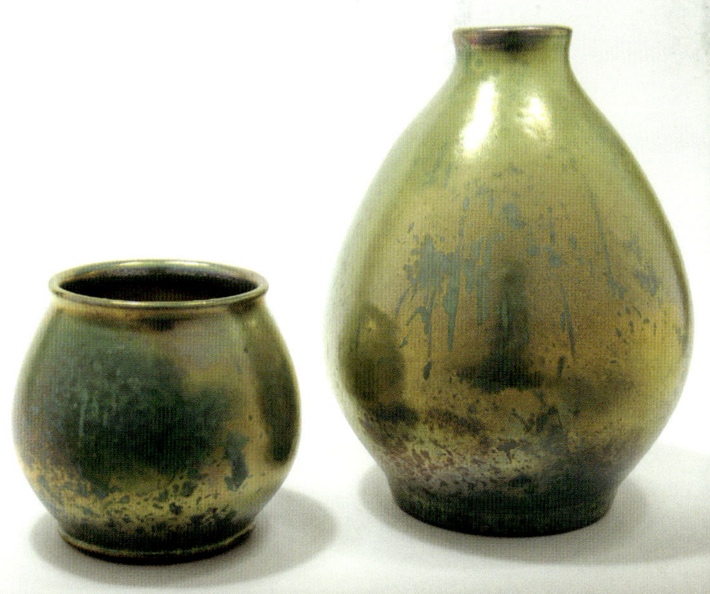

Experimental Glaze Made for Pewabic Pottery. Alex Thullen.
Alex Thullen's investigations into ceramic materials science yield truly Amazing Glazes.

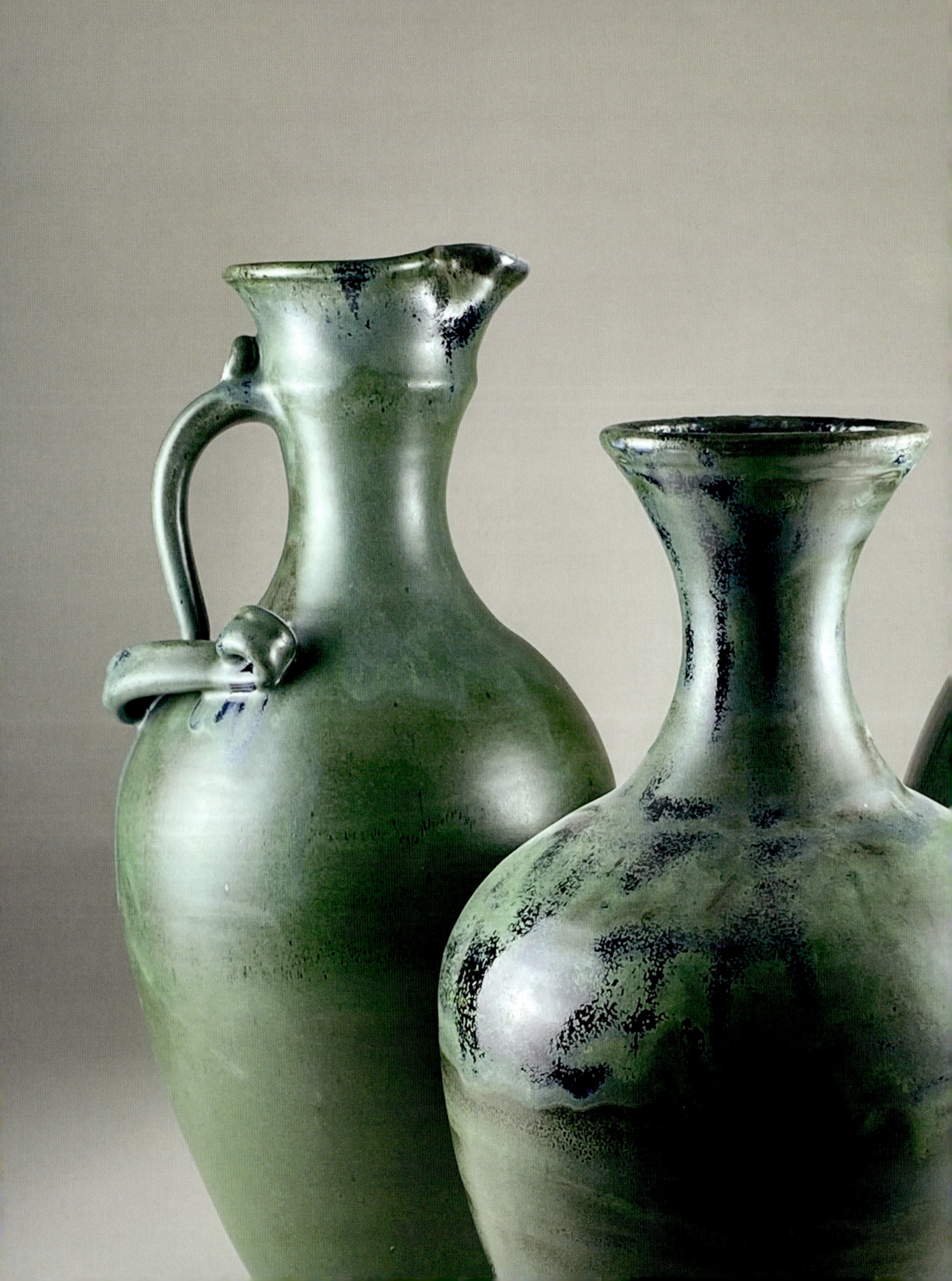

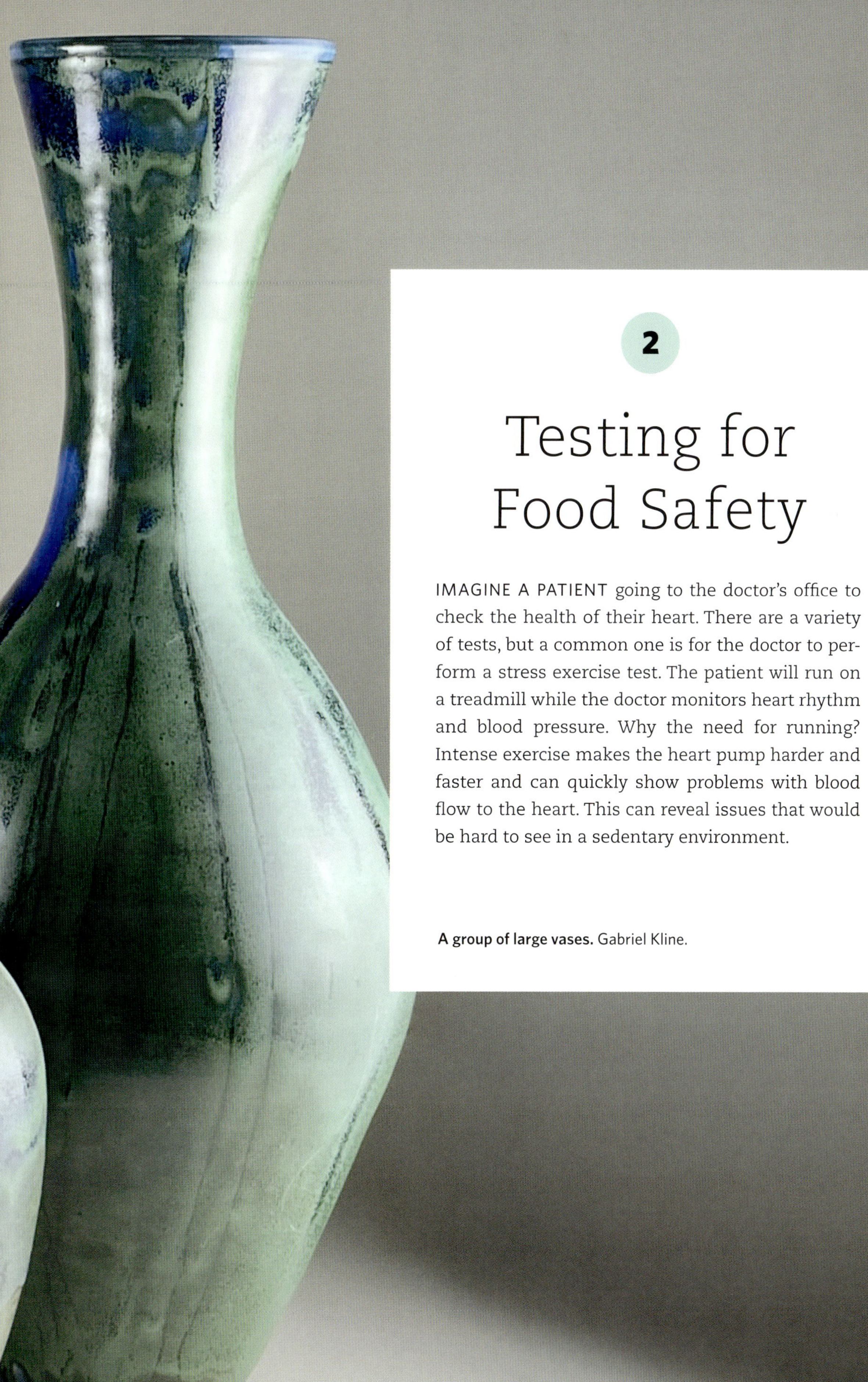

2

Testing for Food Safety

IMAGINE A PATIENT going to the doctor's office to check the health of their heart. There are a variety of tests, but a common one is for the doctor to perform a stress exercise test. The patient will run on a treadmill while the doctor monitors heart rhythm and blood pressure. Why the need for running? Intense exercise makes the heart pump harder and faster and can quickly show problems with blood flow to the heart. This can reveal issues that would be hard to see in a sedentary environment.

A group of large vases. Gabriel Kline.

HOW WE TEST OUR GLAZES

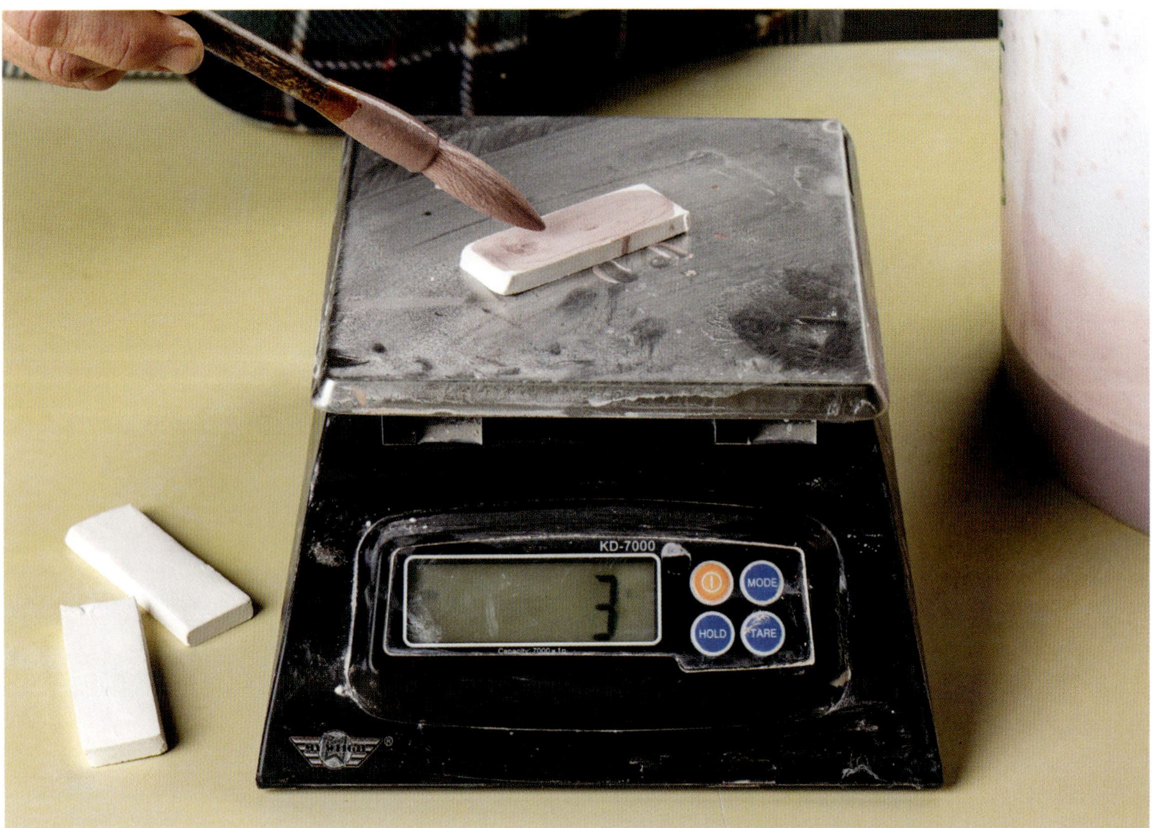

Adding 3 g of glaze to a bisque-fired tile.

Just as a stress test can reveal heart health issues, we reveal issues in a fired glaze by bathing them in an acid. The acid (4 percent acetic acid, a chemically balanced form of vinegar) speeds up the breakdown of the bonds in the glass. After 24 hours, we test the acid solution to determine if any metals have leached out.

But wait, you might be saying, I don't drink acetic acid out of my mugs. Wouldn't doing this test in water be better? The answer is yes and no. Like the stress exercise test for our heart, using acid speeds up a process that happens slowly at neutral pH and allows us to quickly identify problematic glazes. Also, it's important to realize that not all our food is at a neutral pH. It turns out that many common drinks like coffee, juice, wine, and beer can be quite acidic (see sidebar).

In the tests on the next page, we can see that leaching increases with acidity and that an ideal glaze should be resilient to leaching over a large pH range. By design, we are testing our glazes with 4 percent acetic acid to simulate strongly acidic foods and to determine whether the glaze will be stable regardless of what's on your plate.

For our test, we follow the ASTM standard method (coded C738-94). On bisque-fired, 1 × 3 inch (2.5 × 7.5 cm) porcelain tiles, we apply 3 grams of prepared (wet) glaze evenly across the surface of the tile. This is done in triplicate and the tiles are fired to the desired cone as determined by Orton TempCheks (see chapter 5 on firing for more information on TempCheks vs. cones). After a thorough wash with soap and water, the tiles are completely immersed in 40 milliliters of 4 percent trace-metal acetic acid in deionized water for 24 hours at room temperature. The tiles are removed and the acid is analyzed for metal leaching.

PH AND LEACHING

The pH scale, developed in 1923 by Danish chemist, Søren Sørensen shows whether something is acidic (below 7.0), neutral (7.0), or basic/alkaline (above 7.0). If we vary the pH of the liquid in contact with our glaze, we can change how fast the glaze breaks down and how much metal leaches out. Both acidic and basic environments can degrade the glaze, but we focus on acidic solutions as there are few foods that are basic. To make our study as relevant as possible, we ran an experiment where we used the following commonly consumed liquids to degrade the glaze: neutral water (7.0), black coffee (5.0), apple juice (3.5), and a generic cola soda. (2.5). It should be noted that cola and 4 percent acetic acid (2.4) have almost the same pH.

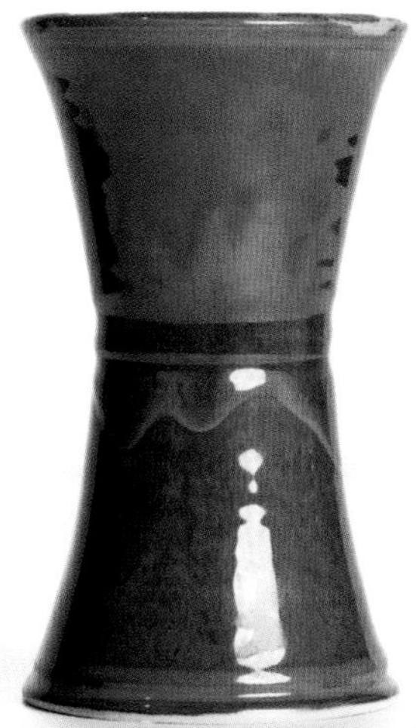

Metallic Teal: This beautiful but unstable glaze uses both cobalt (max 0.5 ppm) and copper (max 1.3 ppm) to get its metallic sheen. When it was tested, we saw that it only barely passed with coffee and that it failed in more acidic solutions. (Cobalt: water 0.06 ppm [pass], coffee 0.13 [pass] ppm, apple juice 0.66 ppm [fail], cola 1.1 ppm [fail]) (Copper: water 0.07 ppm [pass], coffee 1.1 ppm [pass], apple juice 3.8 ppm [fail], cola 7.1 ppm [fail])

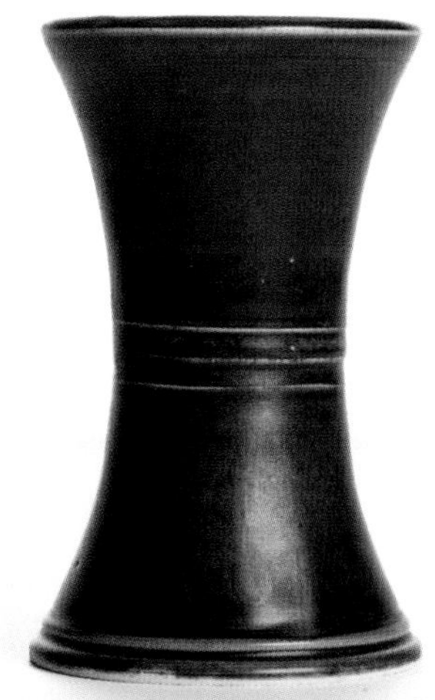

Emily's Purple: We looked at cobalt leaching (max 0.5 ppm) in these various solutions and saw that this glaze passed at all pHs tested. (Cobalt: water 0.04 ppm [pass], coffee 0.05 ppm [pass], apple juice 0.07 ppm [pass], cola 0.13 ppm [pass])

METALLIC TEAL (CONE 6)

INGREDIENTS	AMOUNTS
Minspar Feldspar	41.00
Silica	27.00
Whiting	15.00
Zinc Oxide	12.00
EPK	5.00
Total:	**100.00**

Also Add:

Copper Carbonate	5
Titanium Dioxide	5
Cobalt Carbonate	3

EMILY'S PURPLE (CONE 6)

INGREDIENTS	AMOUNTS
Minspar Feldspar	41.00
Silica	20.00
Talc	15.00
Gillespie Borate	12.00
Dolomite	7.00
Kaolin	5.00
Total	**100.00**

Also Add:

Bentonite	2.00
Cobalt Carbonate	2.00

THE LAB TESTS

After we have prepared our leach solutions, our goal is now to determine how much metal from the glaze dissolved into the solution. These are incredibly small quantities, and to the naked eye the tiles and the solutions look the same before and after leaching. To our benefit, there are several laboratory processes that can detect metals even at ppm levels. The first, atomic emission spectroscopy, detects light coming from the metals. The second technique uses mass spectrometry, which separates the metals using electrical fields. Finally, we can use electron microscopes to see tiny changes in the surface of the tiles.

ATOMIC EMISSION SPECTROSCOPY (AES)

It's a warm summer day on the Fourth of July, and you are staring into the night sky as fireworks explode above you. Rockets filled with strontium fill the heavens with deep red light. Next, in rapid succession, a sodium rocket becomes yellow light, and a barium one becomes bright green. What you are observing is a fundamental chemical process called atomic emission. Whether in a firework detonation or on the surface of the sun, excited elements can release light. Even more importantly, scientists quickly learned that each element gives off a unique "fingerprint" of light. This is how astronomers know the chemical composition of far-off nebulas in space, and it's how we can determine incredibly small quantities of metals in our leach solution.

In our instrument, the leach solution is first sprayed directly into a flame of 10,000°C plasma. This is our laboratory equivalent of a firework explosion, and it excites the elements in the solution causing them to release light. The atomic emission spectrometer then detects the light and matches the elements to each characteristic fingerprint. The detector is extremely sensitive and can sense light even from solutions containing ppm quantities of metals.

MASS SPECTROMETRY (MS)

It's a long, warm weekend, and you're cooling off at the pool. Looking up, you see a group of kids go down a twisty waterslide all at once. Shrieks of joy fill the air as they wind their way down the twists and turns. Amazingly, though, the kids do not come out the bottom all together, but one at a time. The bigger kids sped through the turns while the smaller ones got jostled about, lost momentum, and came out later. The waterslide has separated the group of kids based on their size. This is how mass spectrometry works.

In the mass spectrometer, the elements we are looking at are first turned into charged ions in an incredibly hot torch. Then, like diving down a steep, twisty water slide, they are bombarded by electrical fields from all around as they shoot through the instrument. Depending upon their mass, some elements dive through this electrical obstacle course easily. Other bigger or smaller elements fly off in various directions and crash into the walls. This allows us to detect specific ions based on their mass. If we want, we can then change the speed and the bounciness of the path so that smaller or bigger elements make it through. At the end of this wild ride, the detector counts up how much of a specific element of interest made it through. Comparatively, the mass spectrometer is more sensitive than the atomic emission spectrometer and can quantify the metal concentrations in the leach solutions down to sub-ppm (parts per billion) levels.

SCANNING ELECTRON MICROSCOPY(SEM)

In addition to learning about the metals coming out of our glazes, we also want to see the texture and surface profile of our ceramics. This could be useful in determining if certain glazes are underfired or have nearly imperceptible flaws that could increase the chance of leaching or harboring bacteria. How up-close and personal can we get to our pots?

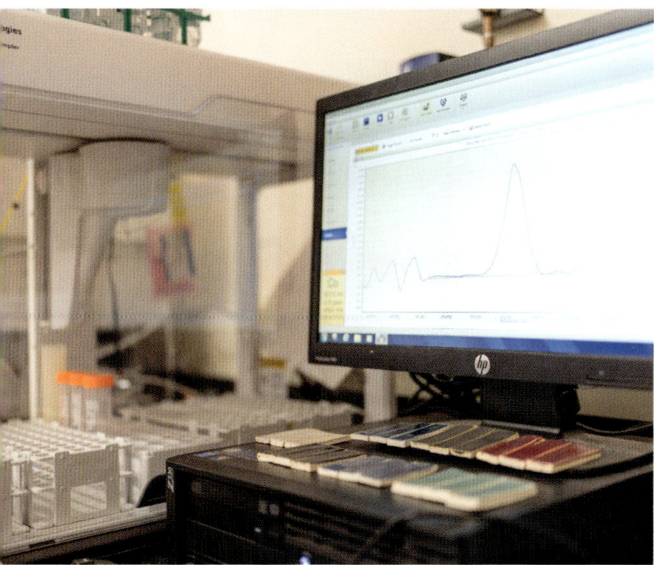

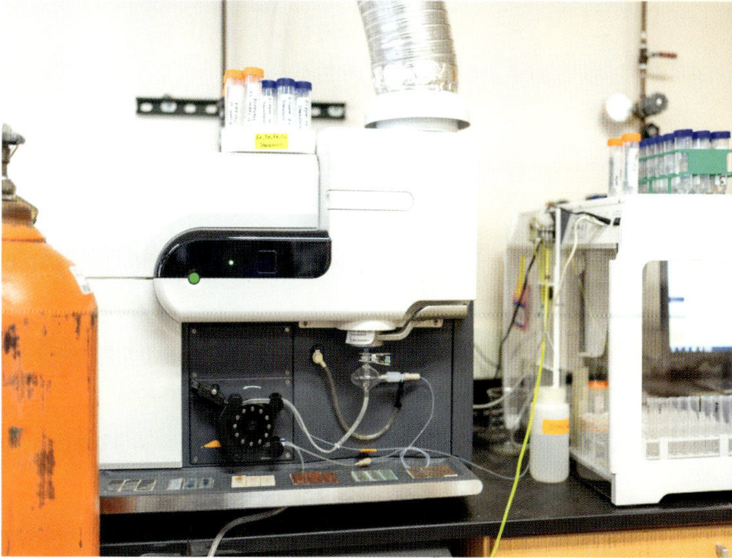

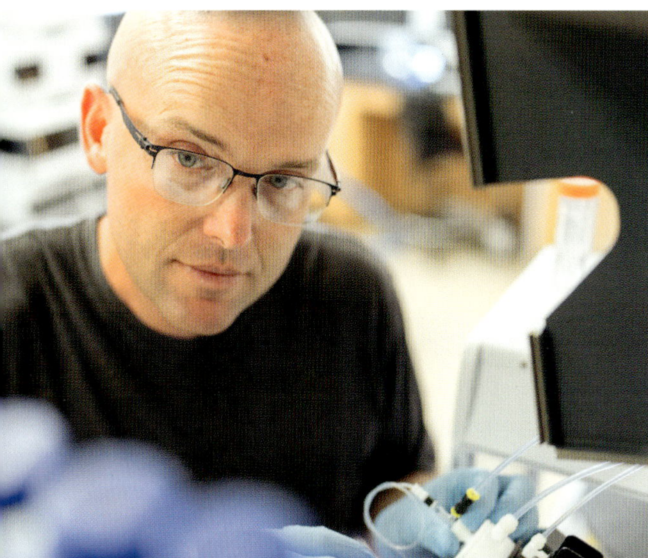

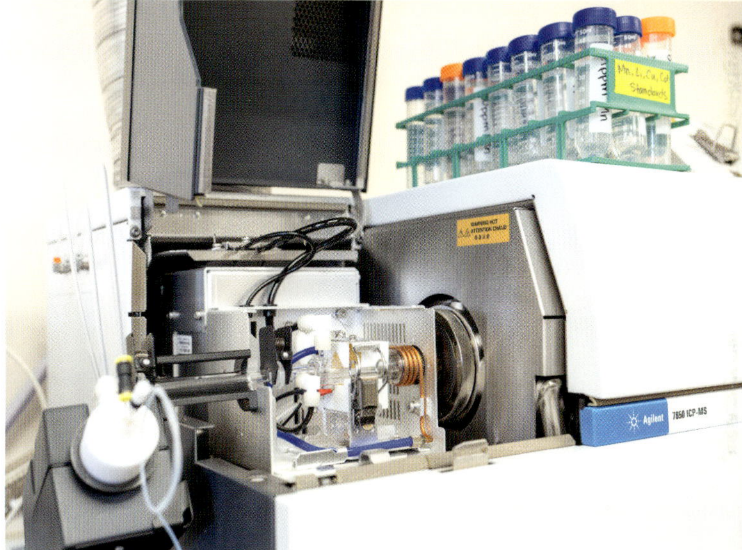

CLOCKWISE FROM TOP LEFT: Detecting fingerprints of light; the atomic emission spectrometer looks at parts per million (ppm) metal concentrations; the mass spectrometer detects incredibly small quantities, down to parts per billion (ppb); Dr. Bill Collins setting up the solution intake on the mass spectrometer.

As it turns out, there are several types of high-powered microscopes that can image objects over one million times smaller than the tip of a pencil. For our purposes, we use scanning electron microscopy, which takes pictures by bombarding the ceramic surface of the object with high-energy electrons. Like colliding billiard balls, the stream of electrons hits and knocks electrons off the surface of the glaze. The detector then captures these electrons and creates an image. This technique allows us to see the world down to 5 nanometers, which is over 250 times higher magnification than the most powerful light microscopes. Perhaps the only downside is that to make the electrons bounce properly, we have to first coat our ceramics in a thin layer of gold with a machine called a sputter coater. Talk about making expensive pots!

WHAT WE TEST FOR (AND WHY!)

Glazes are chemically very complex and are often composed of a half dozen or more elements. **Many of these components are completely harmless when ingested at the concentrations found leaching out of our pottery.** Some are required for proper health. A few can be consumed at low concentration but not high. A couple probably shouldn't be ingested at any concentration. Let's learn about the different elements that we test for and why.

TOXICITY-FREE ELEMENTS: THE ULTIMATE PEACE OF MIND

The biggest chemical contributors to a glaze are the glass formers: silicon and aluminum (and boron for low- to mid-fire). These elements are not required for human health, but, thankfully, they are also nontoxic when ingested at concentrations found in leach solutions. Note that this means after they have been fired. For a discussion on safely handling these materials in their dry form, pre-glaze fire, see pages 60–61. Common primary sources for these elements include silica, clays such as kaolins/ball clay/bentonite, Gerstley Borate, Gillespie Borate, borax, and many frits.

The second biggest contributor to glazes are fluxes, and they usually come from either alkali metals or alkali earth metals. Many of these elements are needed for human health and some can even be found on the back of a food label as part of a healthy diet. The body needs considerable amounts of sodium, magnesium, potassium, and calcium daily to maintain cellular structure and function, build bones, regulate the central nervous system, and perform biochemical reactions. The flux strontium is not needed for the body, but it doesn't seem to have any negative effect either. Common sources for these fluxes are whiting, wollastonite, dolomite, talc, magnesium carbonate, nepheline syenite, Minspar, Custer Feldspar, Mahavir, and G200 Feldspars. Frits often contain mixtures of these fluxes.

Finally, there are several elements that we use in smaller quantities that are also considered nontoxic. Titanium as either titanium dioxide or rutile, tin oxide, and calcium phosphate from bone ash don't leach out elements of concern.

A LITTLE BIT GOES A LONG WAY: IMPORTANT ELEMENTS WITH A LIMIT

Just like a lot of the food that we eat, moderation is key to many of the elements that we consume. Many of the elements that we test for are actually critically important for us to get regularly in our diet . . . we just don't want to overdo it. To our point, humans can overdose on drinking water (e.g., hyponatremia). So it's important to know your dosage. Anything can be toxic in too large an amount.

Let's start with **chromium**, which is responsible for beautiful green, pink, and red glazes. This element primarily exists in two forms: one that is a necessary nutrient and another that is quite dangerous. Thankfully, potters use the form that is crucial for the body. This element plays an important role in energy production, metabolism, and insulin sensitivity, and we get all that we need from a diet full of vegetables and nuts. Getting too much can impact the liver and kidneys and may create insulin resistance. Common sources are chrome and chromium (III) oxide.

Next up is **iron**, the element responsible for the color of blood, the red soil of Mars, and orange/red/brown tones in pottery. As expected, iron is a critical component of red blood cells and helps transport oxygen through the body. It is also found in many important enzymes, and we meet our body's iron demands by consuming meat products, legumes, dark leafy greens, and nuts. Excessive iron consumption can create joint pain and fatigue. Common sources are red iron oxide, black iron oxide, and yellow ochre.

Manganese, responsible for browns and blacks in pottery, is an incredibly important nutrient in the formation of connective tissues and is necessary for the healing of wounds. It also helps the generation of new neurotransmitters and plays a role in the regulation of neuronal activity. Manganese is found in a plethora of vegetables as well as tea. Manganese toxicity impairs many of the systems that it helps. Common sources are manganese dioxide and manganese carbonate.

Copper creates greens in oxidation and, in reduction, reds on our pots. It also does a lot in the body, including acting as an antioxidant, helping in the production of antibodies in the immune system, and participating in the metabolism of nutrients into usable energy. Like manganese, copper plays a crucial role in the nervous system as it helps in the formation of myelin, the protective covering of nerves. Copper can be found in dark chocolate, shellfish, nuts, and legumes. Also, because many pipe systems/cookware have copper in them, drinking water can provide some copper to the diet. Because we consume so much copper, our body has developed efficient ways to regulate and excrete this element, and copper toxicity is uncommon. When it does happen, excess copper can upset the liver and nervous system. Common sources are copper carbonate and copper oxide.

Like the alkali earth metals, **zinc** is considered a flux and used to help melt glazes at lower temperatures. Zinc is necessary for the immune system, the sense of taste and smell and, perhaps most important of all, zinc is required for DNA synthesis and cell division. We meet most of our dietary demands for this element in the meat, dairy, nuts, and legumes that we consume. High levels of zinc can weaken the immune system and interfere with the absorption of micronutrients. A common source is zinc oxide.

ELEMENTS WE DON'T NEED TO CONSUME: HOW MUCH IS TOO MUCH?

There are several metals that we use in ceramics that we simply don't need in our body. Some of these metals absorb into our bodies more easily from food and drink than others. Once inside the body, some of these metals are excreted from our bodies relatively quickly (like lithium or barium) and some slowly (like cadmium). When combined with the inherent toxicity of the metal, public health scientists are able to develop safe levels of consumption below which the human body is minimally affected.

Cobalt makes our beautiful blues and purples, but its role in the body can be a little confusing. We critically need cobalt in the unique form of vitamin B12 to maintain our nervous system, but we do not need any other type of cobalt in our diet. This means that there is no health benefit from consuming the cobalt that might leach from our pottery, and having too much cobalt in your diet can affect the cardiovascular system. Common sources are cobalt carbonate and cobalt oxide.

Like its alkali metal cousins, **lithium** acts as a flux. Unlike sodium and potassium, lithium is not needed in the body and over time can destabilize the kidneys and affect the central nervous system. Common sources are spodumene and lithium carbonate.

Ranging from oranges to purples to browns, **nickel** can be found in a variety of different glazes as a colorant. Nickel is carcinogenic. Common sources are nickel carbonate and green/black nickel oxide.

Barium, another alkali earth metal flux, is responsible for assisting in the creation of unique colors and textures in glazes. Insoluble forms can be ingested to assist in medical procedures; however, soluble forms of barium are poisonous and even used as a rodenticide. Barium that leaches from pottery is soluble. A common source is barium carbonate.

As mentioned before, there are only two FDA regulated metals in pottery: **lead** and **cadmium**. Lead is found in lead silicate glazes but is not commonly used anymore by studio potters. Cadmium is a colorant in pottery that makes unmatched reds, oranges, and yellows. However, because of its considerable toxicity, cadmium is most often used as an "encapsulated stain" to reduce leaching.

THE PERIODIC TABLE OF ELEMENTS

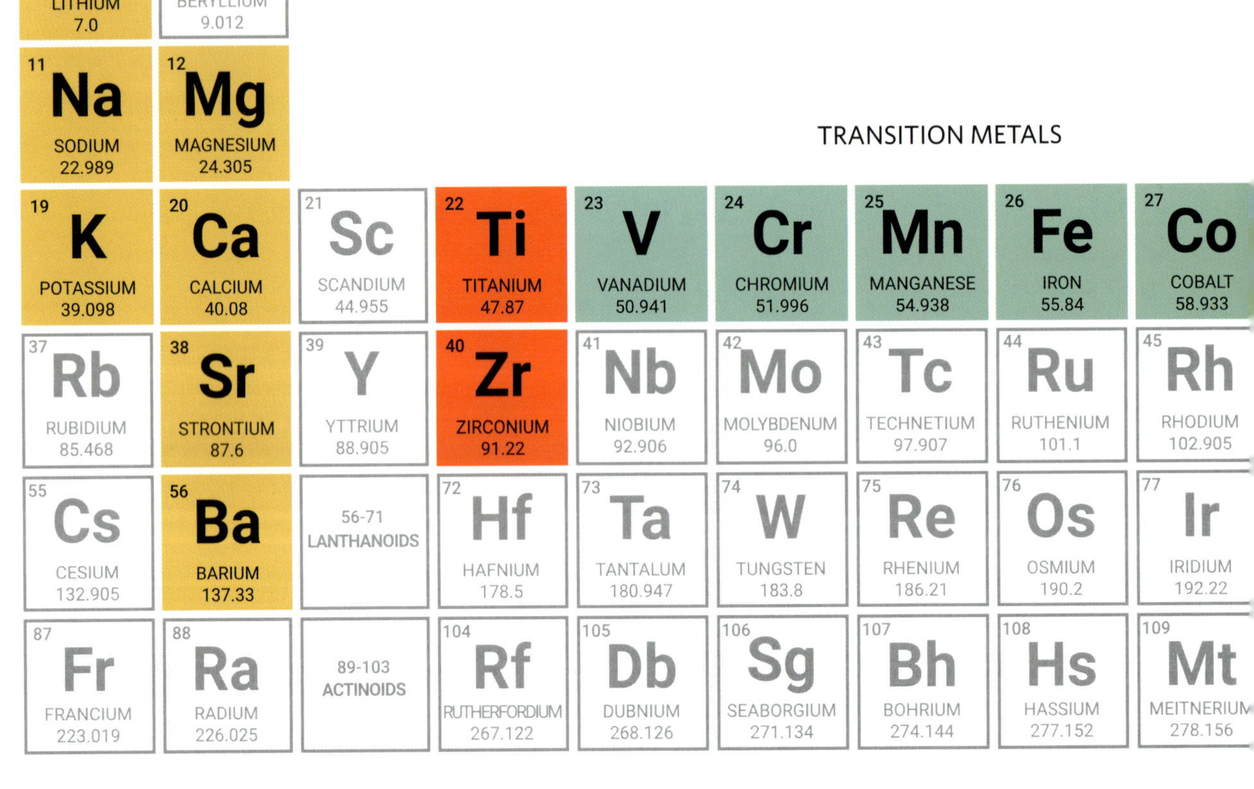

FLUX

GLASS FORMER

COLORANT

MODIFIER

								2 He HELIUM 4.002
			5 B BORON 10.81	6 C CARBON 12.011	7 N NITROGEN 14.007	8 O OXYGEN 15.999	9 F FLUORINE 18.998	10 Ne NEON 20.180
			13 Al ALUMINUM 26.981	14 Si SILICON 28.085	15 P PHOSPHORUS 30.973	16 S SULFUR 32.07	17 Cl CHLORINE 35.45	18 Ar ARGON 39.9
8 Ni NICKEL 58.693	29 Cu COPPER 63.55	30 Zn ZINC 65.4	31 Ga GALLIUM 69.72	32 Ge GERMANIUM 72.63	33 As ARSENIC 74.921	34 Se SELENIUM 78.97	35 Br BROMINE 79.90	36 Kr KRYPTON 83.80
6 Pd PALLADIUM 106.4	47 Ag SILVER 107.868	48 Cd CADMIUM 112.41	49 In INDIUM 114.82	50 Sn TIN 118.71	51 Sb ANTIMONY 121.76	52 Te TELLURIUM 127.6	53 I IODINE 126.904	54 Xe XENON 131.29
8 Pt PLATINUM 195.08	79 Au GOLD 196.966	80 Hg MERCURY 200.59	81 Ti THALLIUM 204.383	82 Pb LEAD 207	83 Bi BISMUTH 208.980	84 Po POLONIUM 208.982	85 At ASTATINE 209.987	86 Rn RADON 222.017
10 Ds ARMSTADTIUM 281.165	111 Rg ROENTGENIUM 282.169	112 Cn COPERNICIUM 285.177	113 Nh NIHONIUM 286.183	114 Fl FLEROVIUM 289.191	115 Mc MOSCOVIUM 290.196	116 Lv LIVERMORIUM 293.205	117 Ts TENNESSINE 294.211	118 Og OGANESSON 294.214

4 Gd ADOLINIUM 157.2	65 Tb TERBIUM 158.925	66 Dy DYSPROSIUM 162.50	67 Ho HOLMIUM 164.930	68 Er ERBIUM 167.26	69 Tm THULIUM 168.934	70 Yb YTTERBIUM 173.04	71 Lu LUTETIUM 174.967
6 Cm CURIUM 247.070	97 Bk BERKELIUM 247.070	98 Cf CALIFORNIUM 251.079	99 Es EINSTEINIUM 252.083	100 Fm FERMIUM 257.095	101 Md MENDELEVIUM 258.098	102 No NOBELIUM 259.101	103 Lr LAWRENCIUM 262.110V

STAINS: A SAFER WAY TO COLOR YOUR POTS

Stains are an alternative to the metal oxide colorants listed above, and they often leach considerably less metal. While their formulation is proprietary, they are generally composed of one or more metal oxide colorants that are premelted with extremely stable and high-melting glaze materials. The resulting solid is then crushed into an extremely fine powder that can be subsequently used to color other glazes.

Why the extra step? Unlike metal oxide colorants, at cone 04 to 10 firings, stains do not melt very easily and thus do not become chemically incorporated into the glass during firing. This is because they have a new molecular form that does not melt at normal kiln temperatures. In effect, the stain is a superfine material suspended within another glaze. This largely prevents the chemical breakdown and release of the metal colorant into food. It is in fact possible to decompose a stain with enough flux and cause it to leach metal colorant out of a glaze. However, this is the exception, not the rule, and it's because of this stability and reliability that stains are widely used in industrial and commercial glazes. This stability is also why the particularly toxic cadmium is almost exclusively used as a stain in ceramics.

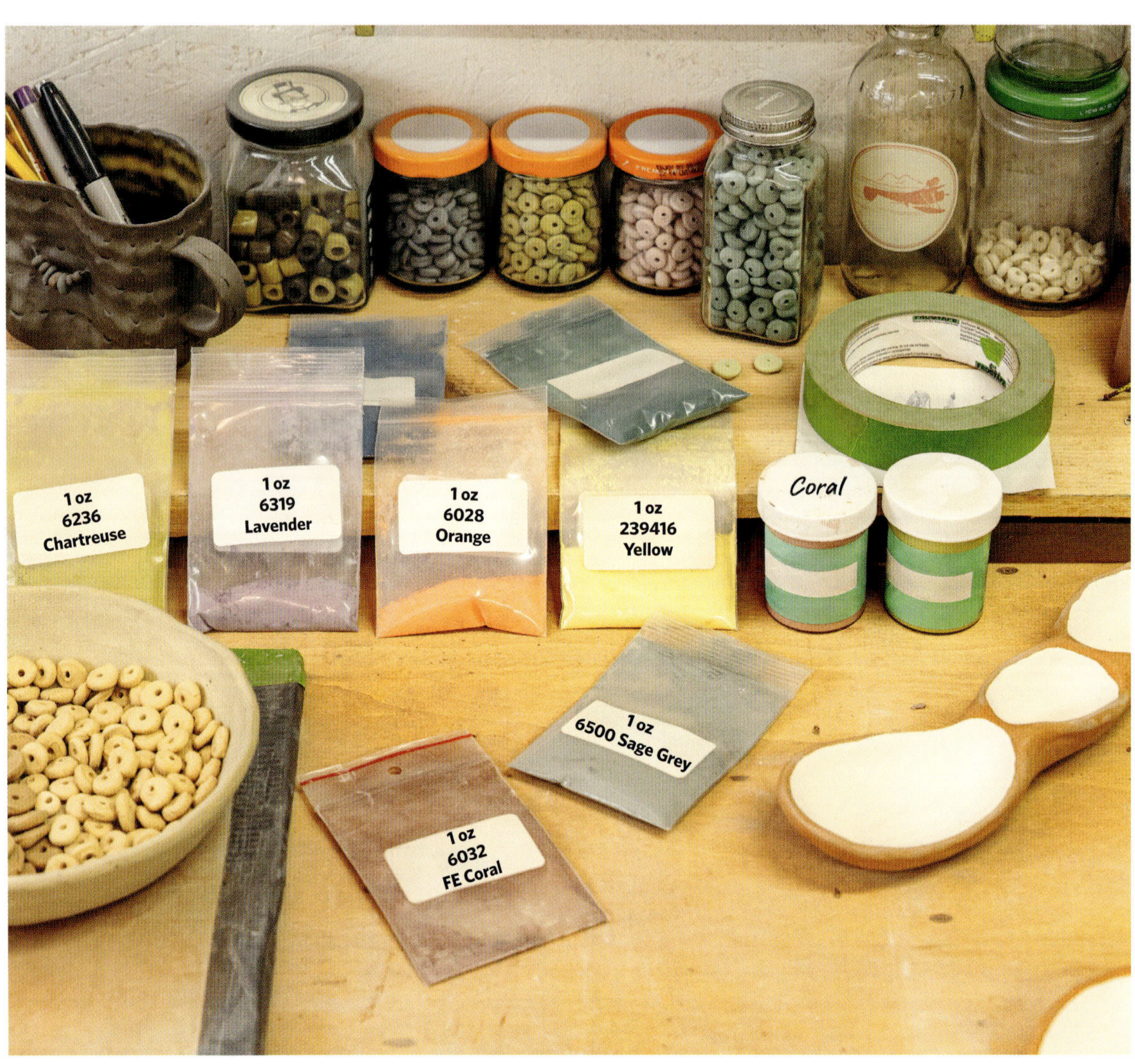

Mason stains are not just for glazes. Here, Stephanie Gesswein tests mason stains to color her clay body.

THE LEMON TEST DEBUNKED

You may have heard of a common studio experiment to determine whether a glaze is stable. In "The Lemon Test," a small puddle of lemon juice or a lemon slice is left on the surface of the work for 24 hours. The tile is then visually inspected to see if any changes have taken place where the acidic lemon has touched the surface. Unfortunately, this test is problematic as it will only reveal the most extreme glaze failures. To the naked eye, most glazes do not show any changes before and after leaching.

As an example, let's return to the metallic teal glaze analyzed earlier in this chapter. We already know that this glaze leaches unacceptable amounts of cobalt and copper over a range of acidic pHs. If we make a test tile, we see that before and after leaching there is no observable change. If we leave a lemon wedge in a puddle of lemon juice on this overnight, there is still no difference, even though lemon juice has a pH of 2.0! Ultimately, it has been our experience testing hundreds of glazes that few change appearance and that the lemon test is probably not a reliable way to determine if a glaze is food safe.

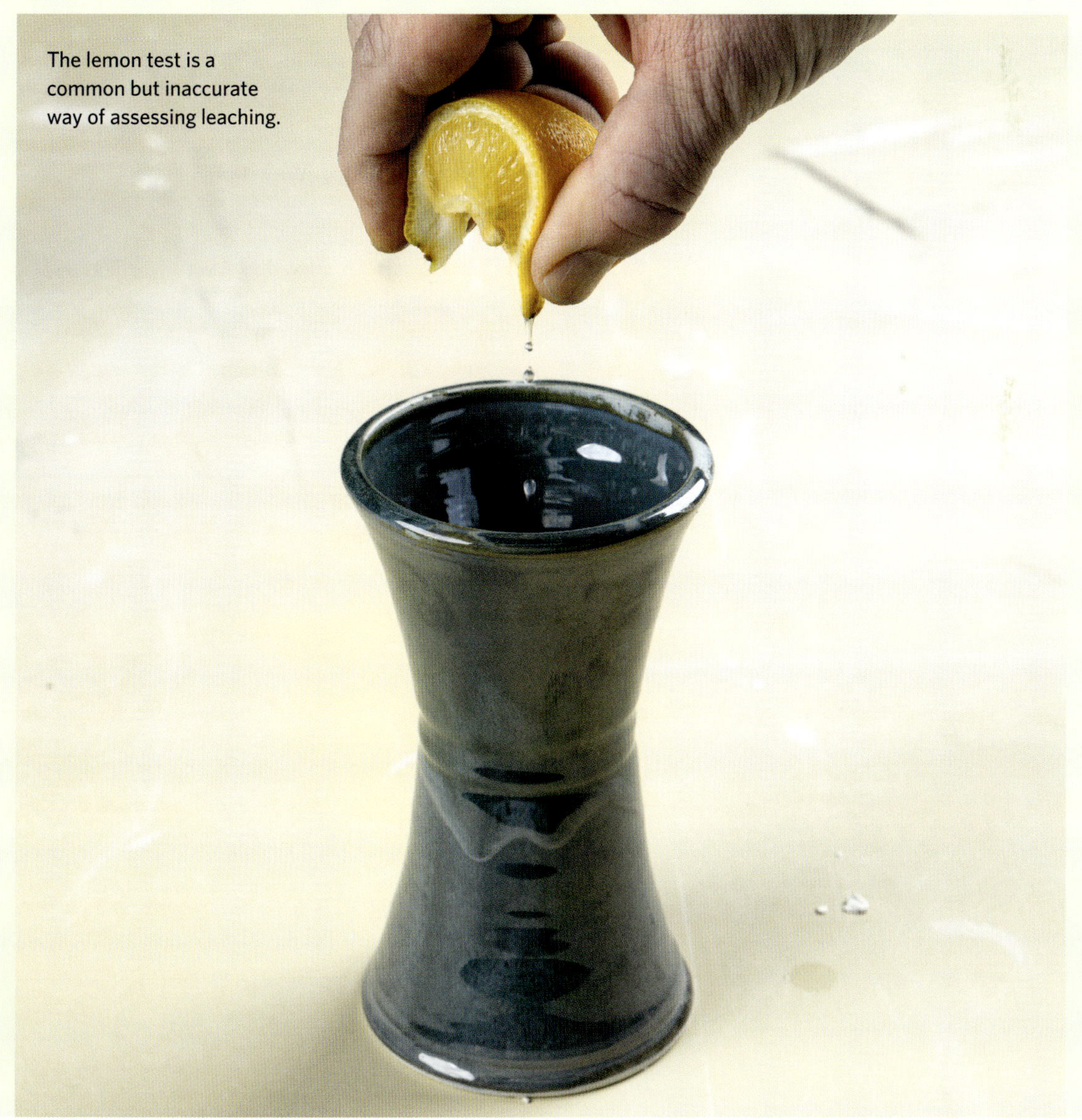

The lemon test is a common but inaccurate way of assessing leaching.

THE ART OF SCIENCE

Linda Bloomfield

lindabloomfield.co.uk   Instagram @LindaThePotter

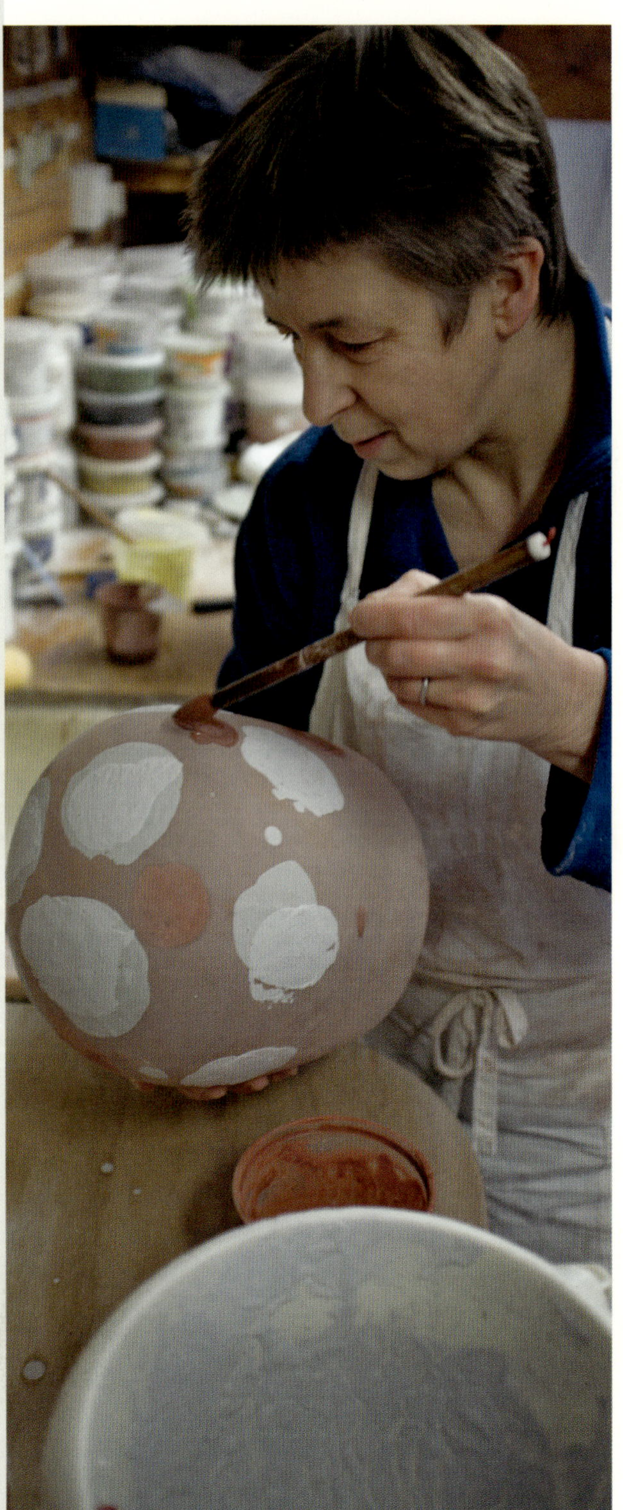

Linda Bloomfield applying lichen glaze to a closed form.

Linda Bloomfield produces two wonderful lines of porcelain: one functional, the other a series of installations that transform landscapes into immersive art experiences. She has also written seven (!) books on ceramics, including five books that deal specifically with glazes. Both her titles *Science for Potters* and *Special Effects Glazes* are in our libraries. Linda is a social media star who shares her work and process freely and widely, as she does here with us in this interview.

AMAZING GLAZE FOOD-SAFE RECIPES: *Why is it important for you to teach others glaze chemistry?*

LINDA BLOOMFIELD: Many potters start out learning about clay and glazes at art school, where there is not often much teaching about glaze chemistry. I feel lucky to have had a grounding in engineering and materials science before becoming a potter. Having an understanding of how glaze chemistry works enables much better control of your glazes and ultimately helps you make better work.

AGFSR: *As more people learn to develop, take control, and experiment with their glaze chemistry, how will that change our art form? In what ways do you see the ceramic community evolving in the future?*

LINDA: New glazes are constantly being discovered, for example, gloop glazes and foam glazes are recent developments. It's great to see the recipes being shared in books and online communities such as Glazy.org. Coming from a science background, I feel it is important to share our knowledge so that others can benefit and in turn develop their own new work. We are all standing on the shoulders of giants.

AGFSR: *Ceramics is becoming more accessible to a greater number of people with commercially available clay, glazes, and programmable electric kilns. As barriers come down and more people get into this field, what opportunities and challenges do you see this creating?*

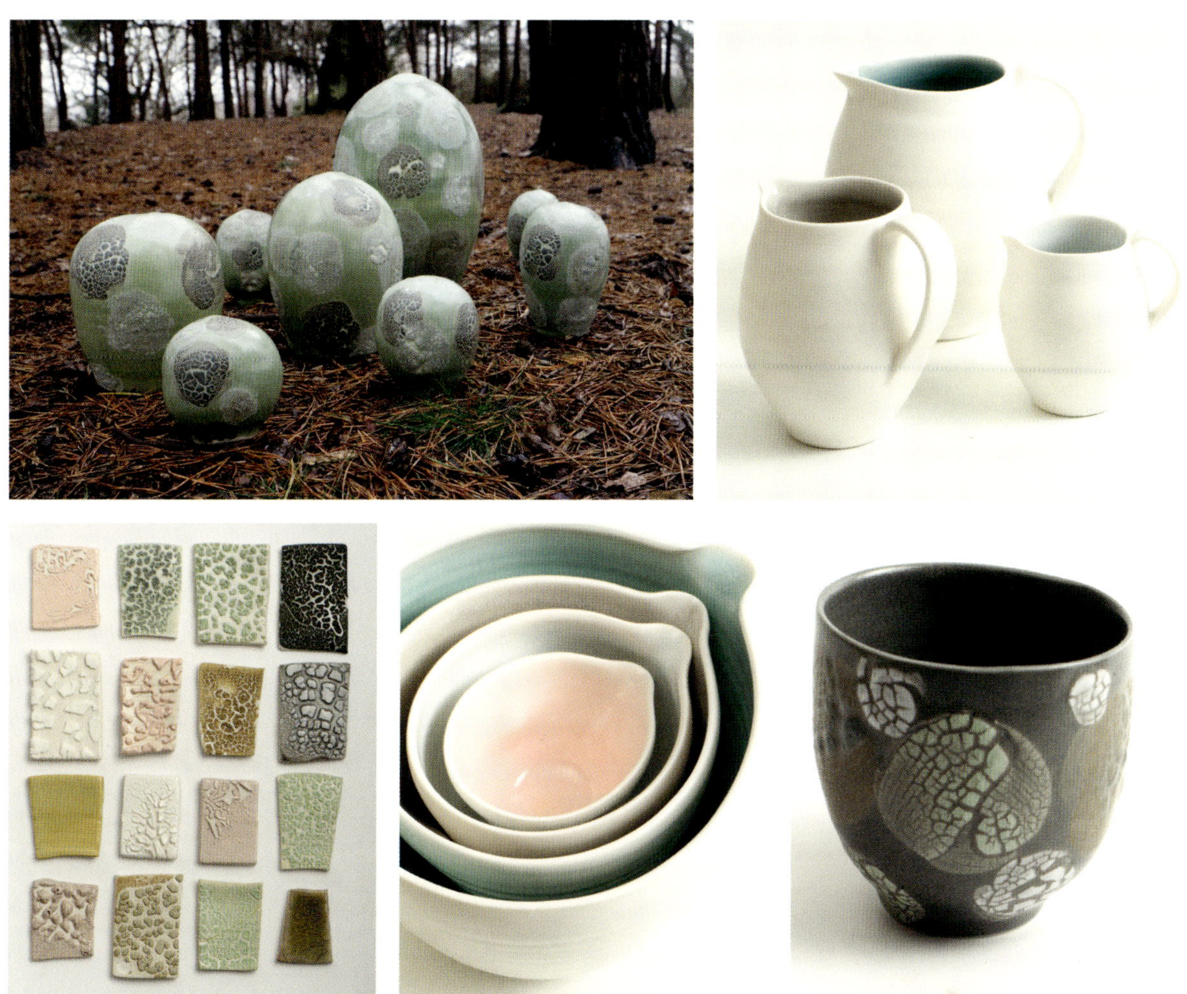

CLOCKWISE FROM TOP LEFT: An outdoor installation of works; a trio of pitchers eager to be used; the combination of a satin glaze with textured alligator glazes provides contrast and visual interest; different liner glazes provide variations on a theme in this set of nested bowls; experiments with alligator crawl glazes.

LINDA: I think it can only be good for the ceramics community that so many people are becoming interested in pottery. We are all relying on the ceramics industry that supports us by supplying materials, tools, and equipment and on educational opportunities to attend courses, workshops, and residencies. Without this support, it would be difficult for everyone to continue making pottery on their own. The bigger the pottery community, the more the support industries can thrive. There is a stark difference between the huge, thriving pottery community of the US and the much smaller one in the UK, where a great number of university ceramics courses have closed owing to lack of funding. Many emerging potters now learn their skills at community pottery studios.

AGFSR: *What does food safe mean to you? When developing your own glazes, how does food safety influence your decision making process?*

LINDA: Food-safe glazes are very important when making functional ware . . . It is also important to use glossy or satin matte glazes on food surfaces to avoid cutlery marking; my tableware is glossy on the inside and satin matte on the outside. When using different glazes on the inside and outside of pots, it is really important to get a good fit between the glaze and clay body to avoid cracking. I test by pouring in boiling water and if there is any cracking, I adjust the expansion of the glaze by reducing the silica.

GALLERY

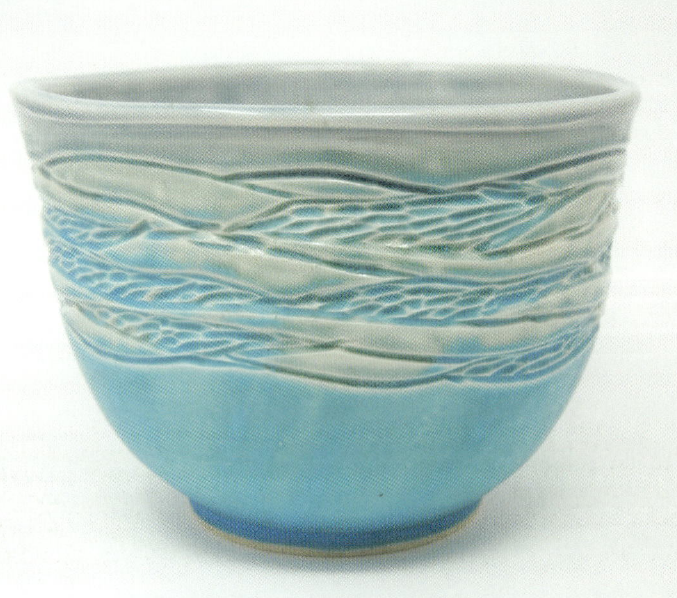

Oceanside Bowl. Trish Cutler.
A matte glaze on the outside of the bowl gives a lovely feel, while the glossy liner glaze is easy to clean.

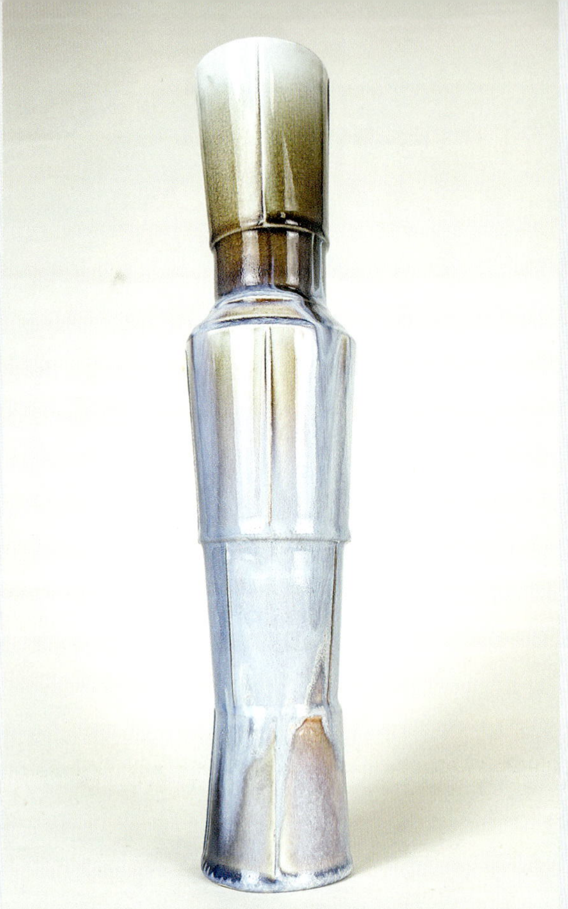

Modular Vase. Tyler Anderson.
This tall vase was slip-cast and sprayed with multiple glazes. A liner glaze allows it to serve as a carafe.

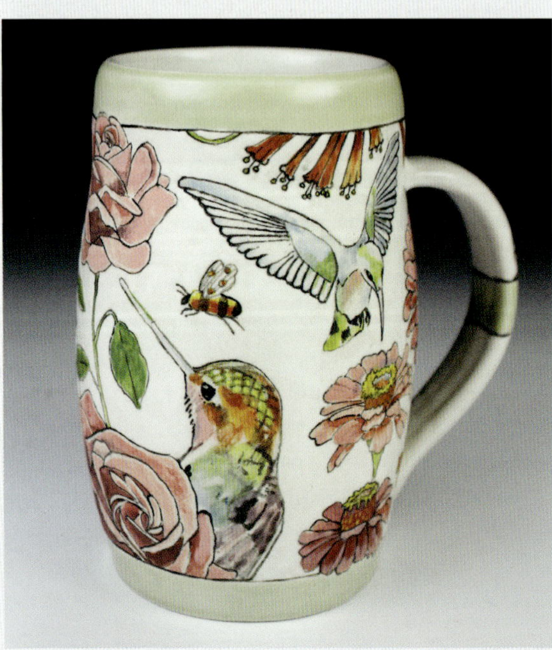

Mug. Ann Ruel.
The wonderfully decorated exterior of this mug elevates the humble form to a fine objet d'art.

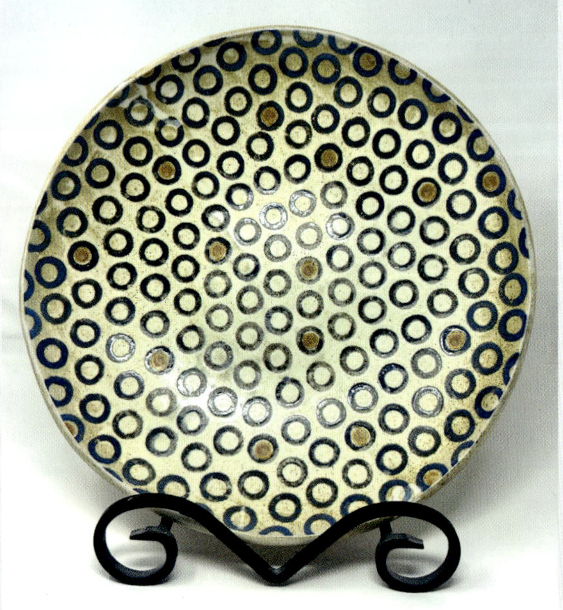

Circle Bowl. Lauren Breitling.
This large bowl features cleanly executed decoration using stamps and sponges.

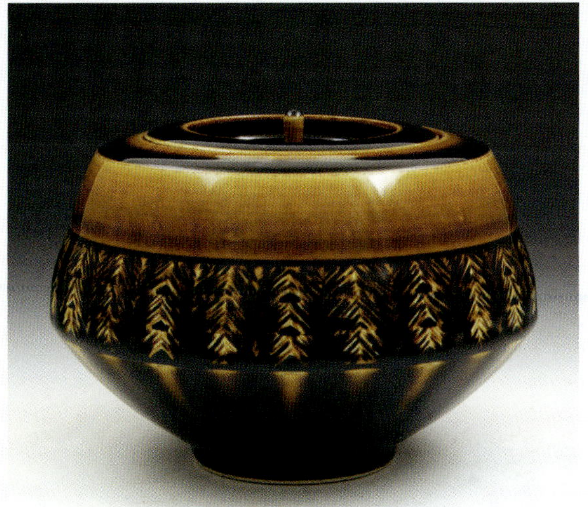

Covered Jar. Alex Thullen.
Exquisitely thrown and assembled with a perfectly fitted lid, this vessel doesn't just wear a glaze, it showcases it.

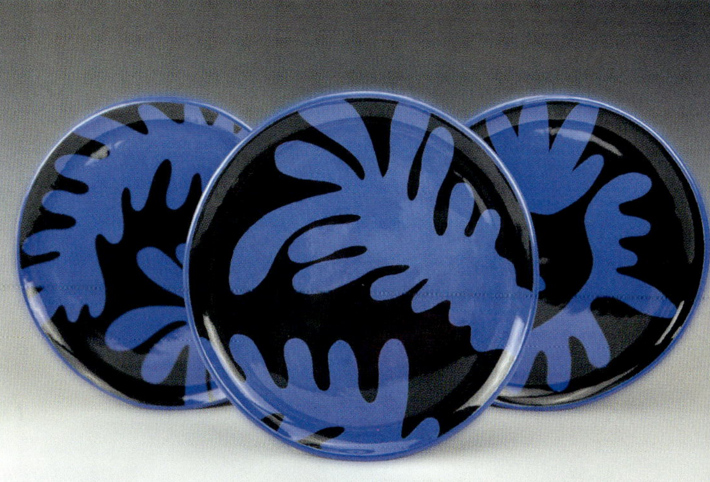

Blue and Black Porcelain Dinner Plates. Jennifer Rosseter.
Jennifer shows her versatility in this series, which contrasts with the style of her sgraffito work.

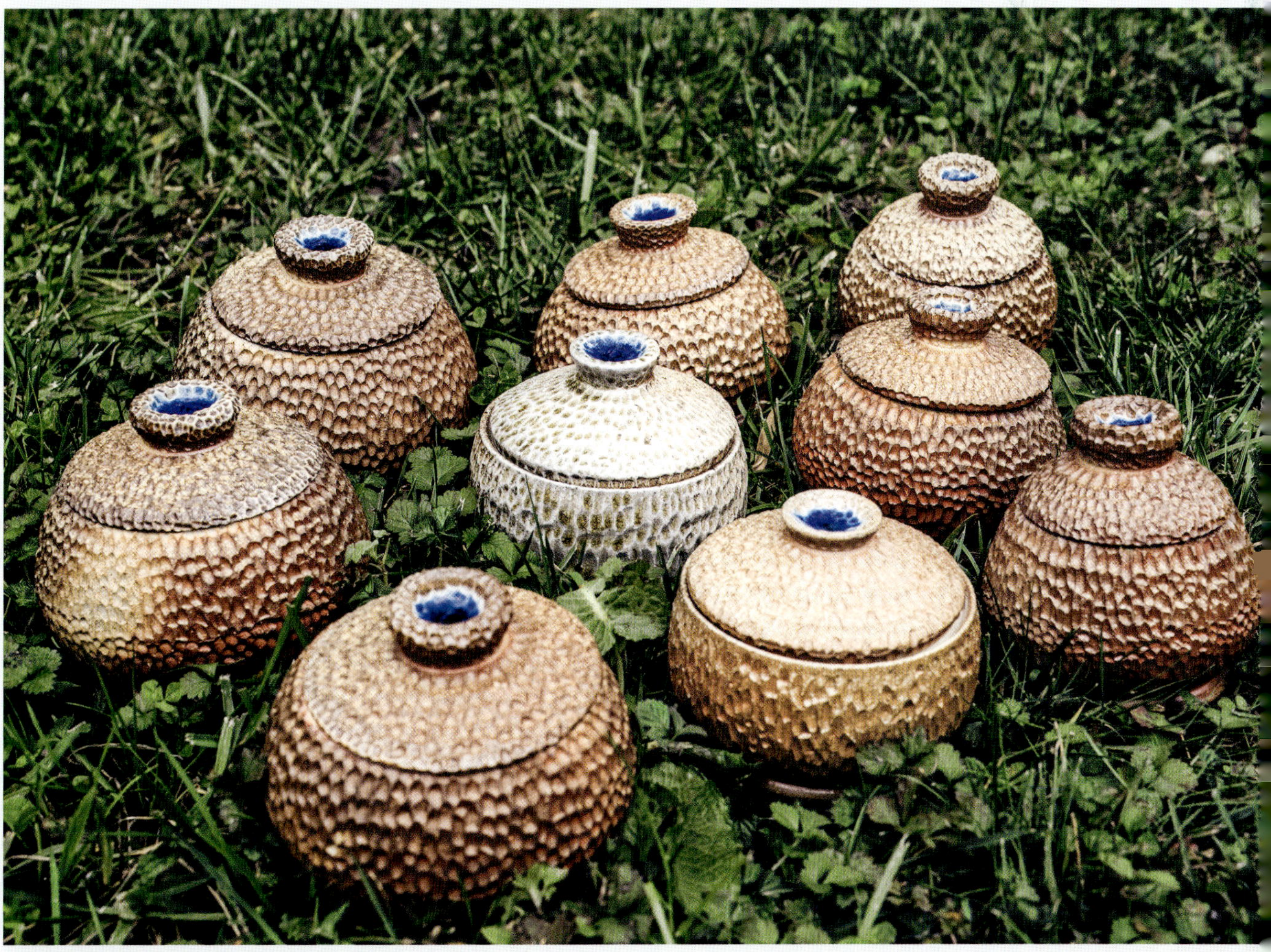

Bottle Grouping. Eva Hart.
A blue liner glaze means these bottles could store spirits, medicines, or syrups. Cork it up!

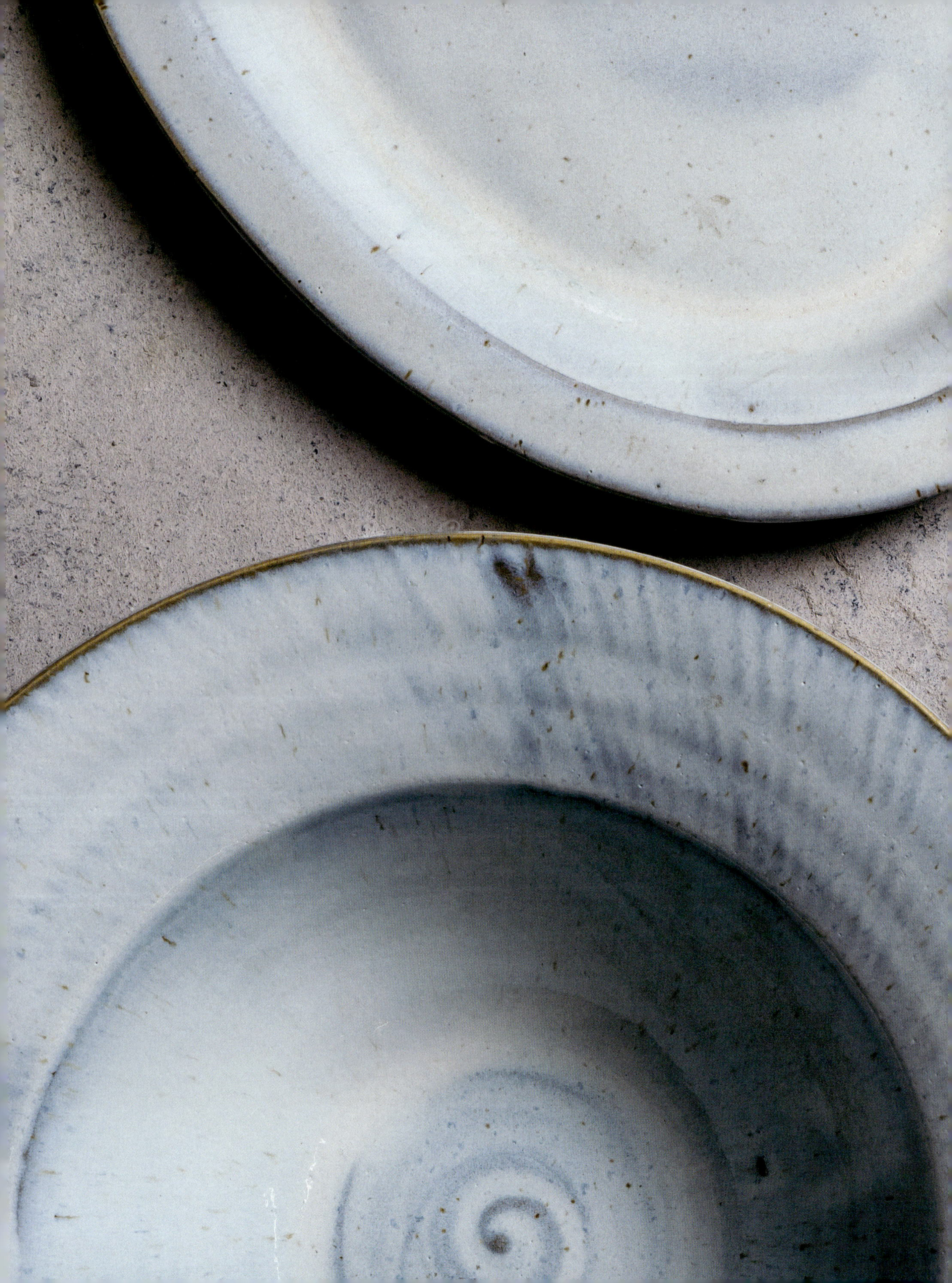

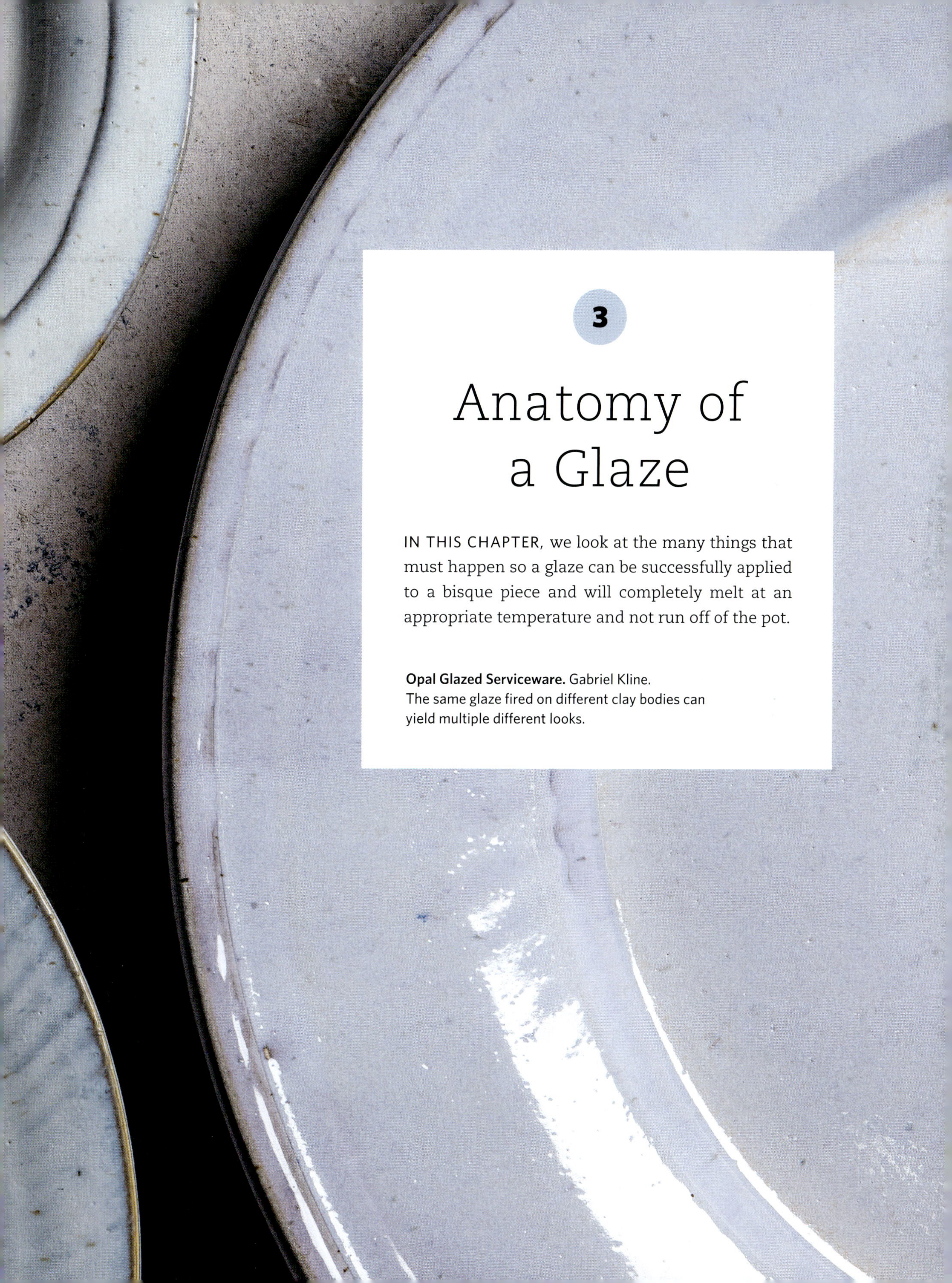

3

Anatomy of a Glaze

IN THIS CHAPTER, we look at the many things that must happen so a glaze can be successfully applied to a bisque piece and will completely melt at an appropriate temperature and not run off of the pot.

Opal Glazed Serviceware. Gabriel Kline. The same glaze fired on different clay bodies can yield multiple different looks.

WHAT'S IN A GLAZE?

Before we begin discussing the various components of a glaze, we should start with why we are applying a glaze in the first place. When a clay body is initially fired to create the brittle but hardened state called bisqueware, it undergoes a series of chemical changes called sintering. In this process, minute amounts of silica and other chemicals within the clay body are melted to create an interconnected network of fused particles. This new form of silica acts as a "molecular glue" that creates rigidity and strength and ultimately holds the clay body together. Indeed, you can even hear harmonic vibrations generated from this new glassy structure when you ping bisque pieces with your finger (listen as the pitch changes from cone 08 bisque pieces compared to the more glasslike cone 04).

At a micrometer level (one hundredth the width of a human hair), bisqueware's true structure looks much more like Swiss cheese than the solid pot that you're holding. While a small amount of glass interconnects the body, much of the silica and clay remain unfused together. This is why we immerse a clay body in boiling water to determine if it has undergone vitrification. The unfused pores within the body absorb and retain water, so the less absorption, the better. This also gets to the root of why undervitrified and unglazed pieces are generally not considered food safe. Without a way to seal the porous network of holes, it's possible for bacteria (approximately 0.5 to 1 micrometers in diameter) or viruses (approximately 0.01 to 0.5 micrometers in diameter) to enter, thrive inside the ceramic, and be protected from future cleaning efforts.

Glazes are an effort to solve this problem by creating an impenetrable barrier between the clay body and the food touching the piece. The main way this is done is simply to apply another layer of silica (with modified chemistry) on top of the clay body that completely melts at the temperature of the firing, thus closing any pores and eliminating possible sites of ingress for pathogens. Additionally, because only a thin barrier covering the entire piece is required for food safety, the glass covering generated by a glaze needs to be only 50 to 200 micrometers thick (1 to 2 human hairs).

GLASS FORMERS: HOLDING A GLAZE TOGETHER

Imagine that you are caramelizing sugar in the kitchen. You take the white sugar in your pot and heat it above 338°F (170°C). The solid sugar melts into a free-flowing liquid that you can pour out into molds to let set into hard candies. During this process, you have used heat to transform highly ordered, crystalline sugar molecules into an amorphous sugar solid, devoid of molecular organization. Believe it or not, this is exactly what is happening when you melt powdered silica from a glaze into a glass.

Silica is a common, crystalline solid of silicon and oxygen and is the most significant structural component of a glaze. When silica is heated hot enough, the highly ordered molecular structure breaks down and the molecules begin to slip and slide past each other and flow freely. But like the caramelized sugar, the silica is cooled too quickly for the molecules of silica to reorganize themselves back into a crystalline state. Instead, they are frozen as a random network of silicon and oxygen atoms. We refer to this amorphous solid as a glass.

The fact that molten silica readily freezes as a glass is hugely significant to how it is used in ceramics. Similar to how the caramelized sugar can be poured and shaped into molds, liquid silica can flow in and around 3-dimensional clay bodies to coat and interpenetrate the porous holes within the bisqueware. This fuses the glass onto the clay body, both sealing it and making the combined structure stronger.

So, why isn't silica the only ingredient in our glazes? It seems like it solves all our problems. Do we even need additional ingredients? Well, there are two big problems. First, silica has a high melting point of 3,110°F (1,710°C), which is 750°F (399°C) higher than cone 10. This means that no studio kiln can even get close to melting pure silica. In fact, outside of an industrial glass making furnace, the only time you probably can see pure silica melting is when a lightning bolt hits beach sand.

The second issue with silica-only glazes is that it flows quickly when melted. This means that as it turns into a liquid it runs like water off vertical surfaces. This isn't necessarily a problem if your pieces are flat tiles, but for many ceramicists, their glaze would be a solid puddle at the bottom of their piece.

CLAYS: KEEPING THINGS TOGETHER

Clay is a complex material, primarily consisting of silica, alumina, and other trace elements. On a microscopic level, clays form highly ordered disc- or sheetlike structures, with particularly high surface areas to volume (imagine stacked molecular plates). Because of the unique structure and chemistry of clays, they possess a static charge on their surface. Due to these properties, when dispersed with other glaze components, clays act as a molecular binder or glue that holds everything together. Perhaps most significantly, this attribute helps the glaze adhere to the ceramic body during the firing process, preventing the melting glass from simply running off of the piece onto the kiln shelf.

Unlike silica, clay minerals do not have a single melting point, but instead undergo complex chemical transformations or decompositions at high temperatures. For example, kaolinite, a common clay mineral used in porcelain and stoneware, does not melt outright but first transforms into another mineral, mullite, and silica. Clay, as well as these new mineral products, help contribute to a glaze's overall melting characteristics and how the glaze interacts with the ceramic body. The overall clay composition and ratio of silica to clay can also determine the final texture (matte versus glossy) of the glaze. We'll discuss this more in the section on the Stull Chart (see page 51).

When water is added to clay, the static-charged, plate structures slide around and incorporate the water to create a gel-like consistency. Why might a studio potter care about making a stable gel? Well, consider that many glaze components are basically crushed up rocks. When rocks are put into water, they often quickly sink to the bottom, which is called *hard panning*. When clay is added to a glaze solution, the resulting gel can trap larger particles and keep them suspended in water for long periods of time. This helps ensure a consistent application and a smooth, even coat when the glaze is applied to bisqueware. For the studio potter, having at least 5 to 10 percent clay is important to maintain the necessary viscosity of the glaze so that particles don't immediately settle out of solution. If the recipe does not have the requisite clay, you can add an additional 1 to 2 percent of bentonite, a highly charged clay good at keeping particles in suspension.

FLUXES: MELTING AT THE RIGHT TEMPERATURE

In science, when one substance goes from solid to liquid, or from liquid to gas (or vice versa), it is called a phase change. For pure materials, these points are defined by a specific temperature. However, you can raise or lower these temperatures by adding small amounts of impurities. We do this in the kitchen when we cook pasta and add table salt (NaCl) to the water. This raises the boiling point of water a few degrees, which helps cook our spaghetti more evenly. Conversely, as roads in winter become icy, we add calcium chloride ($CaCl_2$) or magnesium chloride ($MgCl_2$) to lower the melting point of ice. This means that the solid ice becomes liquid at lower (16°F [–9°C] for $CaCl_2$) and lower (–22°F [–30°C] for $MgCl_2$) temperatures. This is precisely what needs to happen in our glazes. Both silica and alumina have melting points far too high for our kilns. Therefore, we add impurities, called **fluxes**, to the glaze to lower the melting point so that we can melt our glaze at workable temperatures.

The term *flux* is an ancient glassmaking and metallurgical term originating from the Latin word *fluxus*, which means "to flow." In ceramics, the most common fluxes are alkali metal and alkaline earth metals. The alkali metals include lithium oxide (Li_2O), sodium oxide (Na_2O), and potassium oxide (K_2O). These fluxes are highly effective at lowering the melting point of the glaze, but they can actually make the glaze too fluid and can impair its durability. The alkaline earth fluxes are composed of calcium oxide (CaO), magnesium oxide (MgO), strontium oxide (SrO), and barium oxide (BaO). These also lower the melting point, albeit not as strongly as the alkali metals. The alkaline earth metals also help contribute to the stability and hardness of the glaze post firing.

Over time, ceramicists and researchers have experimented with different alkali metal to alkaline earth metal flux ratios to achieve desirable glaze characteristics. It has been found through empirical observation that roughly using 30 percent alkali metal (lithium, sodium, potassium) to 70 percent alkali earth metal (calcium, magnesium, strontium, barium) provides a glaze that melts at a reasonable temperature while maintaining good durability and stability. You can deviate from this ratio to get some interesting special effects (see sidebar on the opposite page), but if you get too far from 30:70, you often begin to lose durability in the process.

Why do we need so many different fluxes? Why can't we find one 30:70 combination that works well? As it turns out, flux choice can have a significant effect on the look and feel of a glaze. All glazes have some silica and alumina (and boron if you are mid- to low-fire). What often makes glazes unique is the alkali metal and alkali earth metal flux choice. Switching out an equivalent amount of calcium oxide for strontium oxide, or from magnesium oxide to barium oxide, can drastically change the appearance, color (if there are additives), flow characteristics, and texture of a glaze. There is considerable room for artistic expression through flux choice.

There are a few additional materials outside of the alkali metal and alkaline earth metals that are added to lower the melting point of a glaze. Specifically, zinc oxide (ZnO) and boron oxide (B_2O_3) are commonly added to get melting temperatures below 2,372°F (1,300°C) (cone 10). In this case, zinc oxide is used in combination with calcium oxide to form what is called a Bristol glaze. Boron is something in-between a glass former and flux. It becomes incorporated into the molecular backbone of the glass (known as a borosilicate glass). It also has a very low melting temperature of 842°F (450°C) and helps significantly reduce the overall melting point of the glaze. Boron oxides are very commonly used in mid- to low-fire glazes.

ADDITIVES

So let's say that you mixed up some silica, alumina, and several fluxes. What would you make? Definitely a clear glaze. Thus far, we have been discussing what components are necessary to make a durable, food-safe glaze that melts at an appropriate temperature, doesn't run off of a pot into a puddle, or hardpan in a glaze bucket. However, when fired, the elements that make up the backbone of our glazes are colorless. If we want our pots to have color, opacity, or special effects, then we need to turn to additives.

Compared to the base recipe, **additives** are listed in addition to the 100 percent total. This allows many of the additives to be swapped out easily without dramatically affecting the chemistry of the glaze. This means a single base glaze recipe can be split up to potentially generate a variety of colors and effects. Additives are also relatively small in quantity when compared to the other ingredients. It is normal to see less than one percent needed for a colorant.

The most common additives are colorants. Potters derive most of their color from metal oxides found in the middle of the transition metals on the periodic table (see page 32). It should be noted that all the elements on the periodic

THE EXTREMES OF SHINOS AND FAKE ASH GLAZES

What happens when you ignore the 30:70 ratio and choose only one type of flux? As it turns out, these glazes are fairly well known: Shinos and fake ash glazes.

Shinos were first developed in the sixteenth century in Japan and were characterized by their thick, milky white appearance, soft velvety texture, and irregular surface patterns and crawling effects. The appeal of Shino glazes often lay in its simplicity and rustic beauty with a *wabi-sabi* aesthetic that emphasized many of the imperfections of the glaze. These traditional Shino glazes have extremely high proportions of alumina and were fluxed almost entirely of potassium oxide and sodium oxide alkali metal with little or no alkaline earth metal.

Fake ash glazes often have a textured surface that resembles the natural deposits, runs, speckles, and rivulets of traditional wood ash glazes. These glazes are often created to replicate the qualities of traditional wood ash glazes with greater consistency and control. To achieve this runny effect, these glazes are fluxed almost exclusively from alkaline earth metals (often calcium or magnesium oxide) without any alkali metal fluxes.

Many Shinos and fake wood ash glazes are often found to be chemically weak and lack the durability of other glazes produced with both types of flux. From a leaching perspective, many Shino recipes are considered food safe as there are no elements of concern that can leach out. Similarly, fake wood ash glazes are only problematic if certain colorants are added. However, both of these glazes often possess physical imperfections such as pinholes, crawling, and crazing, which can potentially impact the food safety of the glaze.

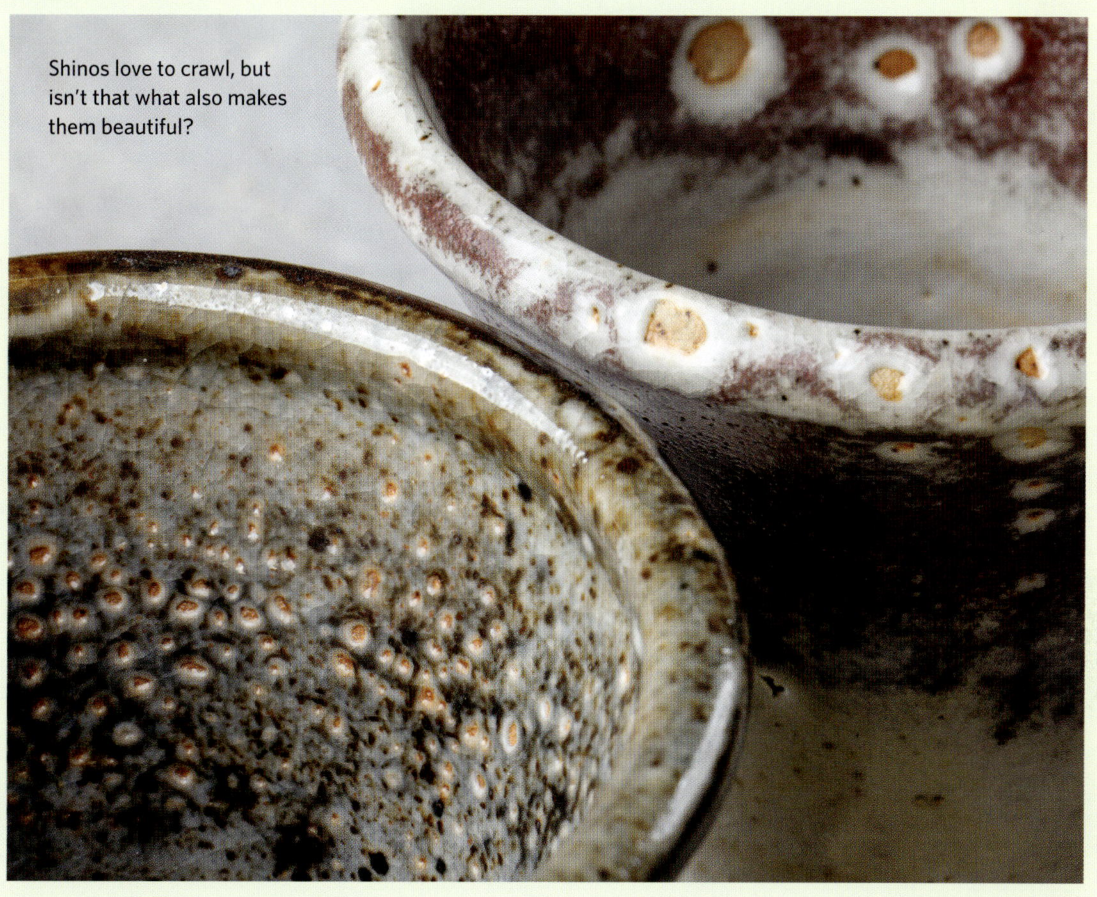

Shinos love to crawl, but isn't that what also makes them beautiful?

table interact with light, but for many metal oxides, those interactions exist in the ultraviolet region making light that we cannot see. However, certain transition metal oxides possess a "goldilocks" arrangement of electrons that can absorb and reflect different types of visible light. This is why chromium oxide (green/pink), manganese dioxide (brown/black), iron oxide (red/brown), cobalt oxide (blue), nickel oxide (purple/brown), and copper oxide (green/red) all exist right next to each other on the periodic table. Metal oxides too far away from this sweet spot lack the proper electron arrangement and cannot interact with visible light in the same way. If you take a look at titanium dioxide (on the far left of the transition metals) and zinc oxide (on the far right), they are too far away from this sweet spot and are colorless to the human eye.

Zirconium oxide sits right below titanium on the left edge of the transition metals and, as such, is also colorless. Potters use this white, high-melting material to their advantage to make their glazes more opaque. Titanium dioxide can also be used to whiten and opacify, but titanium also has a tendency to create unusual, chaotic, and exciting effects to a glaze. You will see both titanium dioxide as well as its mineral form, rutile, as common additives. Rutile is especially interesting, as it is a cheap, chemically impure form of titanium dioxide. Often it's composed of roughly 80 to 85 percent titanium dioxide, with the remainder being iron oxide and other trace elements. It is sold in two forms: dark and light rutile, with dark rutile having a more variable percentage of iron and other metal contaminants. Because these other metals can also be colorants, light rutile is often preferred when consistency is desired (and is the primary form of rutile used in this book's recipes).

Tin oxide is primarily used as an opacifier or in conjunction with certain colorants to create a secondary effect. When it is combined with chrome oxide, a pink or red is created instead of a chartreuse color. Tin can also be used as a whitening agent or opacifier, but this is less common due to its expense.

Bone ash is calcium phosphate, and it's often used in conjunction with iron to create chemically chaotic and beautiful glass structures. Traditionally, cow bones are calcined and crushed to produce bone ash. More recently, synthetic calcium phosphate has become available.

COMPLEX INGREDIENTS MADE SIMPLE

Let's pretend you are baking a cake and that you have various ingredients like whole wheat flour, eggs, butter, sugar, baking soda, and water. Some of these ingredients, like the flour (complex carbohydrates, protein), eggs (protein, fats) or butter (fats, salt), contain multiple important components. Conversely, the sugar (sucrose), baking soda (sodium bicarbonate), and water add only a single piece each to the recipe. Making glazes is similar. Some of the ingredients add one necessary element, while others add several.

Before we get into the weeds of listing everything that can go into a glaze, let's remind ourselves again what are the critical pieces of a glaze: silica, alumina/boron, fluxes, and additives. In an ideal world, each of these four components would be a singular ingredient, and we would be able to add or subtract each piece at will. Want to add a touch more alumina? Sprinkle in a bit more, right? We are going to see that it is not quite that simple. But don't worry, we created charts to simplify things. Let's get into it!

MATERIALS WITH SINGULAR INGREDIENTS

Everything that is a singular ingredient means that you can directly add or remove this component without affecting any other component in your glaze.

GLASS FORMERS	FLUXES	ADDITIVES
Silica	Whiting	Chrome Oxide
	Magnesium Carbonate	Cobalt Oxide
	Strontium Carbonate	Cobalt Carbonate
	Barium Carbonate	Copper Oxide
	Lithium Carbonate	Copper Carbonate
	Sodium Carbonate	Iron Oxide
	Potassium Carbonate	Manganese Dioxide
	Zinc Oxide	Nickel Carbonate
		Nickel Oxide
		Tin Oxide
		Ultrox

Silica: Silica (SiO_2) is our primary glass former and a material with a singular ingredient. Almost every recipe contains silica.

Alumina/Boron: Unfortunately, these are nonavailable as singular ingredients. Aluminum oxide (Al_2O_3) determines whether our glaze is glossy or matte. Boron oxide (B_2O_3) is a glass former and helps lower the overall melting temperature. The sources for both materials contain multiple ingredients.

Fluxes: All of the alkali earth metals can be found as singular ingredients. Whiting ($CaCO_3$), magnesium carbonate ($MgCO_3$), strontium carbonate ($SrCO_3$), and barium carbonate ($BaCO_3$) all release carbon dioxide and are directly converted in the kiln to the desired metal oxides. Magnesium carbonate is not often used, as it is very fluffy when dry and forms thick gels when wet. (Note: There are two multiple-ingredient versions of magnesium oxide called dolomite and talc.)

The alkali metals can be found in a similar fashion, but there is an inherent drawback to using them in glazes. Lithium carbonate (Li_2CO_3), sodium carbonate (Na_2CO_3), and potassium carbonate (K_2CO_3) are all converted in the kiln to the metal oxide just like the above mentioned alkali earth metals. However, these three ingredients all have a physical property that makes them more difficult to apply to pots: These ingredients are all water-soluble to varying degrees. This means that when a potter mixes up a glaze and adds water, these salts begin to dissolve just like table salt dissolves in a glass of water.

This is problematic for two reasons: 1) When the flux is dissolved in the water, its concentration depends on how much water you have in your bucket, and it becomes challenging to know how much is applied when you coat a pot. This means that your recipe might call for 10 percent potassium carbonate, but you might only get 5 percent after the water dries off of your dipped mug and leaves behind the salt residue. 2) The water in a glaze gets drawn into the porous network of holes on a bisque piece through capillary action. When the piece is fired, these alkali metals inside the pot can actually begin to flux the silica and alumina in the clay body. In some cases, this may weaken the piece and/or create structural defects. (Note: There are multiple ingredient versions of all the alkali metals.)

Zinc oxide (ZnO) is also considered a flux, and it is a singular ingredient.

Additives: All of the colorants that we use are considered singular ingredients. This includes chrome oxide (Cr_2O_3), cobalt carbonate ($CoCO_3$), cobalt oxide (CoO), copper carbonate ($CuCO_3$), copper oxide (CuO), iron oxide (Fe_2O_3), manganese carbonate ($MnCO_3$), manganese dioxide (MnO_2), nickel carbonate ($NiCO_3$), and nickel oxide (NiO_2). As you can see, some are supplied as metal oxides and others as metal carbonates, or both. Regardless of the commercial form, they all end up as metal oxides, as metal carbonates release carbon dioxide at high temperatures. Stains are not technically singular ingredients, but because they are designed to not melt at studio kiln temperatures, the additional components do not get incorporated into the glaze, and thus stains should also be thought of as singular ingredient colorants.

Some of the opacifiers, whiteners, and modifiers are also all singular ingredients. This includes Ultrox (zirconium silicate), titanium dioxide, and tin oxide. Ultrox is technically a combination of zirconium and silica, but because of the high melting temperature, Ultrox does not change the amount of silica in a glaze recipe.

MATERIALS WITH MULTIPLE INGREDIENTS

Components with more than one glaze ingredient can be tricky. If you increase or decrease the amount of these materials, you are also changing the amount of another ingredient. This can sometimes create an arithmetic balancing act.

Alumina/Boron: As previously stated, alumina is a critically important glass former and helps determine the texture of the glaze. We get our alumina from two major sources: clays and feldspars.

GLASS FORMERS	FLUXES
All Clays	Wollastonite
Borax	Dolomite
Colemanite	Talc
Ulexite	Spodumene
Gillespie Borate	Feldspars/ Feldspathoids

Interestingly, these two sources are geologically linked. Feldspars are mixtures of three things: alumina, silica, and an alkali metal such as lithium, potassium, or sodium. These minerals make up roughly 50 percent of the composition of the earth's crust. As these rocks are slowly weathered by water, the water-soluble alkali metal (Li+, Na+, K+) is dissolved away into a river or lake, and the feldspar is converted into clay. As such, clays are mixtures of two things: alumina and silica.

Clays are very often evaluated based on their whiteness, with more grey clay sources possessing trace amounts of iron impurities. Many clays are named after the mining company or mine location where the clay deposit is found. For example: EPK stands for the company "Edgar Plastic Kaolin," and OM4 Ball Clay stands for "Old Mine 4."

There are many sources of boron. Borax ($Na_2B_4O_7$) has both boron and a sodium flux and is used in many low-fire glazes. Borax is very water-soluble and can be challenging to effectively use in glazes. Two alternatives with slightly lower solubilities are colemanite ($Ca_2B_6O_{11}$) and ulexite ($NaCaB_5O_6[OH]_6$). Both provide boron along with calcium and/or calcium and sodium.

To get a naturally occurring, ideal boron source with no water solubility, you need to use either Gerstley or Gillespie Borate. These boron sources are complex mixtures of minerals. They are composed of combinations of colemanite, ulexite, and bentonite. This means that they not only add boron, but also silica, alumina, sodium, magnesium, and calcium to a glaze. To the savvy reader, you might realize that Gerstley/Gillispie Borate contain all the necessary components of a glaze (silica, boron, alumina, and two frits). The question might be then: Can we just use this one ingredient? Unfortunately, only at very low-fire temperatures. For these borates, both the silica and alumina content (glass formers) is low compared to the boron and flux (melting agents). This means that the glaze melts at a very low temperature and when heated too high (mid- and high-fire) makes puddles on the kiln shelf. To fix this for mid-fire glazes, it's necessary to add silica and alumina to the recipe.

Fluxes: As previously stated, most of the alkaline earth fluxes are single component ingredients. There are three multi-component fluxes in this category. Talc ($Mg_3Si_4O_{10}[OH]_2$) is a multicomponent magnesium source that also adds silica. Wollastonite ($CaSiO_3$) adds both calcium and silica. Dolomite ($CaMg[CO_3]_2$) adds two fluxes: calcium and magnesium. As magnesium sources, dolomite and talc can be advantageous to using magnesium carbonate, as they are easier to handle and mix into a glaze.

Due to the water solubility issues of some alkali metal fluxes (lithium carbonate, sodium carbonate, potassium carbonate), potters use insoluble feldsparlike minerals as their alkali metal flux source. In all cases, these minerals not only add the flux, but also silica and alumina to the glaze. Spodumene ($LiAl[SiO_3]_2$) is an insoluble lithium flux source. The other feldsparlike minerals are mixes of potassium and sodium fluxes in varying amounts. Even ingredients listed as sodium (soda) feldspar or potassium (potash) feldspar are combinations of both fluxes. For example: Minspar Feldspar is high in sodium and low in potassium, while G-200 Feldspar, G-200 EU Feldspar, and Mahavir Potash Feldspar are high in potassium and low in sodium. Nepheline syenite, a particularly popular flux, adds 75 percent sodium and 25 percent potassium flux.

WHAT EXACTLY IS A FRIT?

Is there a one-stop shop solution to complex ingredients? In a word: frits. Frits are idealized combinations of silica, alumina, boron, and one or more fluxes. They are created by first superheating precise mixtures of raw mineral components until molten glass is formed. Then, the molten mixture is instantly cooled in water. The resulting glass is crushed into a fine, insoluble powder. These frits are designed to be durable glazes that melt at specific temperatures. For example, Ferro Frit 3124 is a glossy glaze that melts perfectly at cone 04. In fact, you can make an entire glaze with just this one ingredient (although it might hardpan without any additional clay).

There are a variety of types of frits for a variety of purposes, and they are often denoted by a string of numbers. This can lead to some confusion, as frits can have similar numbers but are not 1:1 exchangeable as they may not have similar chemistry. Despite this compositional variability for commercial frits, almost all are made up of silica, alumina, boron, and often more than one type of flux. As seen in the recipes in chapter 4, Ferro Frit 3134 is a particularly common boron source seen in mid-fire glazes.

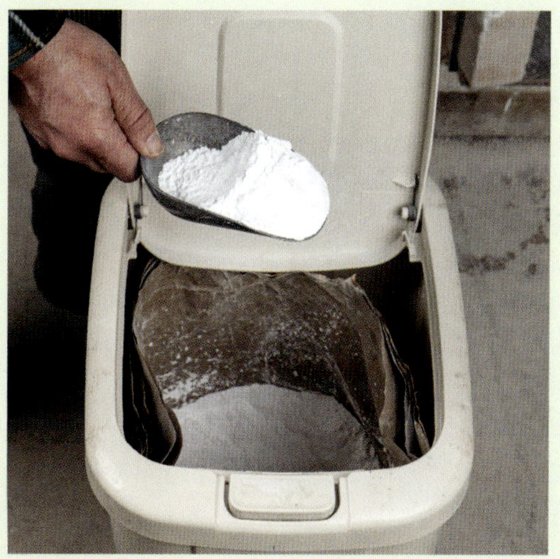

Frits are glazes that have a specifically formulated chemical content that are fired and then pulverized.

UMF FORMULA AND STULL CHARTS MADE SIMPLE

UMF FORMULA: IMPORTANT FEATURES

When you flip over a package of potato chips you get an instant breakdown of the nutritional information (or lack thereof). The carbohydrate, fat, and protein macromolecules are broken down by amounts and daily recommended percentages. This is what the **Unity Molecular Formula**, or **UMF**, does for glazes. It provides a standardized way to understand and compare glaze compositions by expressing the major components of the glaze (silica, alumina, and fluxes) in terms of their molecular equivalents. This allows ceramicists to adjust and compare different glazes more accurately and predict their behavior during firing.

In a nutshell, the UMF simplifies the chemistry of glazes by converting the complex raw material recipe into a standardized format. Here's how it works: First, each raw material is broken down into its constituent oxides. For example, spodumene would contain silica, alumina, and lithium oxide (flux). Using the molecular weights of these elements, they are converted from weight percentages (what you weighed out on a balance) into molecular equivalents (based on how much each atom weighs). All of the flux oxides (like Li_2O, K_2O, Na_2O, CaO, MgO, etc.) are added up and normalized to 1.0. In doing so, a ratio of silica and alumina to flux is determined.

This might seem like a lot of work, and it definitely does require a series of calculations, but by using the UMF a ceramicist can quickly get at several pieces of important information. When the flux is normalized to 1.0, they can easily see whether the alkali metal flux to alkali earth metal flux ratio is close to ideal (0.3:0.7). As mentioned earlier, it is thought that deviating too far from this ratio can affect the durability of a glaze. The UMF can also be used to look at the silica to alumina ratio in a glaze. A higher silica-to-alumina ratio might result in a glossier glaze, while a higher alumina content might make the glaze more matte.

STULL CHARTS: A WAY TO VISUALIZE GLAZE COMPOSITION

A **Stull chart** (opposite) uses the UMF information to provide a visual framework for understanding how silica and alumina ratios influence glaze characteristics. Similar to the UMF, the chart is displayed in molecular equivalents compared to how much flux is in the recipe, with the x-axis showing increasing amounts of silica and the y-axis alumina.

Experimentally, if you keep the flux constant and vary the silica and alumina, you can create a series of unique glazes that could be represented as points over the entire chart. These glazes would teach you three things: First, recipes too high in either silica or alumina don't melt properly and produce underfired, non-food-safe glazes. Second, as the total amount of silica and alumina increases in proportion to the flux, you need higher and higher temperatures to completely melt the glaze. This means that if you have too much glass formers and not enough flux the glaze will be underfired. Conversely, if you have a lot of flux and very little silica and alumina the glaze will melt too vigorously and run off of your pieces.

Third, the center region of the Stull chart where glazes are considered fully melted is actually divided into three unique regions: mattes, semi-mattes, and glossy. For many recipes, having a silica to alumina ratio of 5:1 or greater will produce a glossy glaze. Having slightly less than this ratio (4:1 or less) produces semi-matte and matte glazes.

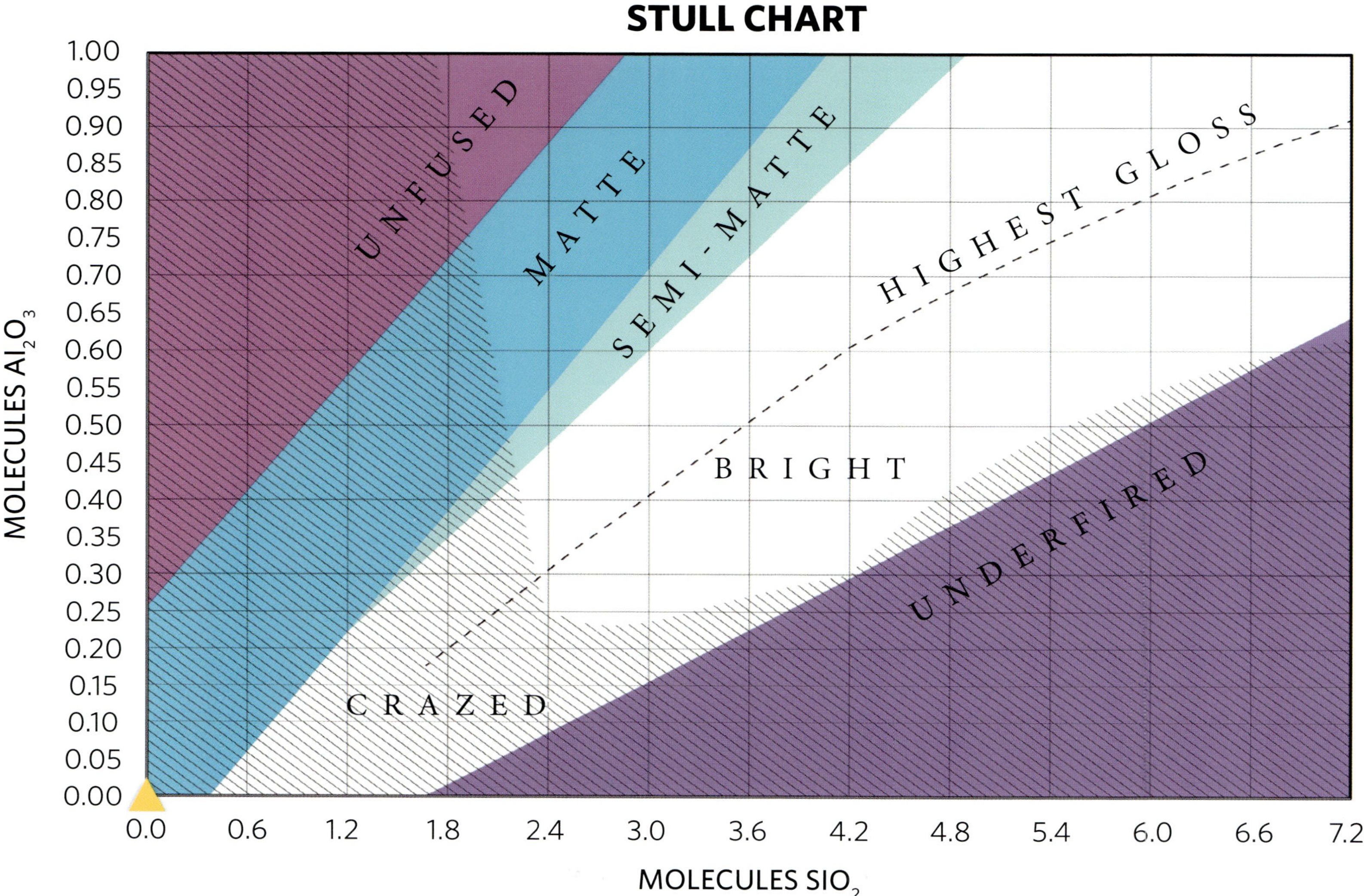
STULL CHART
UNFUSED
MATTE
SEMI-MATTE
HIGHEST GLOSS
BRIGHT
CRAZED
UNDERFIRED
MOLECULES Al_2O_3
1.00
0.95
0.90
0.85
0.80
0.75
0.70
0.65
0.60
0.55
0.50
0.45
0.40
0.35
0.30
0.25
0.20
0.15
0.10
0.05
0.00
0.0
0.6
1.2
1.8
2.4
3.0
3.6
4.2
4.8
5.4
6.0
6.6
7.2
MOLECULES SIO_2

THE CHALLENGES OF MATTE GLAZES

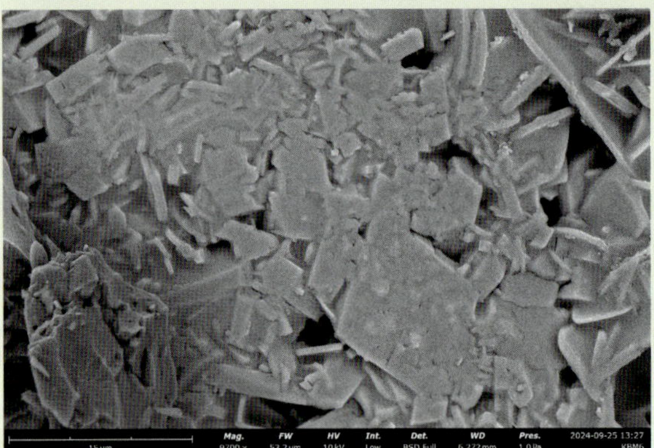

SEM image of a true matte glaze with microcrystals across the entirety of the surface (scale of 15 micrometers).

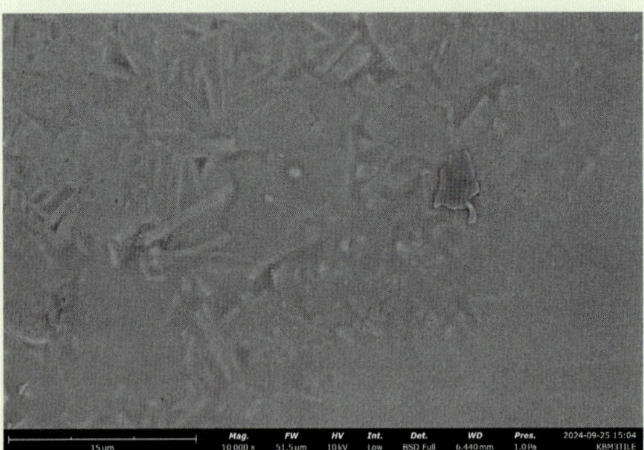

A semi-matte glaze with dispersed crystals and glossy sections.

A glossy glaze with a smooth surface.

Matte glazes are an interesting example of fully melted glazes that form microcrystals on their surface as they cool. Although they feel smooth and silky to our fingers, on the nanoscale they have a broken and cavernous surface. Indeed, when compared to the near-blank landscape of a glossy glaze, the matte glaze contains a mind-boggling number of pockets and nanometer-size canyons. Strangely, this means that the matte glaze actually has considerably more surface area than a glossy glaze. If you had nanotweezers and could grab the edges of a matte glaze and pull it flat like a glossy glaze, you would find that, like unfolding a piece of origami, the surface has grown by several times.

This significantly larger surface area may have a profound impact on the durability of the glaze and chemical leaching. Because there is so much more area to interact with food, there is more opportunity for the glaze to leach out metals of concern. In all our analyses, matte and semi-matte glazes tend to leach out higher amounts of metals than the corresponding glossy glaze would. Indeed, it can be incredibly challenging to find matte glazes that can pass our standards, and we very often resort to using stains as safe alternatives for colorants.

As an example of this, we can look at a modified Katz-Burke Matte (page 76). We created a series of this glaze that sequentially increased the amount of silica but kept everything else the same. Effectively, this made a horizontal line on the Stull chart moving from matte, to semi-matte, to glossy. We colored each of these glazes with 1.0 percent cobalt carbonate to make beautiful blue tiles. At left, you can see the SEM images of the surface of each of these tiles as they transition from matte to glossy. When we analyze the cobalt leach test for each of these tiles, we see that the gloss variant is food safe and leaches only 0.2 ppm (max 0.5 ppm). The semi-matte glaze leaches cobalt above the limit at 0.65 ppm. And the matte glaze tile dramatically increases to 2.1 ppm, four times above the limit. This effect has been replicated with over a dozen different matte glazes at both mid- and high-fire.

THE ART OF SCIENCE

John Britt

johnbrittpottery.com   Instagram @john.britt1

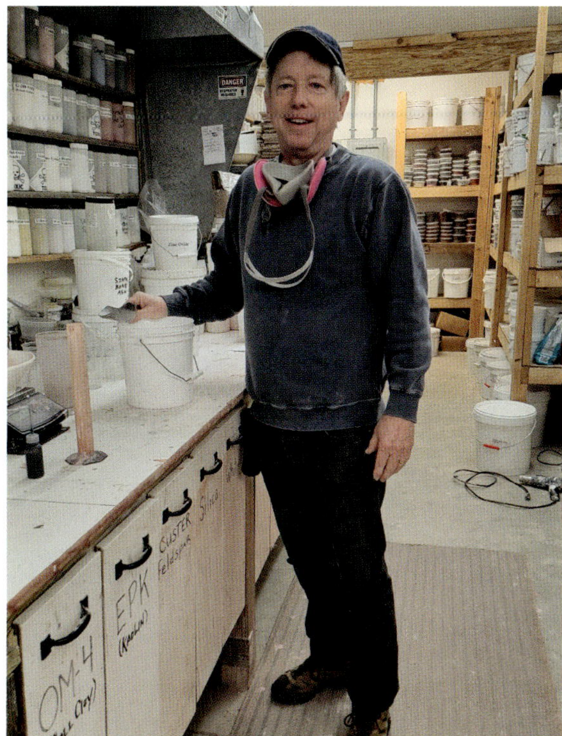

Cooking up something new in the glaze kitchen.

Who says there's no such thing as a free lunch? John Britt has been feeding the masses for years. John has given away more educational content on the internet than anyone else we know. With an irreverent style and the ability to explain complex concepts in easy-to-understand terms, John's videos are informative, fun, and illuminating. Since we've known John, we've seen him push the whole field forward through his in-person classes and workshops, online presentations, and writing for periodicals, not to mention his own books. *The Complete Guide to Mid-Range Glazes* and *The Complete Guide to High-Fire Glazes* should be staples in every studio. We were honored to have John as our Tech Editor for the first two books in the series, but it's time he got his much-deserved feature. While his career is far from over, we believe John Britt should be a first ballot inductee in the Glazing Hall of Fame.

(Note that this interview was done in conversational form and transcribed.)

AMAZING GLAZE FOOD-SAFE RECIPES: *What does food safe mean to you?*

JOHN BRITT: The first thing I always ask is: what's the definition? Food safe technically means: no lead or cadmium. So technically all the glazes in my book, without inclusion stains, are food safe. But that's not what potters want. They want glazes that are stable, that don't leach, cutlery mark, craze, et cetera. This is a very high bar that is not even met by producers of store-bought glazes. But this is what potters want. First, I always encourage them to use liner glazes. That means that there is nothing to leach out. I use a lot of iron glazes and those are not very toxic, in comparison to other colorants. So, that keeps things fairly easy. Then I try to use glazes that are high in silica and alumina so the coloring oxides are held in the glaze matrix and won't leach. The third caveat is that I try to keep the coloring oxides as low as possible to still get the colors I want. Finally, if you're a potter, you should always practice safe lab technique; wear a dust mask (or fume mask if you are doing lusters) and gloves when making glazes. Keep the dust down in your studio by regularly washing your apron/clothes, use a damp towel, and wet mop (no sweeping).

If you do those things then I think pottery is extremely safe. I try to use the knowledge we've gained: no lead, no cadmium, and try to keep things like barium carbonate and colorants as low as possible. I would read the SDS sheets for the materials in my studio and try to keep out any that are too dangerous.

AGFSR: *With all the information currently available, where do you think the ceramic community is going in the future?*

JOHN: I don't know where it's going, but it's going there fast! When you start looking on social media, Instagram, et cetera, and you see all the stuff that's just flooding in there every day it is amazing. But it is just a massive amount of totally unmoderated content that can be overwhelming. Which is good

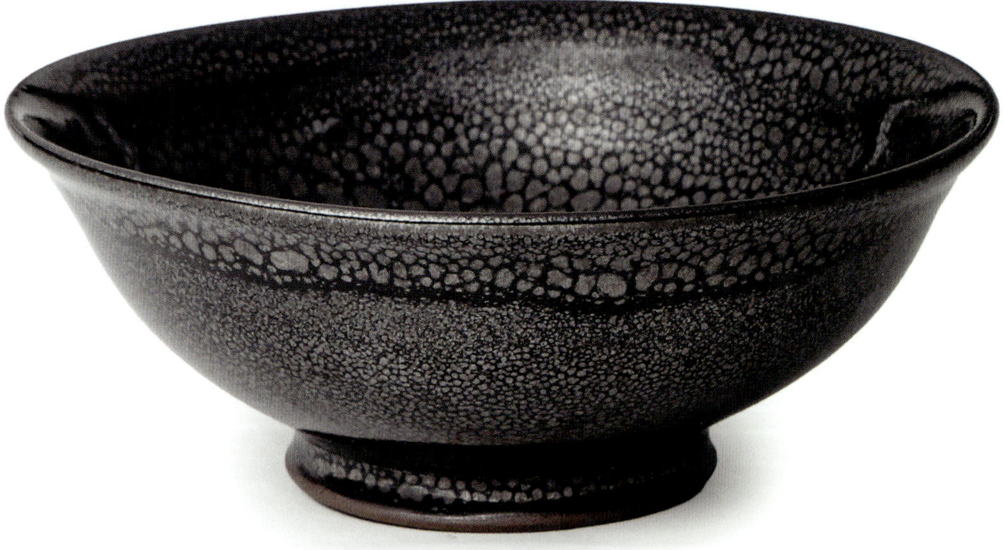

Classic oil spot effect on this footed bowl. Notice the double dip at the top.

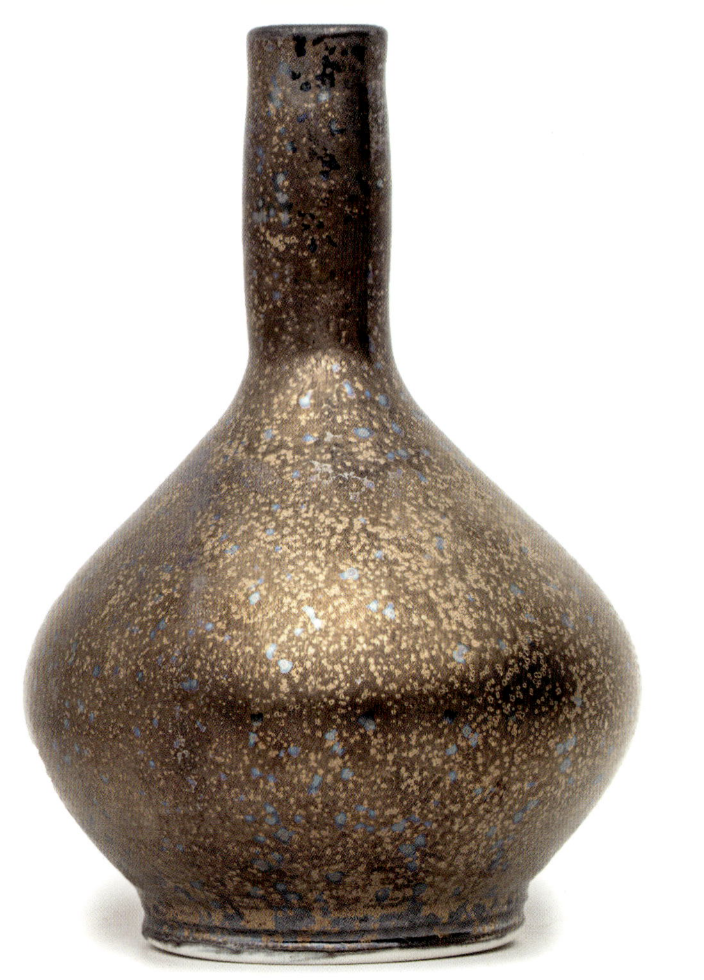

With careful formulation, glaze can imitate precious metals like copper and bronze.

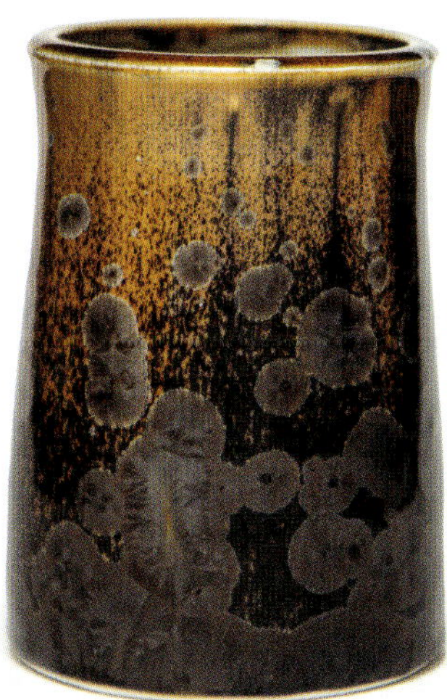

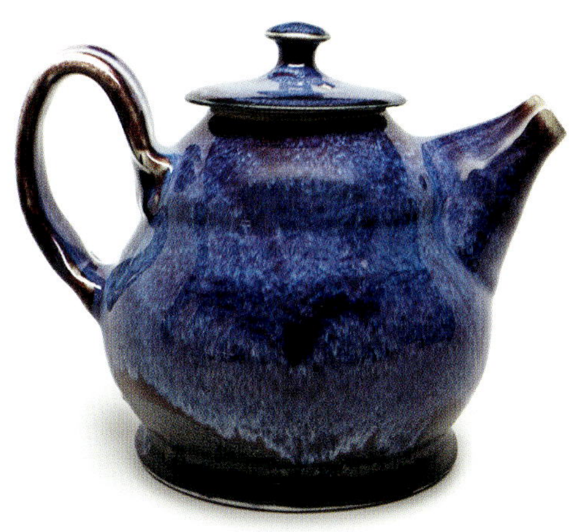

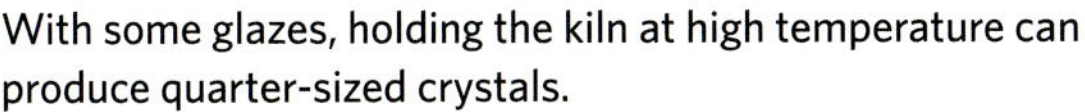

With some glazes, holding the kiln at high temperature can produce quarter-sized crystals.

This teapot uses a food-safe liner glaze.

information? And which is not? So maybe that is where this book comes in. It will be nice to have something that's saying, here, this is what we've tested, and this has good science behind it. It's not just somebody randomly saying it a thousand times, and then people believing it.

AGFSR: *Glaze and clay body chemistry sit at the intersection of science and art. So for you, what do you think are some of the challenges that this creates, and how do you overcome these barriers when it comes to communicating more scientific ideas to nonscientists?*

JOHN: You have two schools of thought: One school is using the approach of industrial ceramics, and then the other school is using the artistic approach to create beautiful things. So now there is a trend to use the industrial side as the standard and trying to impose that on the whole field. Then I'm over here with all the artists. When you say blue to them, they know that there are 10,000 shades of blue, but they want a specific type of blue. Some of these artists will see and actually feel the colors. So, it is not just "blue." This is the other side of the industrial approach.

You can't expect everybody to be a scientist and a mathematician. But you also don't want to just say, "Oh, it doesn't matter and just do whatever you want." Artists, also, just want good stable glazes that pass standards. But because it is so complicated, sometimes the artists feel like they don't know enough so that freezes them, and then they throw their hands up. I try to come down somewhere in between. Give the artists some base glazes and concepts of how to make stable glazes without requiring them to become mathematicians and industrial ceramicists. Then show them where to have their glazes tested so they know for sure.

Education is critical to give artists knowledge and agency. It helps to be able to say what sodium oxide does but sometimes I feel like we get too deep into the technical stuff. We don't need to get into valence and electron shells, but we do want them to know that sodium oxide has the highest expansion/contraction and can be the cause of crazing, or that barium carbonate gives brightly colored matte glazes but can be toxic. That is helpful. We want students and artists to make informed decisions about safety and yet feel free to get the colors and textures they want. I try to give people enough information to function safely and also show them places to go to if they want to delve deeper.

AGFSR: *You've given away so much free content on YouTube, and pottery videos are notoriously difficult to monetize. It's obviously such a passion project for you. What motivates that?*

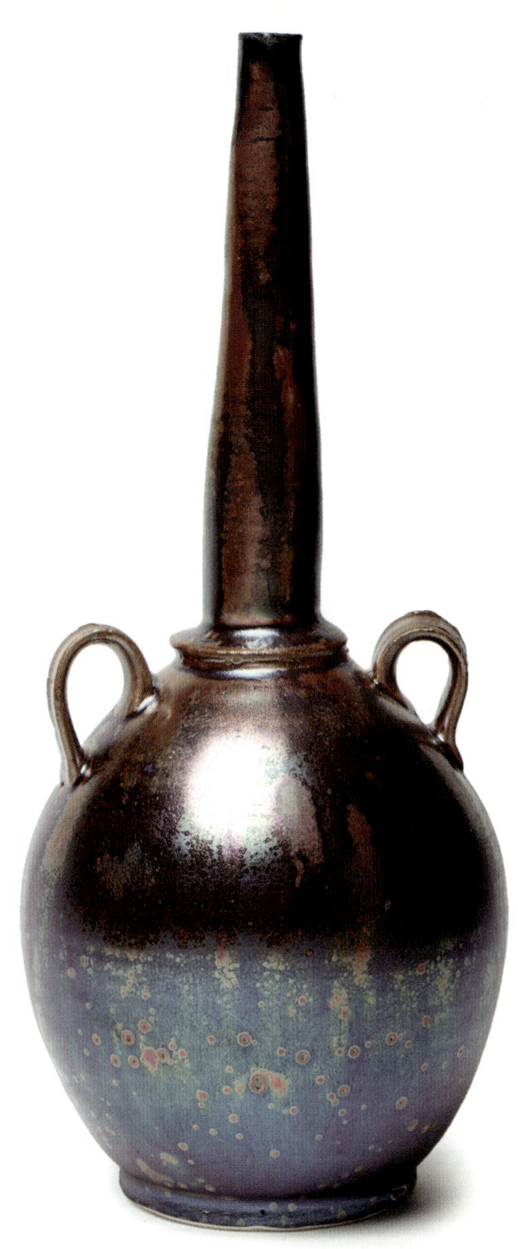

A bit of iridescence makes this piece exciting.

JOHN: When I started in pottery, and since I didn't go to school for it, there was no one to talk to. I don't know if you remember the old days, but I can put on my grandpa hat here. We either submitted questions to Ceramics Monthly and waited a month or two to get the answer, or we would wait for a whole year to go to NCECA (National Conference on Education in the Ceramic Arts) and ask questions to the Glaze Doctors. It was just really kind of lean out there.

I had read that William Howson Taylor of Ruskin Pottery discovered a sang-de-boeuf glaze (notoriously difficult at that time) in the early 1900s but had burnt all his recipes and notes before his death. I thought that was a tragedy and so was the common practice of secrecy and hiding information about glazes and firing. So, I decided right then and there that I would freely share everything. When the internet came along in the 1990s, I just decided, I'm going to tell people the things to learn and try to spread glaze knowledge that way.

And I have a philosophical point of view that knowledge is a fundamental human right. It creates a level playing field, and it shouldn't be only for those who can afford it. So, I started making YouTube videos, and I had a blog early on. Now content has shifted to each person's social media pages, and you can get outstanding content in a 2-minute "story."

I don't know if my content is important in the grand scheme of things, the meaning of life, et cetera, but if you are doing pottery, I think it's important to be able to find good information. Knowledge gives people agency and helps them be able to do stuff themselves, instead of being always afraid and looking for an "expert" to tell them what to do. That's the main thing. When I took a glaze class at Alfred from Val Cushing in the summer of 1994, the biggest thing was that it made me feel free to change some ingredients, add some things, do something different, and know the world's not going to come to an end. Then, once you're on that sort of stairway, you can move up and the amazing world of glazing opens up to you.

GALLERY

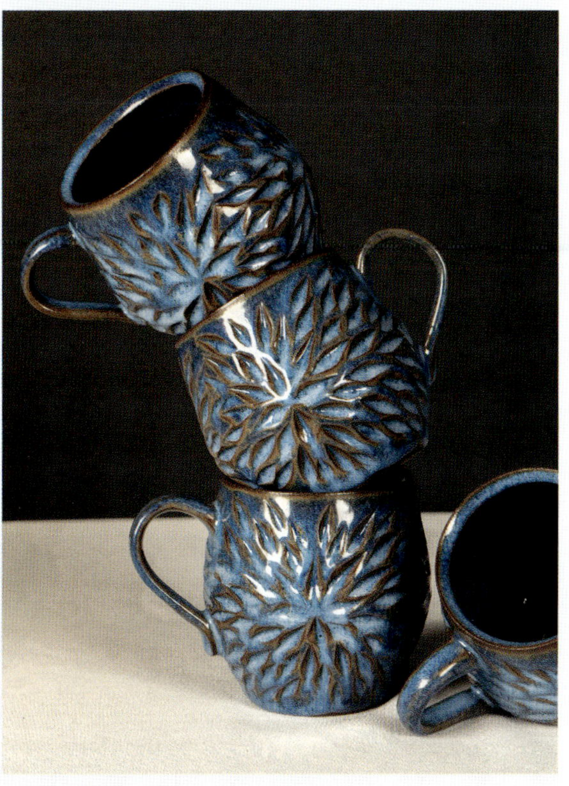

Carved Mug Stack. Channa Alterman.
A food-safe glaze is a must for mugs. Finding one that pools beautifully is a bonus.

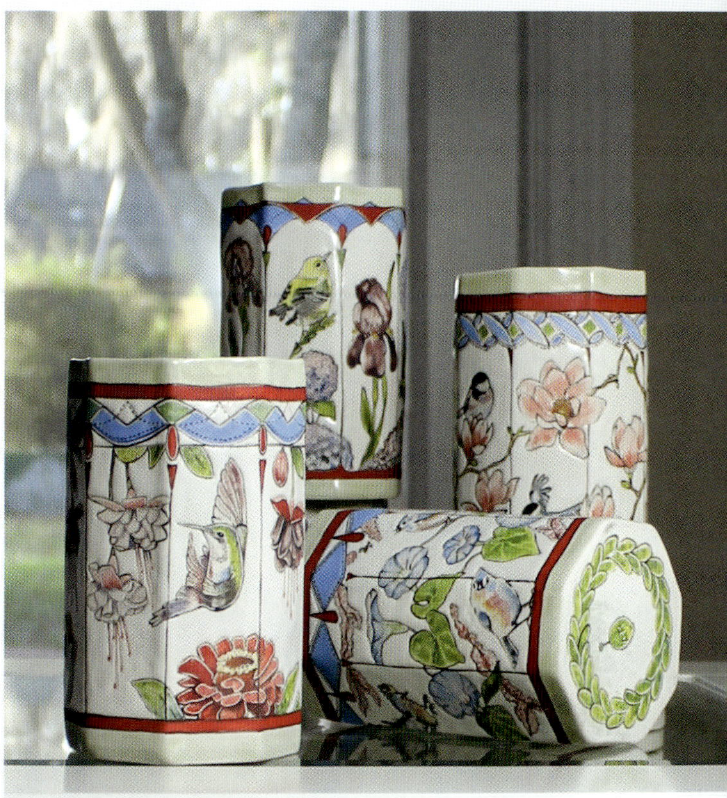

Vase Grouping. Ann Ruel.
Ann creates a narrative across the surface of these classic, angular forms.

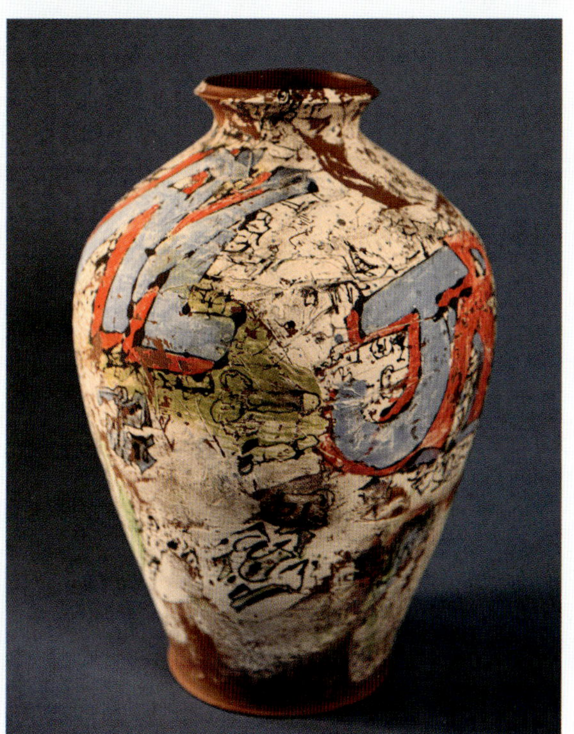

Vase. Alex Thullen.
A bit of texture. A bit of smooth. This glaze works well over both.

Graffiti Vase. Jason Rojas.
As long as you glaze the interior of a piece, the exterior can be unglazed without compromising function.

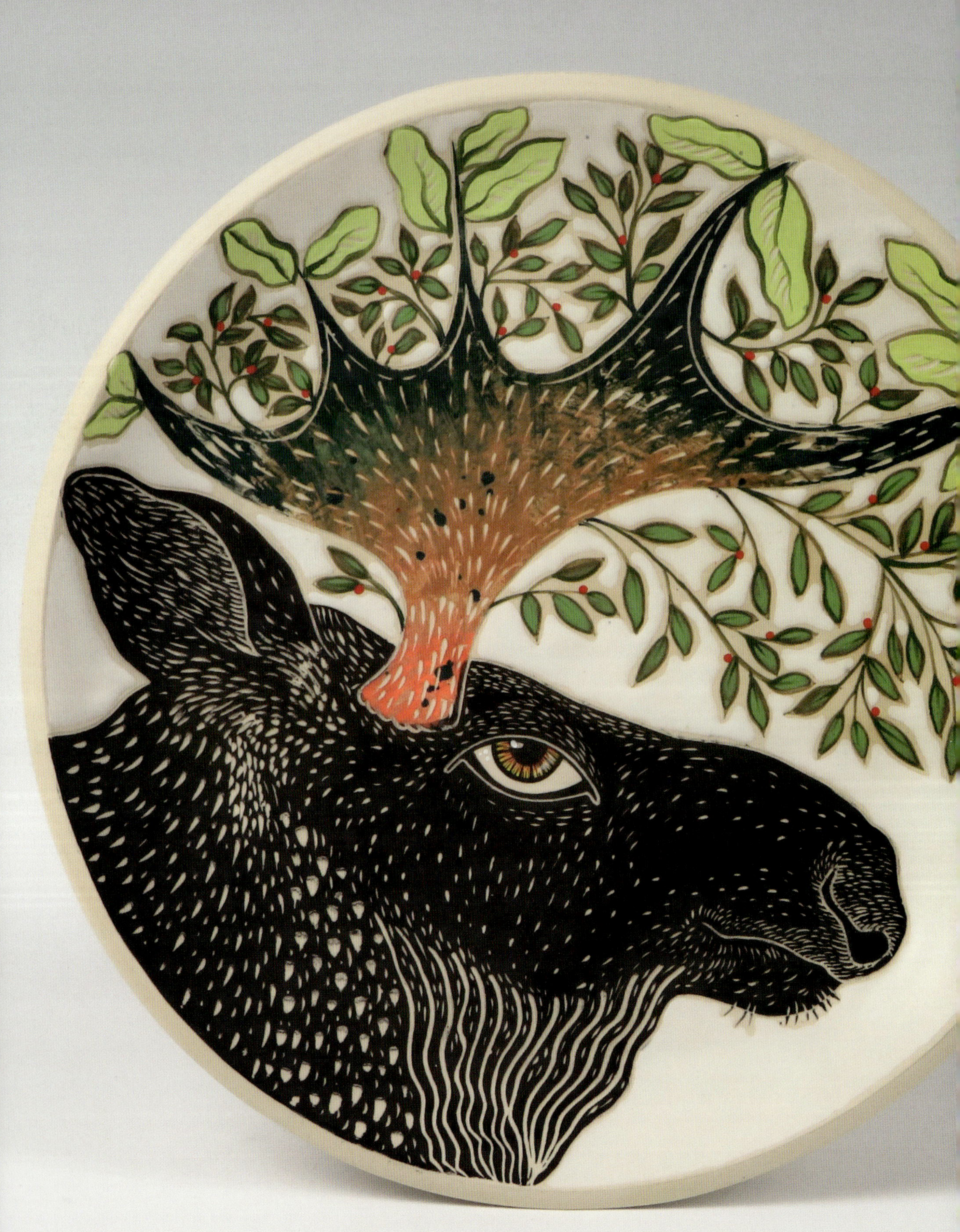

4

Food-Safe Glaze Recipes and Combinations

AT LONG LAST, here it is! Now that we've developed a deeper understanding of what makes up a glaze, we'll move on to the tested food-safe recipes themselves. But first, let's take a look at the best practices for how to mix up these glazes.

Moose Platter. Jennifer Rosseter.

MIXING GLAZES SAFELY

Our exploration of food-safe glazes would not be complete without going over the best practices for safely mixing and applying glazes. It does little good to produce a food-safe product if we expose ourselves to the same chemicals we are trying to avoid in our finished product while creating it in the studio.

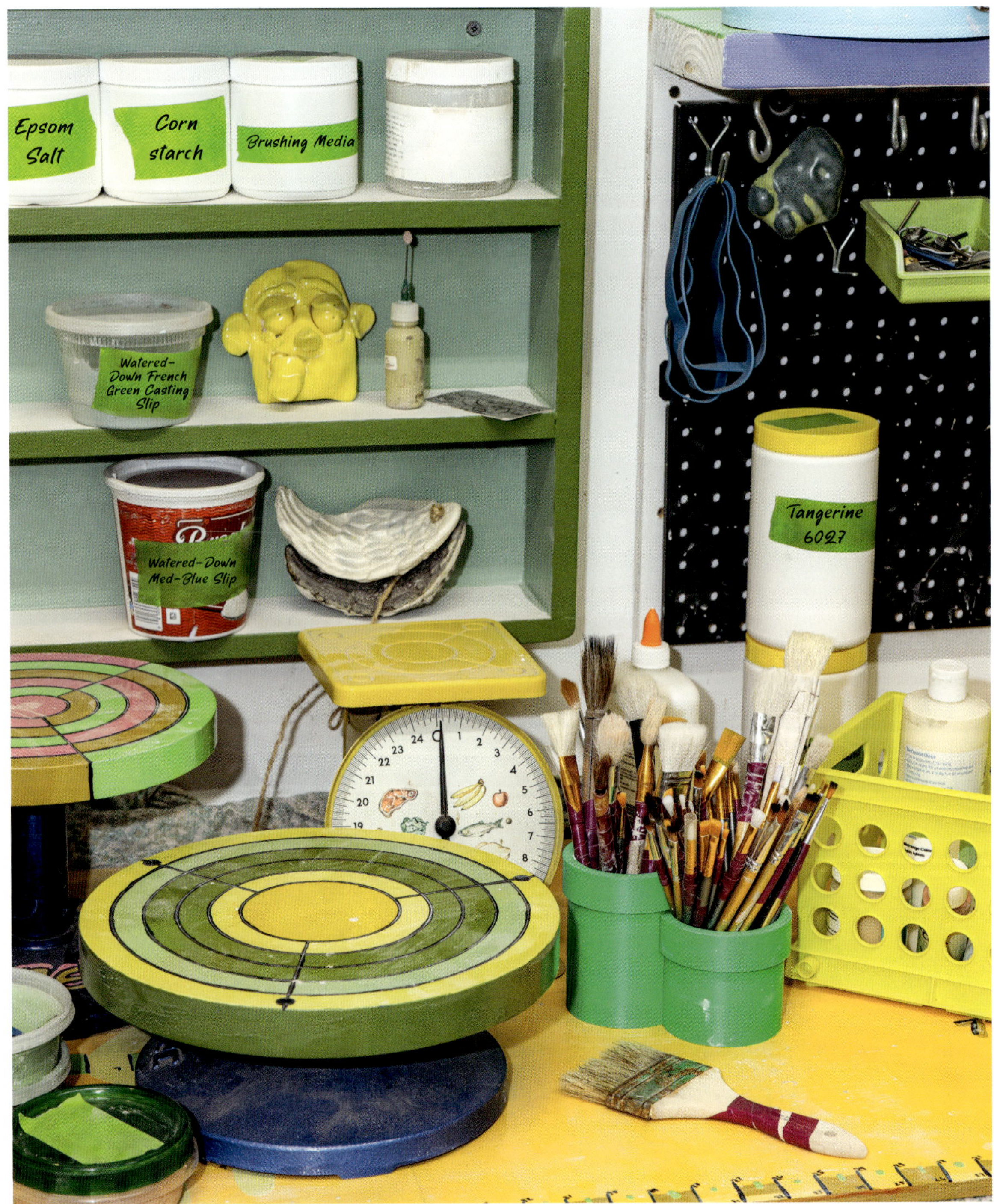

Pez Rivera's studio at Odyssey ClayWorks is neatly organized and aesthetically pleasing.

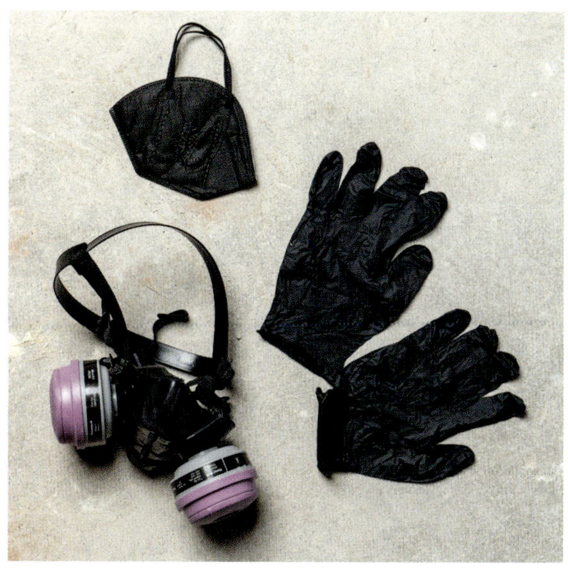
A KN-95 dust mask, nitrile gloves, and a respirator with filters.

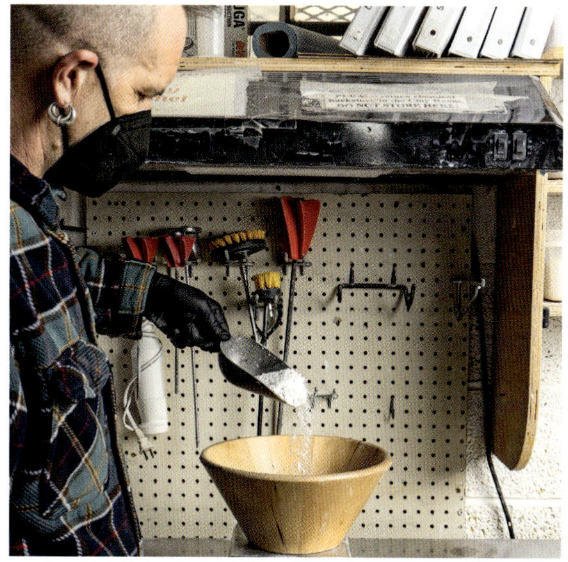
Wear PPE and weigh out glaze materials underneath a fume hood or spray booth.

Let's start with the types of contact you may have with glaze materials in their dry and wet forms. If you mix your own glazes, you'll be transporting dry materials from your supplier, storing them at your studio, and finally weighing them out into your mixing bucket. The dry, pulverized powders easily disperse into the air, so transport them in the trunk of your car or the bed of your truck, not in the cabin of your vehicle. Once at the studio, store these materials in clearly labeled containers with sealed lids or that otherwise limit dust.

You must wear a KN-95 mask or a filtered respirator whenever weighing out materials or transferring dry materials from one container to another. You can also wear nitrile gloves to keep the materials off your skin, though we would estimate that 99 percent of clay artists don't wear gloves. Do all the measuring and transferring of materials in a well-ventilated area, either outside or under a fume hood. If you have a spray booth with a fan vent, it can double as a nice place to mix and slake your glazes without creating a localized dust cloud.

Once your glaze is slaked with water and thoroughly mixed, you can take off the mask. Note that in a room that does not have a vent specifically for mixing glazes, the particulate matter can remain in the air for up to six hours, in which case you would want to leave it on! You may also want to continue to wear the gloves. You'll always want to avoid exposing any cuts or scrapes to avoid unnecessary exposure.

Despite the name, there should be no food or drink in the glaze kitchen! And make sure you wash your hands whenever you take a break to have a snack.

And a word to the wise: When applying glazes, fill up a bucket of water and keep a large automotive sponge on hand to quickly clean up the inevitable spills and drips and bloops. If glaze does splash and hit you in the eye or in your mouth, immediately rinse with as much water as you can. Dilution is the solution. This rarely happens, but many studios keep an eye rinse station next to the sink as a precaution.

There is often a fear of doing long term damage to our health when we hear terms like silicosis, but it is actually extremely rare and mostly affects mine and industrial workers, not studio potters. Heed the precautions in this chapter and you'll be golden. Common sense and a "Safety First!" attitude will ensure that we are able to spend a long and lovely life in the studio.

LINERS AND THE SAFE USE OF UNSTABLE GLAZES

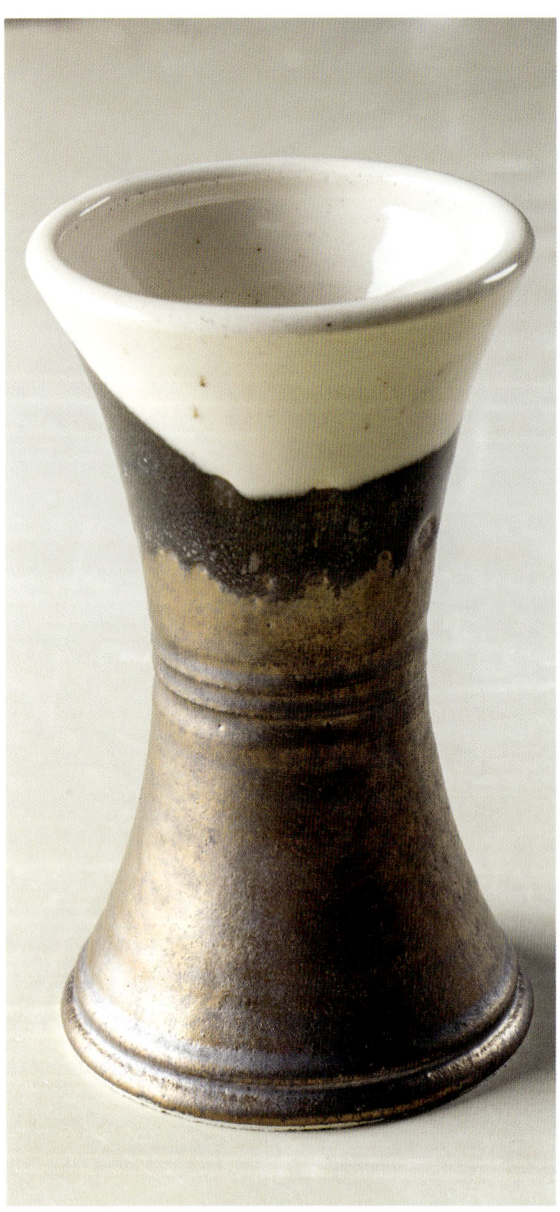

Gold Metallic failed our tests but is an Amazing Glaze, so we lined this tumbler with Donte's Lumos and overlapped the two, creating an exciting third color to complete the combo.

This chapter is full of recipes that passed our stringent testing standards. When mixed and fired appropriately, these glazes can be used anywhere on your work, including as a "liner" glaze, a proven food-safe glaze that fits the clay body and doesn't leach. There are also a couple glazes we tested that failed our standards. Our view is that there are no bad glazes, and ones that fail our tests can still be safely used on the outside or non-food bearing surfaces of our work. Importantly, there is no evidence that you can absorb heavy metals in a fired glaze simply by picking the piece up and putting it to your lips.

To get the best results when using a liner glaze, we highly recommend breaking your glazing into two sessions. In order to glaze only the inside of the piece, pour glaze, using a funnel, if necessary, into the pot and pour back out while rotating the piece to get an even coat.

Wait overnight! When you glaze the inside of a piece, the glaze (and therefore the water in the glaze) migrates through the porous bisque and can affect the amount of glaze that can be absorbed when you glaze the outside. The key is to let the piece dry overnight. You can force dry it with a fan, too, if you are in a hurry, but it still might take an hour. Once the water from the glaze has evaporated out, you can glaze the outside of the piece. You can decide if you want the liner glaze to cover the lip of your pot, in which case you may want to wax over it before glazing the outside to get a clean line.

"Unstable" glazes may be used on the outside or non-food bearing surfaces of the work. We love the metallic sheen of the Cone 6 Gold Metallic glaze, but it was one of our worst offenders in the leaching category. However, we lined this cup and dipped the top third with Donte's Lumos, allowed that to dry, then dipped the bottom three-fourths of the outside in Gold Metallic. The overlap created a dynamic shiny black that made for a great two-glaze combination.

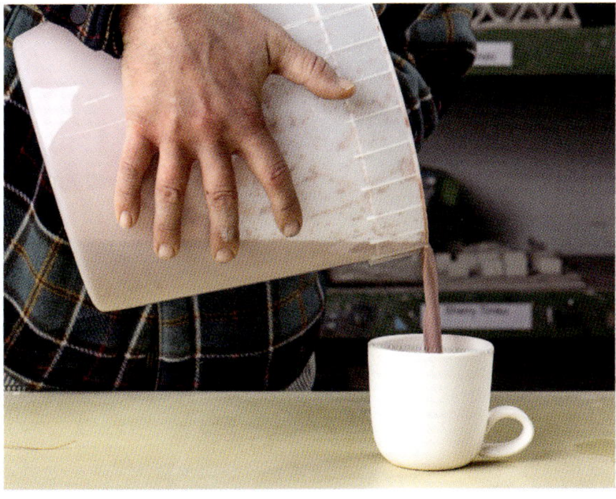

1. Pouring the liner glaze into the pot.

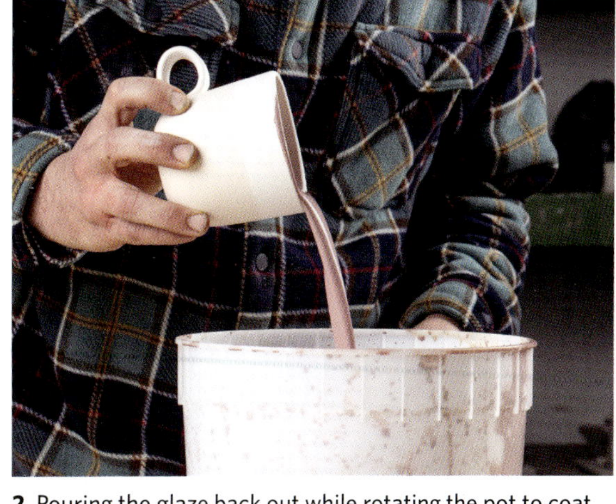

2. Pouring the glaze back out while rotating the pot to coat the entire interior.

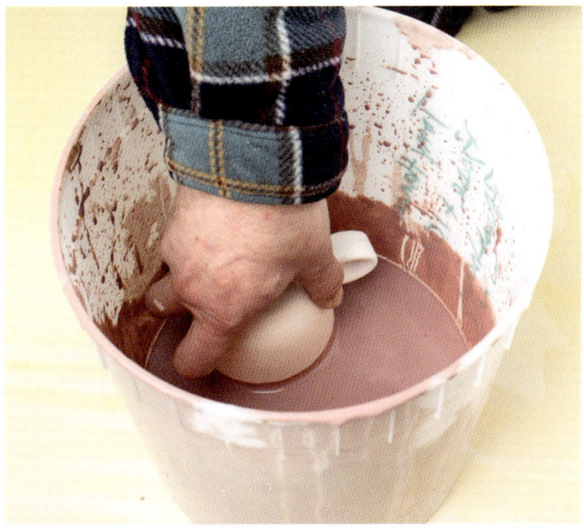

3. Dipping the rim in liner glaze. You can decide how far down you want to go.

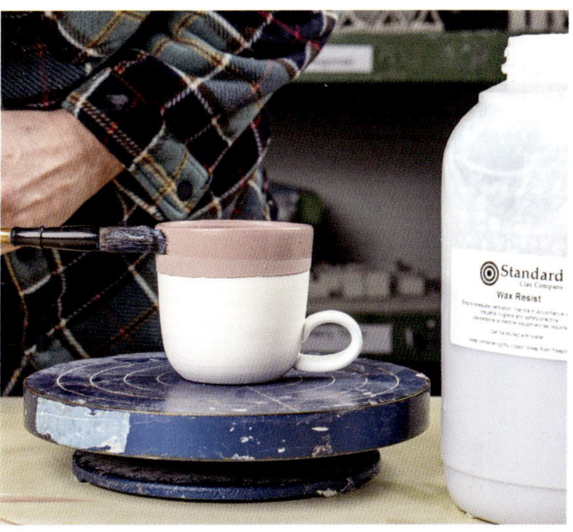

4. If you want a clean line between the two glazes, carefully wax over the first glaze with a soft bristle brush and let dry for at least 15 minutes.

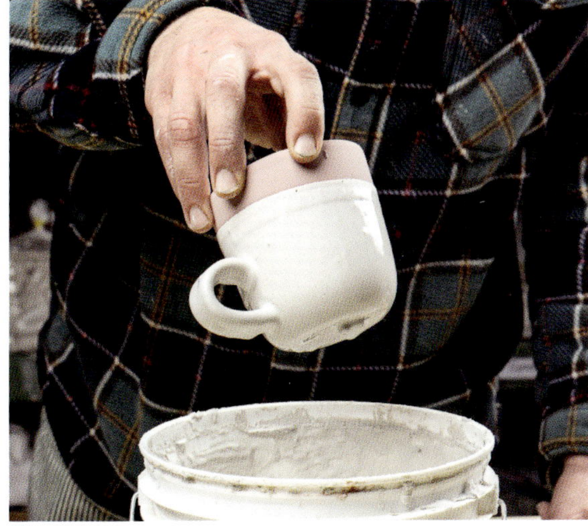

5. Dipping the exterior. In this case, we did not apply wax and are overlapping the two glazes to create a third color.

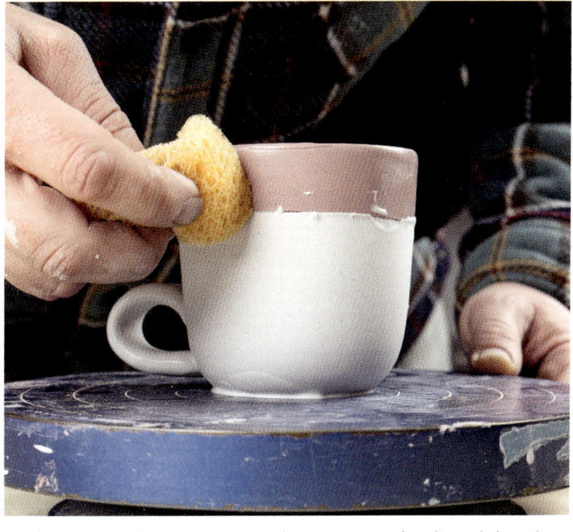

6. If you waxed your piece, make sure to go back and detail the waxed area with a sponge to remove any unwanted glaze.

BEAUTIFUL GLAZES THAT FAILED

Some of the glazes that did not pass our tests were just too pretty to not include in this book. All of these should be used with a liner glaze.

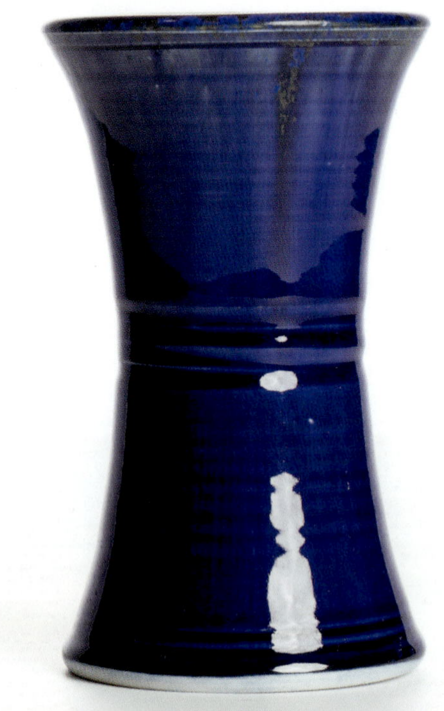

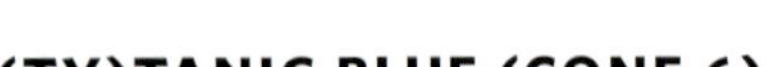

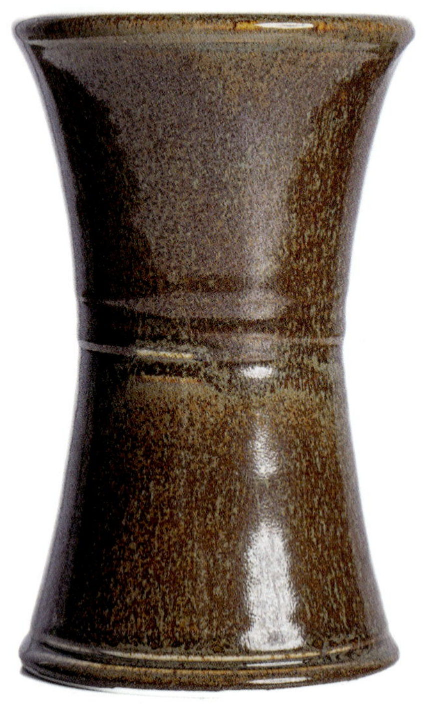

(TY)TANIC BLUE (CONE 6)

INGREDIENTS	AMOUNTS
G-200 Feldspar	31.00
Zinc Oxide	25.00
Whiting	17.00
Silica	15.00
OM4 Ball Clay	8.00
Ferro Frit 3134	4.00
Total	**100.00**

Also Add:

Cobalt Oxide	3.00
Lithium Carbonate	3.00
Titanium Dioxide	3.00

NOTES:
Chemical Analysis:
Cobalt: 8.7 ppm (max 0.5 ppm)—Fail
Lithium: 2.1 ppm (max 0.06 ppm)—Fail
Zinc: 11.6 ppm (max 0.5 ppm)—Fail
This formed a deep, dark cobalt blue that ran over on top of other glazes, creating rivulets that resembled ash glaze.

REOSTAT RED (CONE 6)

INGREDIENTS	AMOUNTS
G-200 Feldspar	44.00
Silica	16.50
Bone Ash	14.00
Kaolin	10.50
Talc	10.00
Lithium Carbonate	3.00
Bentonite	2.00
Total	**100.00**

Also Add:

Black Iron Oxide	11.00

NOTES:
Chemical Analysis:
Lithium: 0.6 ppm (max 0.06 ppm)—Fail
Iron: 0.19 ppm (max 0.2 ppm)
This pretty iron saturate red barely failed!

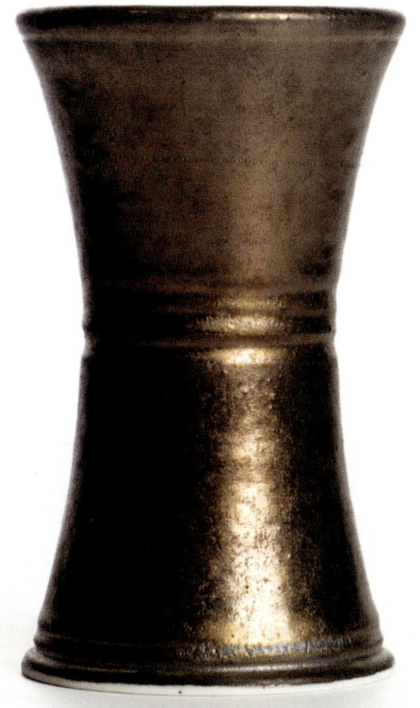

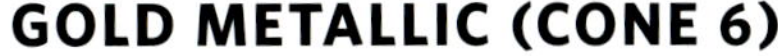

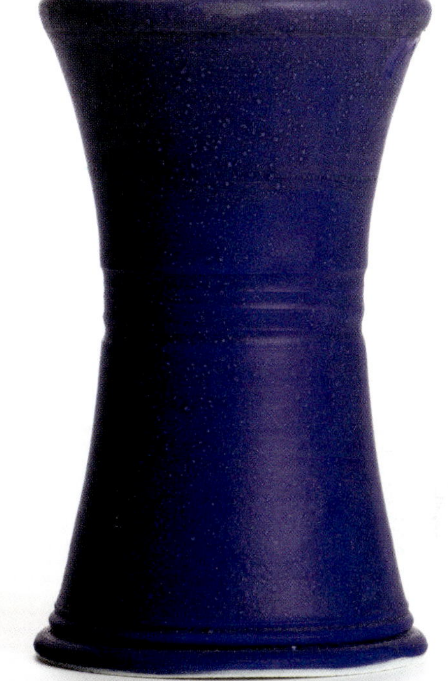

GOLD METALLIC (CONE 6)

INGREDIENTS	AMOUNTS
Redart	86.00
OM4 Ball Clay	7.00
Silica	7.00
Total	**100.00**

Also Add:

Manganese Dioxide	64.00
Black Copper Oxide	7.00
Cobalt Oxide	4.30

NOTES:

Chemical Analysis:
Copper 3.3 ppm (max 1.3 ppm)—Fail
Manganese 41.2 ppm (max 0.05 ppm)—Fail
Cobalt 1.9 ppm (max 0.5 ppm)—Fail
Okay, this one mega failed. Any glaze that is 40 percent manganese is probably not going to pass . . . but it is also one of the most dynamic glazes in the book, an alchemical achievement that turns dirt to gold.

INTENSE BLUE (CONE 6)

INGREDIENTS	AMOUNTS
Nepheline Syenite	47.30
Barium Carbonate	36.60
Silica	7.50
OM4 Ball Clay	6.60
Lithium Carbonate	2.00
Total	**100.00**

Also Add:

Cobalt Carbonate	3.00
Bentonite	2.00

NOTES:

Chemical Analysis:
Barium 7.8 ppm (max 1.0 ppm)—Fail
Cobalt 0.2 ppm (max 0.5 ppm)
Lithium 0.12 ppm (max 0.06 ppm)—Fail
Barium blues are like no other—deep and meaningful. While a glaze made from over 30 percent barium carbonate may not be appropriate for the food and drink bearing surfaces, you can use it elsewhere to great effect.

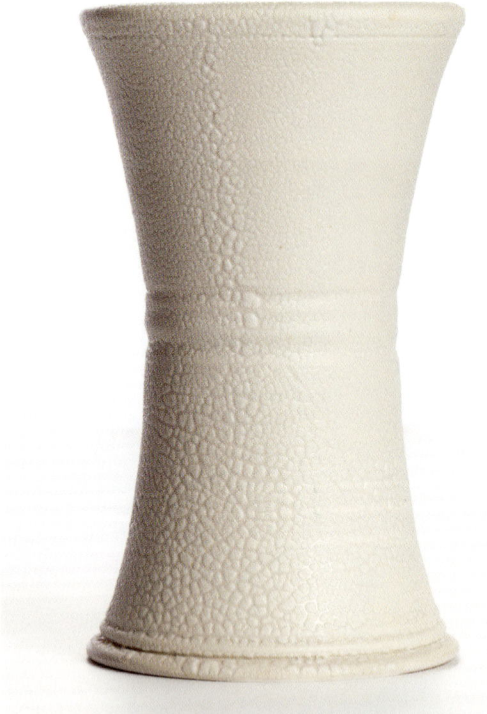

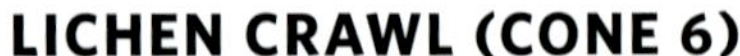

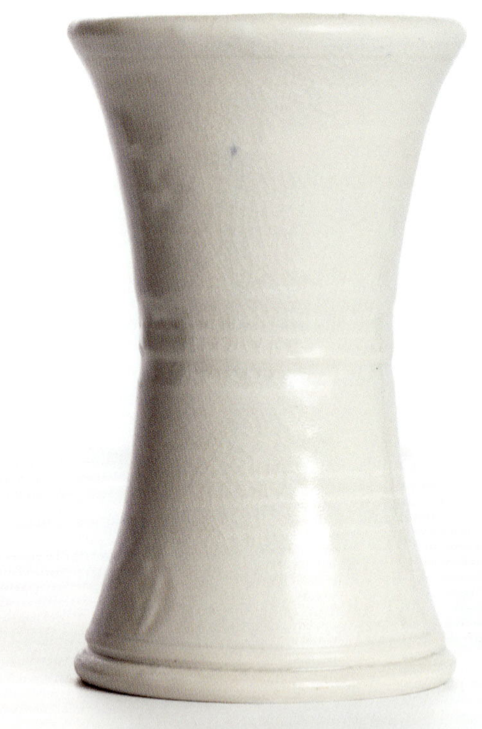

LICHEN CRAWL (CONE 6)

INGREDIENTS	AMOUNTS
Nepheline Syenite	48.00
Magnesium Carbonate	35.00
Gillespie Borate	9.50
Whiting	7.50
Total	**100.00**

NOTES:

Chemical Analysis: No chemicals of concern in the base recipe. However, when colored with 1 percent cobalt carbonate, the chemical analysis was cobalt 2.8 ppm (max 0.5 ppm). Even without the colorant, a crawl glaze is just not suited for food and drink. Can you imagine trying to clean that?

MARINAFLAKE 3 (CONE 6)

INGREDIENTS	AMOUNTS
Nepheline Syenite	79.50
Wollastonite	14.00
Ferro Frit 3110	6.50
Total	**100.00**

NOTES:

Chemical Analysis: There are no elements of concern. However, when colored with 1 percent cobalt carbonate, the chemical analysis was cobalt 1.3 ppm (max 0.5 ppm). Similarly to Lichen crawl, Marinaflake 3 is a dynamic-looking glaze, but its look relies on heavy crazing, which makes it inappropriate for use on food-bearing surfaces.

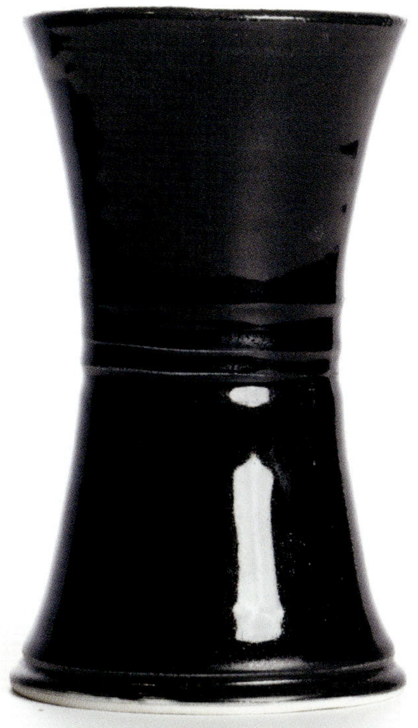

GLOSS OIL SPOT (CONE 6)

INGREDIENTS	AMOUNTS
Nepheline Syenite	46.80
Ferro Frit 3195	19.60
EPK	14.00
Whiting	7.00
Cobalt Carbonate	7.00
Talc	5.60
Total	**100.0**

Also Add:

Cobalt Carbonate	5.00
Red Iron Oxide	6.50

NOTES:
Chemical Analysis:
Cobalt 1.1 ppm (max 0.5 ppm)—Fail
5 percent cobalt, hmmm? That makes for an expensive glaze. It's pretty, if you own a platinum mine.

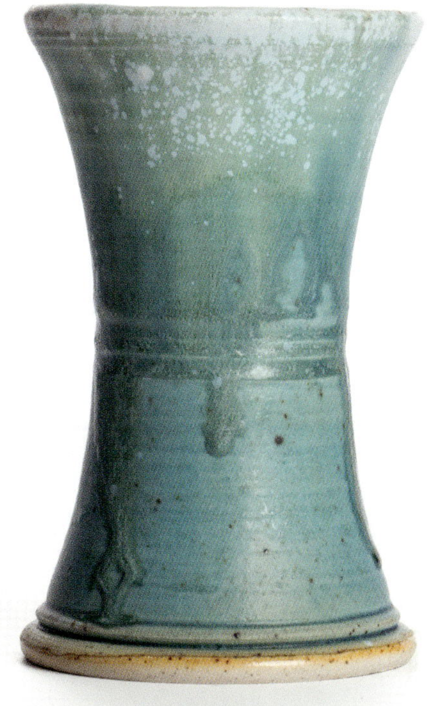

BARIUM MATTE (CONE 10)

INGREDIENTS	AMOUNTS
Nepheline Syenite	56.00
Barium Carbonate	41.90
OM4 Ball Clay	1.40
Lithium Carbonate	0.70
Total	**100.00**

Also Add:

Copper Carbonate	3.00

NOTES:
Chemical Analysis:
Barium: 32.1 ppm (max 1.0 ppm)—Fail
Copper: 19.8 ppm (max 1.3 ppm)—Fail
Lithium: 1.6 ppm (max 0.06 ppm)—Fail
Here's another great barium blue, this time in turquoise. But since it failed our tests, we suggest that it should be used everywhere except the food and drink bearing surfaces of your work.

CONE 6 RECIPES

Now that we have a deeper understanding of the materials in our glazes, including the roles they play and which ones we need to test for, let's take a look at some recipes and combinations. We've tried to offer up a variety of colors and textures to provide as many variations as possible. Please note that glazes sometimes have multiple names, and you may run into a recipe that is "also known as" something else. What is most important is the recipe and the result. A glaze by any other name would fire as sweet.

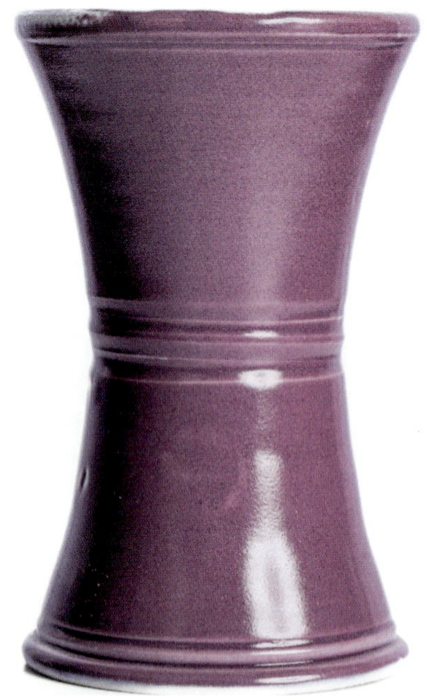

OLD FORGE BLURPLE

INGREDIENTS	AMOUNTS
Nepheline Syenite	32.50
Ferro Frit 3134	30.00
Silica	15.00
Whiting	12.50
Bone Ash	7.50
EPK	2.50
Total	**100.00**

Also Add:

Bentonite	2.00
Tin Oxide	2.00
Cobalt Carbonate	0.25
Chrome Oxide	0.10

NOTES:
Chemical Analysis:
Chromium 0.01 ppm (max 0.05 ppm)
Old Forge Blurple is a consistent purple with some blue undertones that don't move.

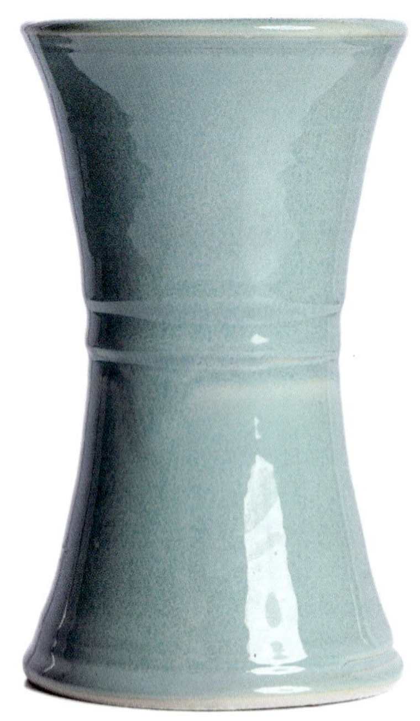

SWEET MINTY TURQUOISE

INGREDIENTS	AMOUNTS
Minspar Feldspar	41.00
Silica	28.00
Whiting	12.00
Gillespie Borate	10.00
Strontium Carbonate	7.00
Magnesium Carbonate	2.00
Total	**100.00**

Also Add:

Titanium Dioxide	3.00
Copper Carbonate	2.00
Rutile	1.50
Zircopax	1.00

NOTES:
Chemical Analysis:
Copper 0.60 ppm (max 1.3 ppm)
An opaque and smooth turquoise, this glaze pinholes in some combinations but dazzles in others.

These recipes were fired to cone 6 in oxidation on Highwater Clays' Helios Porcelain or Standard Clays' Angel White. We used the medium cone fire schedule on a Skutt 1227 (see page 126). The lab results from the leach analysis are listed in the notes beneath each glaze.

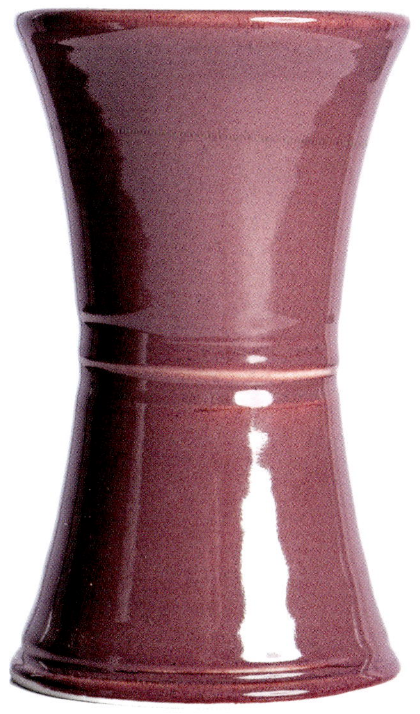

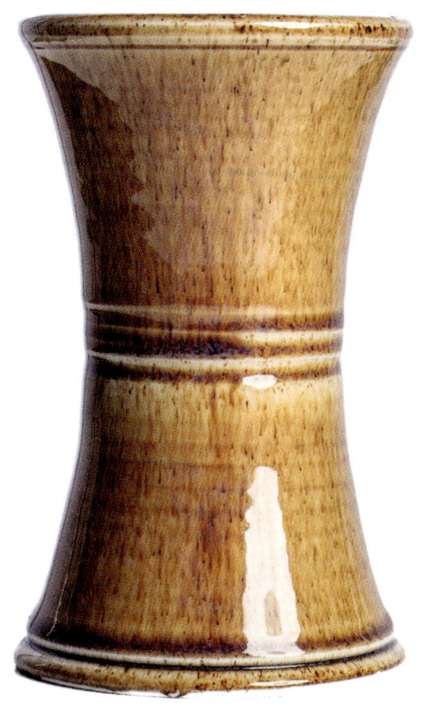

JUNE PERRY RED

INGREDIENTS	AMOUNTS
Silica	42.40
Gillespie Borate	17.80
Whiting	16.90
Nepheline Syenite	13.60
EPK	9.30
Total	**100.00**

Also Add:

Tin Oxide	5.00
Chrome Oxide	0.15

NOTES:
Chemical Analysis:
Chromium: 0.00 ppm (max 0.05 ppm)
June Perry Red is a deep opaque red that likes layering.

OLD FORGE SUNSET

INGREDIENTS	AMOUNTS
Nepheline Syenite	37.00
Gillespie Borate	24.00
Silica	21.00
EPK	12.00
Whiting	4.00
Talc	2.00
Total	**100.00**

Also add:

Manganese Dioxide	4.00
Rutile	4.00
Bentonite	2.00
Red Iron Oxide	2.00

NOTES:
Chemical Analysis:
Iron: 0.06 ppm (max 0.2 ppm)
Manganese: 0.00 ppm (max 0.05 ppm)
Iron and manganese give this glossy glaze a winning variegated brown that looks dapper in combination with some of the black glazes.

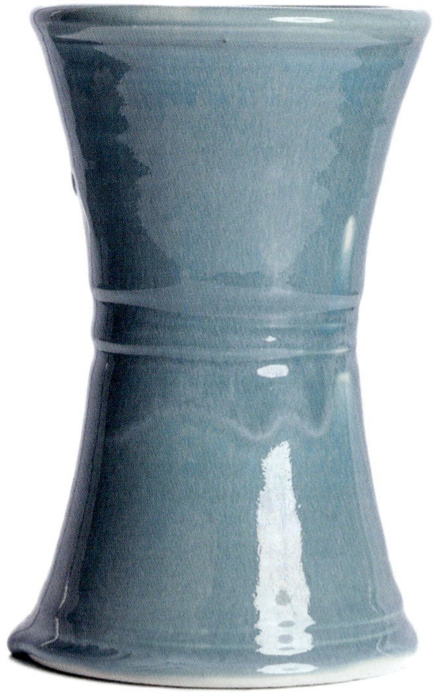

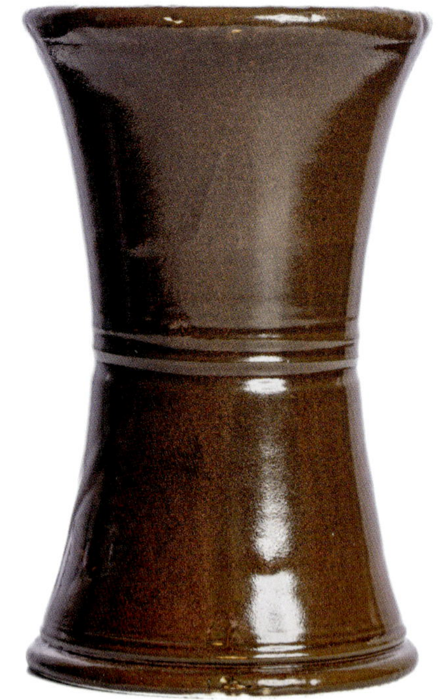

VAL'S TURQUOISE

INGREDIENTS	AMOUNTS
G-200 Feldspar	35.60
Silica	27.50
Gillespie Borate	21.80
Whiting	11.40
Dolomite	3.70
Total	**100.00**

Also Add:

Copper Carbonate	2.90
Bentonite	1.00

NOTES:

Chemical Analysis:
Copper: 0.25 ppm (max 1.3 ppm)
Val's Turquoise is a classic copper cone 6 glaze. A little bentonite helps the glaze adhere to the clay body.

RUST RED

INGREDIENTS	AMOUNTS
Gillespie Borate	31.70
Silica	29.70
G-200 Feldspar	19.80
Talc	13.90
EPK	4.90
Total	**100.00**

Also Add:

Red Iron Oxide	13.50
Bentonite	2.00

NOTES:

Chemical Analysis:
Iron: 0.18 ppm (max 0.2 ppm)
An iron saturate glaze that passed our strict test, Rust Red is a deep brown that goes redder the thicker it is applied. Try a double dip!

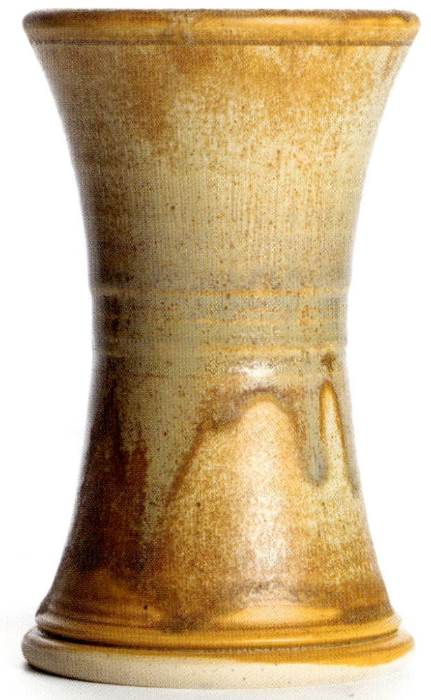

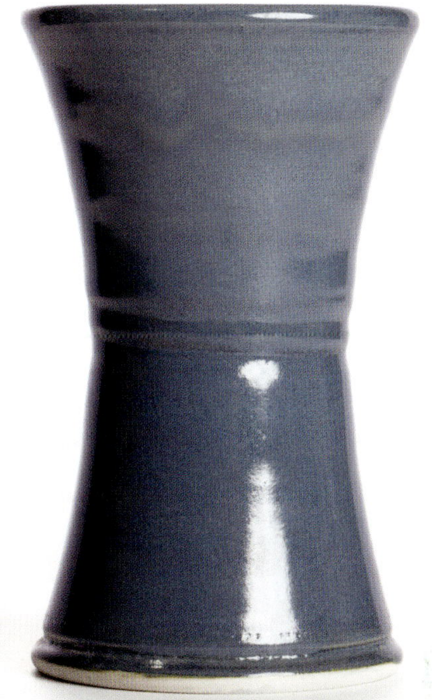

BRITT'S PRETTY MATTE MUSTARD

INGREDIENTS	AMOUNTS
G-200 Feldspar	48.10
Dolomite	24.00
Ferro Frit 3134	12.70
EPK	10.40
Whiting	4.80
Total	**100.00**

Also Add:

Titanium Dioxide	10.00
Black Nickel Oxide	2.20
Bentonite	2.00

NOTES:
Chemical Analysis:
Nickel: 0.02 ppm (max 0.02 ppm)
Very runny in combinations, but this is also one of the most dynamic modifier glazes in the book. Definitely use a kiln cookie underneath this glaze, but be prepared to be amazed.

OVERCAST BLUE

INGREDIENTS	AMOUNTS
Silica	33.10
Minspar Feldspar	20.70
EPK	17.20
Whiting	15.20
Gillespie Borate	13.80
Total	**100.00**

Also Add:

Light Rutile	6.00
Copper Carbonate	3.00
Cobalt Carbonate	1.50

NOTES:
Chemical Analysis:
Cobalt: 0.17 ppm (max 0.5 ppm)
Copper: 1.13 ppm (max 1.3 ppm)
A smooth, opaque light blue, Overcast Blue makes a wonderful two glaze combination over (Ty)tanic blue. It's moody all by itself, but aren't we all sometimes?

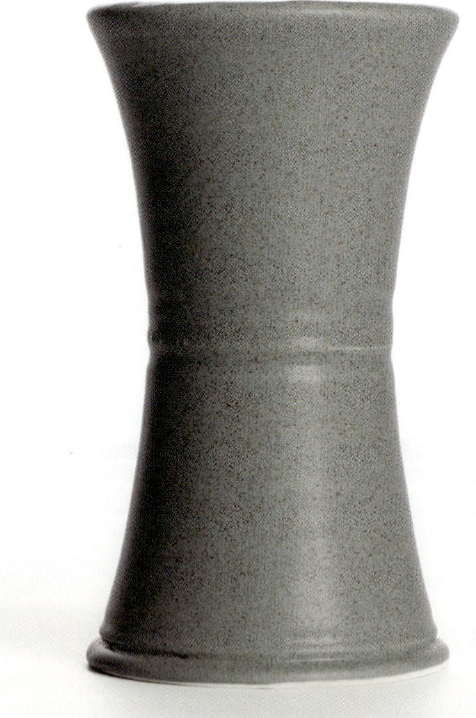

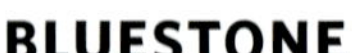

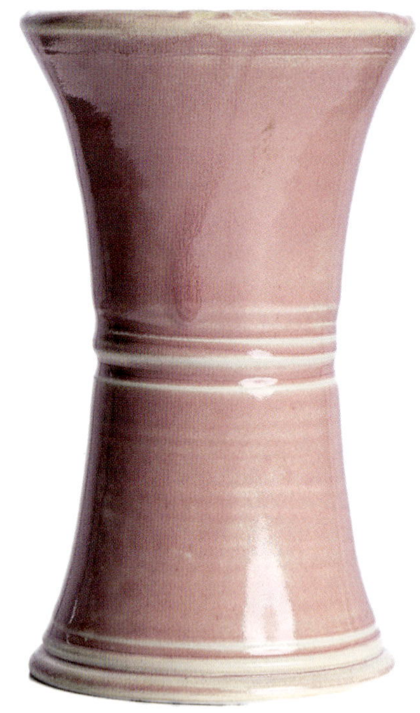

BLUESTONE

INGREDIENTS	AMOUNTS
Nepheline Syenite	36.40
EPK	24.00
Gillespie Borate	12.90
Dolomite	10.50
Zircopax	7.40
Silica	7.20
Talc	1.60
Total	**100.00**

Also Add:

Red Iron Oxide	1.00
Cobalt Carbonate	0.50
Chrome Oxide	0.10

NOTES:

Chemical Analysis:
Cobalt: 0.12 ppm (max 0.5 ppm)
Chromium: 0.02 ppm (max 0.05 ppm)
Iron: 0.10 ppm (max 0.2 ppm)
Pleasantly stony, and as its name would suggest, Bluestone looks geological in nature, a light grey-blue semi-matte that intermingles nicely over a glossy glaze.

OLD FORGE FLOATING PINK

INGREDIENTS	AMOUNTS
Ferro Frit 3134	30.00
Nepheline Syenite	20.00
Silica	20.00
EPK	15.00
Whiting	15.00
Total	**100.00**

Also Add:

Titanium Dioxide	2.50
Tin Oxide	2.50
Bentonite	2.00
Chrome Oxide	0.01

NOTES:

Chemical Analysis:
Chromium: 0.02 ppm (max 0.05 ppm)
Pink is a rare color in ceramics but an exacting combination of tin and chrome yields this fine pastel. We like it in combination with other red and purple glazes.

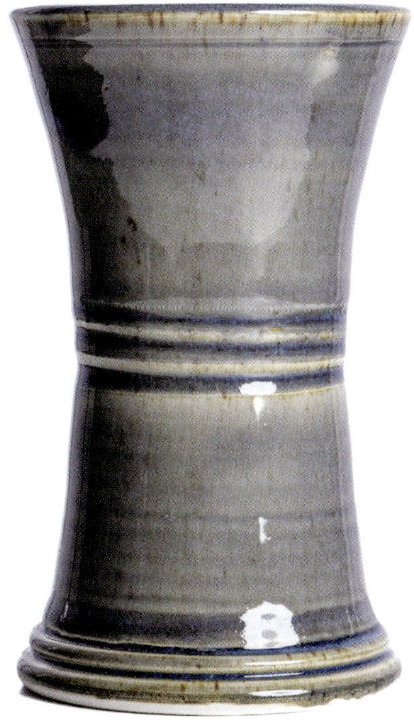

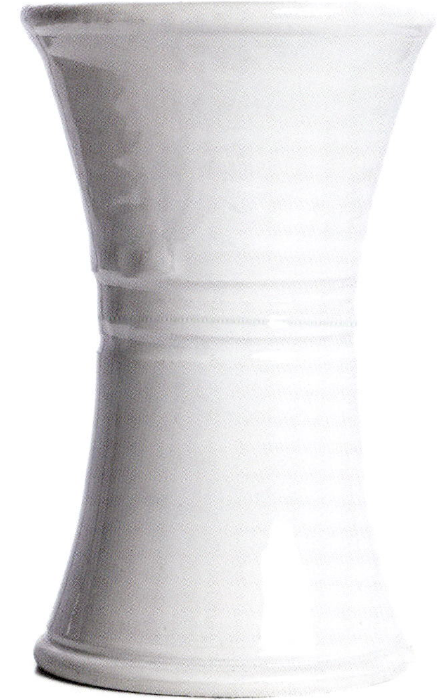

RMC GREY

INGREDIENTS	AMOUNTS
G-200 Feldspar	29.00
EPK	16.00
Silica	15.00
Ferro Frit 3124	13.00
Whiting	11.50
Talc	8.50
Ferro Frit 3134	7.00
Total	**100.00**

Also Add:

Rutile	6.00
Manganese Dioxide	3.00
Cobalt Carb	0.40

NOTES:
Chemical Analysis:
Cobalt: 0.31 ppm (max 0.5 ppm)
Manganese: 0.00 ppm (max 0.05 ppm)
RMC Grey is a translucent grey that fits both porcelain and stoneware nicely.

DONTE'S LUMOS

INGREDIENTS	AMOUNTS
Ferro Frit 3134	37.30
Silica	25.60
G-200 Feldspar	17.30
Whiting	8.30
EPK	6.40
Zinc Oxide	5.10
Total	**100.00**

Also Add:

Tin Oxide	6.60

NOTES:
Chemical Analysis:
Zinc: 0.22 ppm (max 0.5 ppm)
An opaque, creamy off-white, Donte's Lumos makes a great two-glaze combination with Golden Metallic.

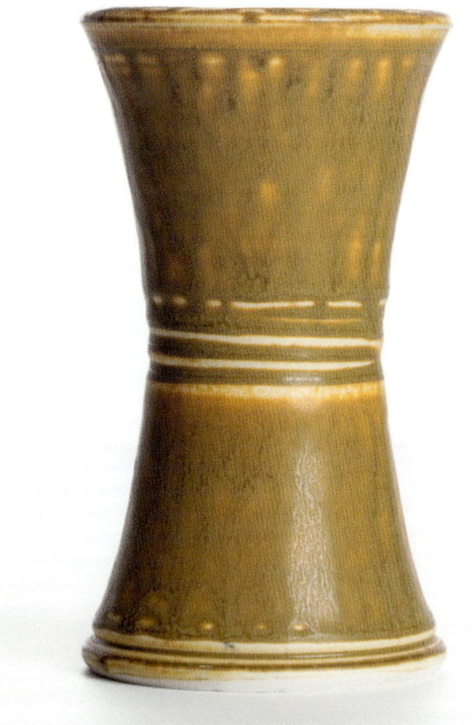
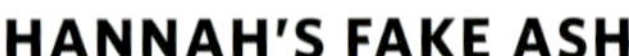
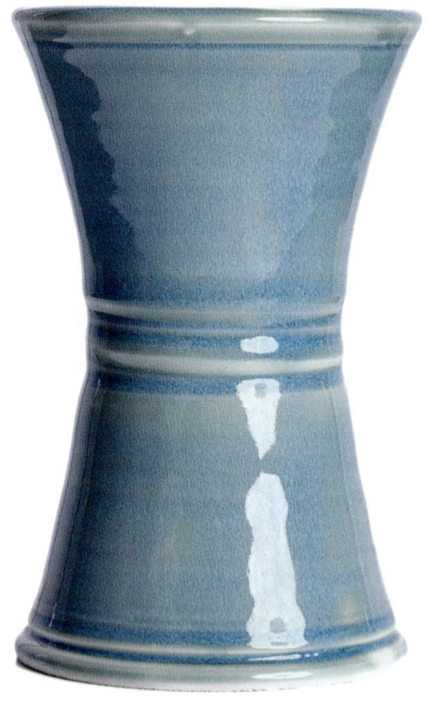

HANNAH'S FAKE ASH

INGREDIENTS	AMOUNTS
Redart	60.00
Whiting	30.00
Strontium Carbonate	10.00
Total	**100.00**

NOTES:
This is great in combinations to provide movement. In our tests, when applied in combination at the top of a piece, Hannah's Fake Ash ran 3 to 4 inches (7.5 to 10 cm) and created a lot of action. We realized a little too late that we should have tested for iron, a component in Redart! We recommend you get your version of Hannah's Fake Ash tested independently.

BLUE EGG

INGREDIENTS	AMOUNTS
G-200 Feldspar	51.00
Gillespie Borate	21.00
Silica	19.00
Whiting	7.00
OM4 Ball Clay	2.00
Total	**100.00**

Also Add:

Copper Carbonate	2.00

NOTES:
Chemical Analysis:
Copper: 0.21 ppm (max 1.3 ppm)
A translucent copper glaze that looks turquoise over porcelain and light green over stoneware, Blue Egg is smooth and glossy.

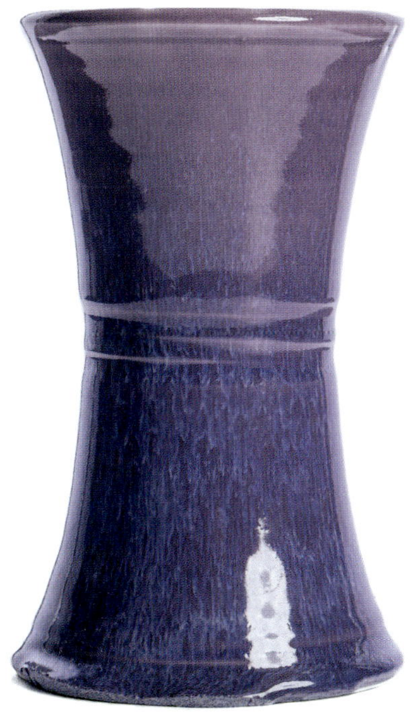
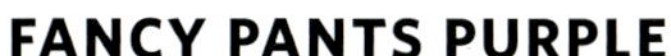

FANCY PANTS PURPLE

INGREDIENTS	AMOUNTS
Wollastonite	25.00
EPK	20.00
Ferro Frit 3134	20.00
Silica	20.00
Gillespie Borate	15.00
Total	**100.00**

Also Add:

Tin Oxide	5.00
Titanium Dioxide	1.00
Cobalt Carbonate	0.25
Copper Carbonate	0.25
Chrome Oxide	0.02

NOTES:

Chemical Analysis:
Cobalt 0.07 ppm (max 0.5 ppm)
Copper 0.00 ppm (max 1.3 ppm)
Chromium 0.00 ppm (max 0.05 ppm)
A beautifully variegated purple that looks great all by itself, Fancy Pants Purple also made some of our most dynamic combinations.

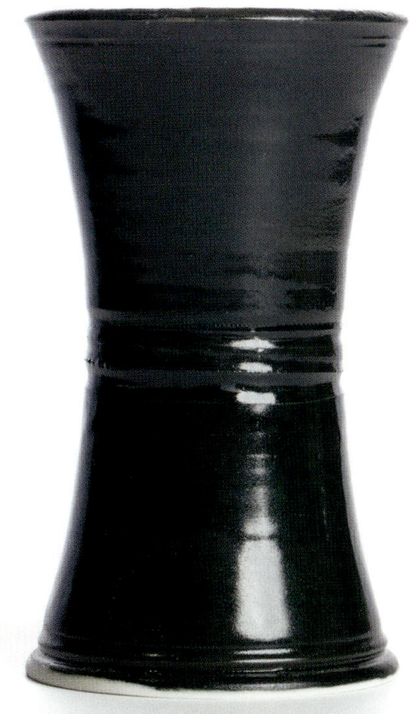

CHROMATIC BLACK

INGREDIENTS	AMOUNTS
Nepheline Syenite	38.40
Wollastonite	18.20
EPK	17.20
Silica	14.10
Ferro Frit 3134	12.10
Total	**100.00**

Also Add:

Red Iron Oxide	2.50
Chrome Oxide	1.25
Cobalt Oxide	0.60

NOTES:

Chemical Analysis:
Chromium: 0.03 (max 0.05 ppm)
Cobalt: 0.06 ppm (max 0.5 ppm)
Iron: 0.12 ppm (max 0.2 ppm)
Chromatic black is very dark, but this particular black has lots of green undertones from the addition of chrome oxide.

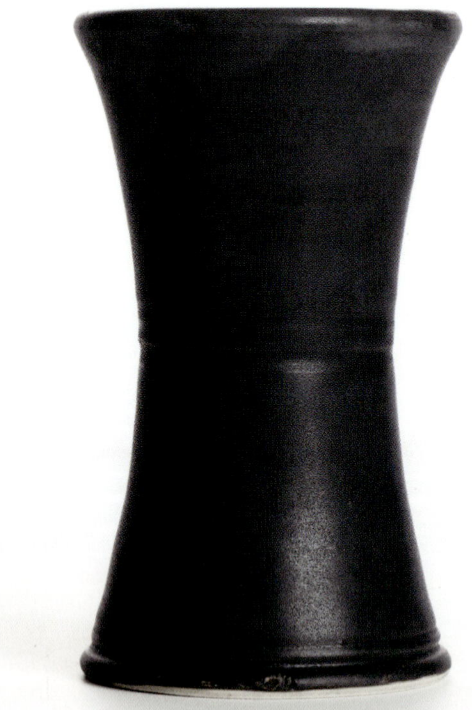

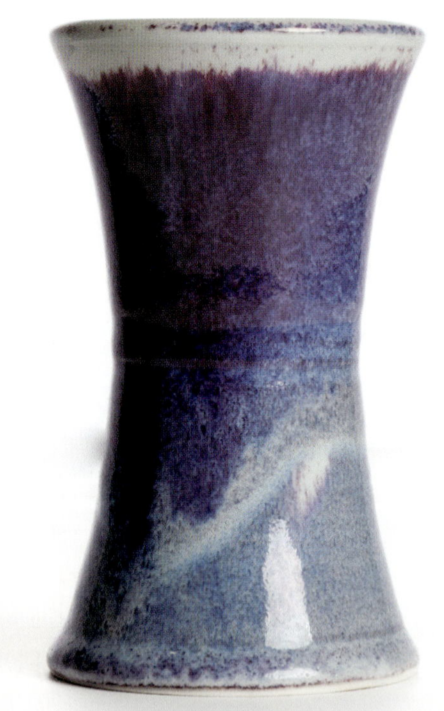

KATZ-BURKE MATTE WITH BLACK STAIN

INGREDIENTS	AMOUNTS
Ferro Frit 3124	30.00
EPK	30.00
Nepheline Syenite	15.50
Whiting	15.50
Silica	9.00
Total	**100.00**

Also Add:

Mason Stain 6600 Best Black	6.00

NOTES:

Chemical Analysis:
Chromium: 0.00 ppm (max 0.05 ppm)
Cobalt: 0.02 ppm (max 0.5 ppm)
Iron: 0.01 ppm (max 0.2 ppm)
Manganese: 0.00 ppm (max 0.05 ppm)
A texturally pleasing glaze, Katz-Burke Matte feels great in the hand. It also loves to be layered underneath Britt's Pretty Matte Mustard.

SIC(K) RED

INGREDIENTS	AMOUNTS
Minspar Feldspar	47.00
Gillespie Borate	14.00
Silica	13.00
Wollastonite	13.00
EPK	9.00
Zinc Oxide	4.00
Total	**100.00**

Also Add:

Tin Oxide	2.00
Copper Carbonate	1.00
220 Mesh Silica Carbide	1.00

NOTES:

Chemical Analysis:
Copper 0.32 ppm (max 1.3 ppm)
Zinc 0.2 ppm (max 0.5 ppm)
For localized reduction in an oxidizing atmosphere, this glaze will give you a copper red in an electric kiln. A double dip will yield the best results. Also, our tests looked decidedly better on porcelain than stoneware.

CONE 10 RECIPES

These glazes were fired in reduction in a downdraft gas kiln. See page 127 for our firing schedule.

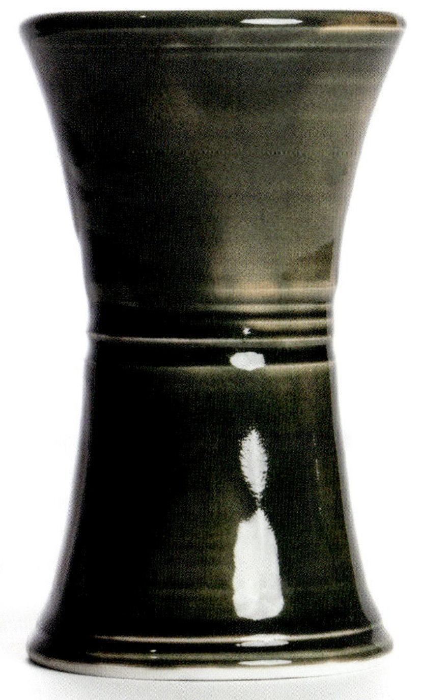

SUPER CANDY APPLE

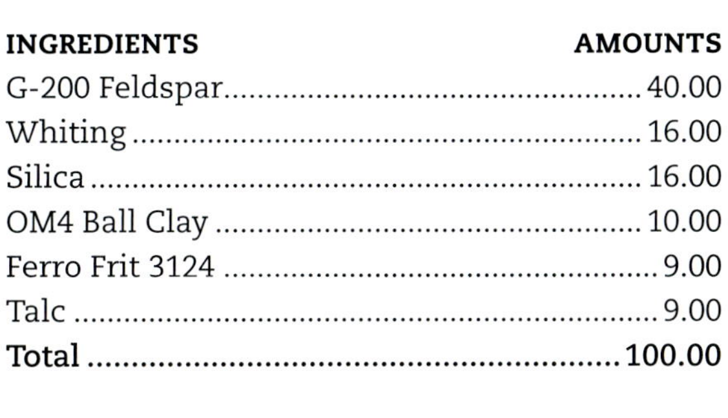

INGREDIENTS	AMOUNTS
G-200 Feldspar	40.00
Whiting	16.00
Silica	16.00
OM4 Ball Clay	10.00
Ferro Frit 3124	9.00
Talc	9.00
Total	**100.00**

Also Add:

Mason Stain 6204 Victoria Green	8.00

NOTES:
Chemical Analysis:
Chromium: 0.00 ppm (max 0.05 ppm)
Copper: 0.00 ppm (max 1.3 ppm)
This produces a really remarkable green that looks like sour apple hard candies—the kind that use Blue #40 and Yellow #1 to make green. Super Candy Apple yields a unique look out of the reduction kiln.

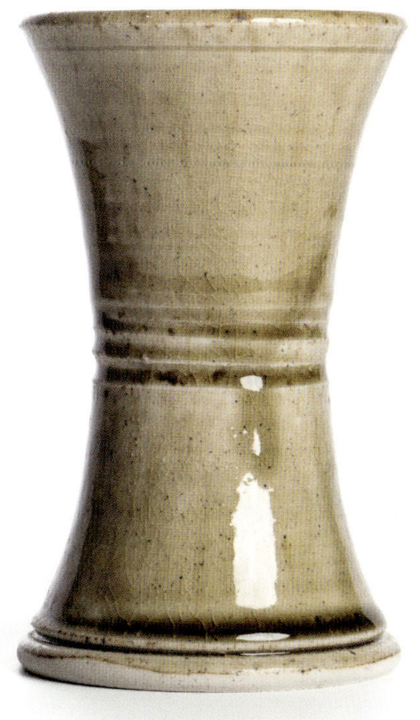

PHIL ROGERS ASH

INGREDIENTS	AMOUNTS
Wood ash	53.00
G-200 Feldspar	29.00
Silica	7.00
Tile #6 Kaolin	6.00
Whiting	5.00
Total	**100.00**

NOTES:
Chemical Analysis:
Iron: 0.07 ppm (max 0.21 ppm)
A classic light brown ash recipe, your particular results will depend upon the nature of the ash you are using. Gabriel's master, Hank Goodman, imported ash from New Mexico. When he switched, the glaze was never the same again.

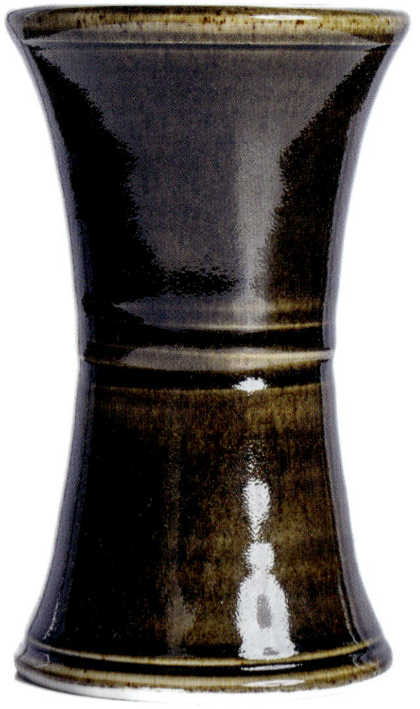

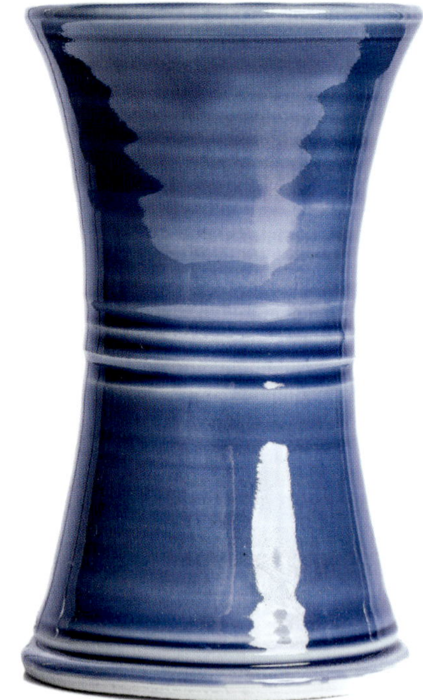

HAMADA RUST

INGREDIENTS	AMOUNTS
G-200 Feldspar	78.00
Gillespie Borate	12.00
Whiting	6.00
EPK	4.00
Total	**100.00**

Also Add:

Red Iron Oxide	7.50

NOTES:
Chemical Analysis:
Iron: 0.15 ppm (max 0.2 ppm)
You can imagine Shoji Hamada squatting on the ground and ladling this glaze into a teabowl, swiftly coating the inside with a graceful flick of his wrist. It's a legendary glaze that stands the tests of time.

TIN PURPLE

INGREDIENTS	AMOUNTS
Silica	34.00
G-200 Feldspar	25.00
Whiting	24.00
EPK	13.00
Gillespie Borate	2.00
Zinc Oxide	2.00
Total	**100.00**

Also Add:

Copper Carbonate	2.00
Tin Oxide	2.00
Cobalt Carbonate	0.50

NOTES:
Chemical Analysis:
Cobalt: 0.07 ppm (max 0.5 ppm)
Copper: 0.83 ppm (max 1.3 ppm)
Zinc: 0.16 ppm (max 0.5 ppm)
Our results came out very blue with slight purple undertones, but we found it made a super-duper two-glaze combination with Watral Purple.

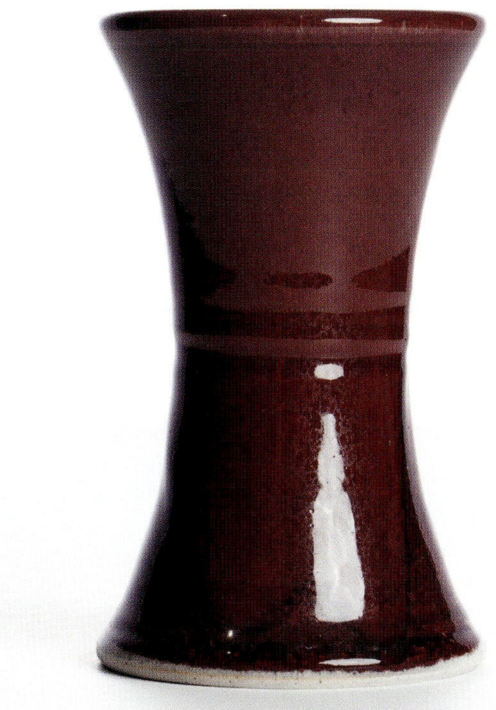

CRANBERRY

INGREDIENTS	AMOUNTS
G-200 Feldspar	73.80
Whiting	11.10
Gillespie Borate	10.20
Silica	4.90
Total	**100.00**

Also Add:

Tin Oxide	1.00
Copper Carbonate	0.30

NOTES:
Chemical Analysis:
Copper: 0.42 (max 1.3 ppm)
Cranberry is a proper, stately copper red that benefits from thick application and looks great in combination with white, blue, black, and purple glazes.

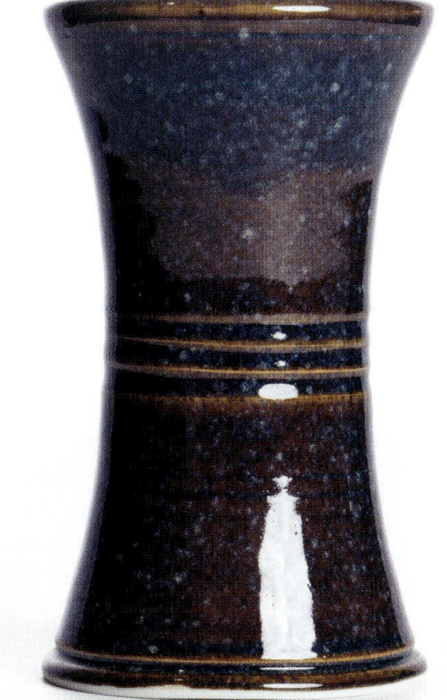

GAVIN'S PURPLE

INGREDIENTS	AMOUNTS
G-200 Feldspar	53.70
Silica	22.40
Whiting	12.90
EPK	6.00
Gerstley Borate	2.50
Zinc Oxide	2.50
Total	**100.00**

Also Add:

Black Iron Oxide	3.0
Rutile	3.0

NOTES:
Chemical Analysis:
Iron: 0.02 ppm (max 0.2 ppm)
Zinc: 0.01 ppm (max 0.5 ppm)
Gavin's Purple is a variegated glaze with lots of blue, purple, and orange highlights. It's dynamic on its own but super funky when combined with Apricot.

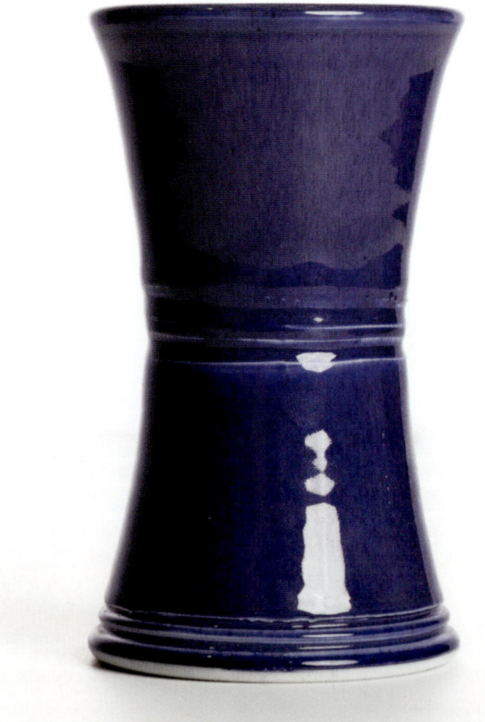

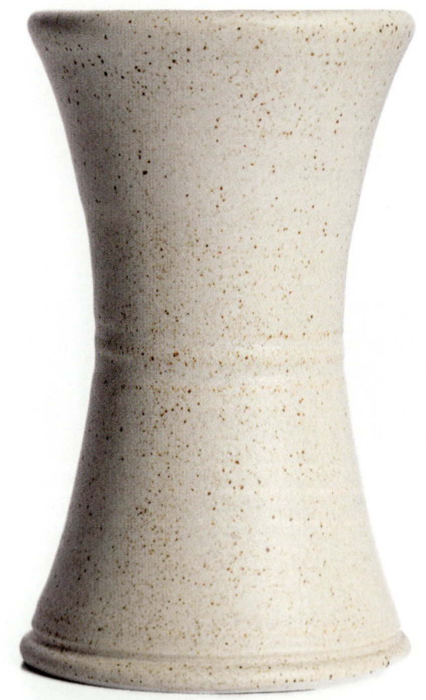

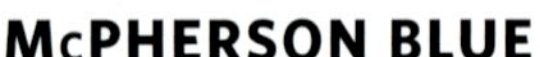

McPHERSON BLUE

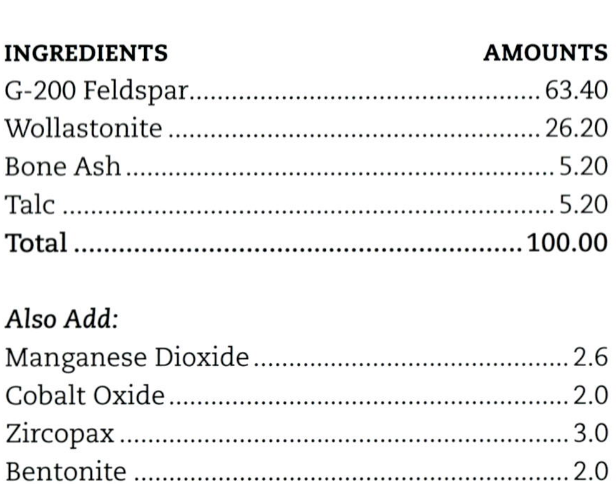

INGREDIENTS	AMOUNTS
G-200 Feldspar	63.40
Wollastonite	26.20
Bone Ash	5.20
Talc	5.20
Total	**100.00**

Also Add:

Manganese Dioxide	2.6
Cobalt Oxide	2.0
Zircopax	3.0
Bentonite	2.0

NOTES:
Chemical Analysis:
Cobalt: 0.16 ppm (max 0.5 ppm)
Manganese: 0.03 ppm (max 0.05 ppm)
McPherson Blue is a winner! Use it above or below other glazes. It plays well with others.

WINOKUR YELLOW

INGREDIENTS	AMOUNTS
G-200 Feldspar	53.20
EPK	22.90
Dolomite	19.40
Whiting	4.50
Total	**100.00**

Also Add:

Zircopax	16.90
Tin Oxide	3.50
Red Iron Oxide	1.40

NOTES:
Chemical Analysis:
Iron: 0.14 ppm (max 0.2 ppm)
A buttery yellow more on the matte side, we loved it in combination with other rutile and iron glazes.

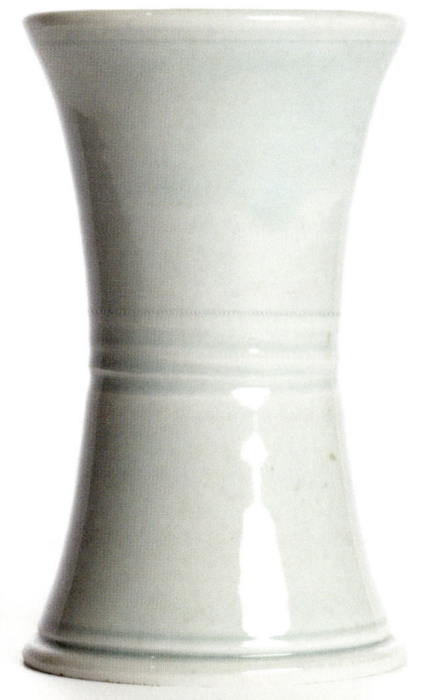

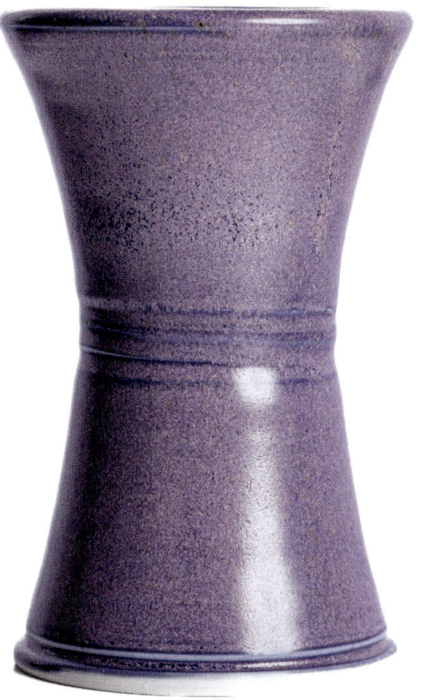

FRASIER CELADON

INGREDIENTS	AMOUNTS
G-200 Feldspar	34.00
Wollastonite	27.00
Silica	21.00
Grolleg Kaolin	15.00
Talc	3.00
Total	**100.00**

Also Add:

Red Iron Oxide	1.0

NOTES:
Chemical Analysis:
Iron: 0.09 ppm (max 0.2 ppm)
Light blue over porcelain, translucent green over stoneware, Frasier Celadon is an exceptionally smooth feeling glaze. It's classy by itself but adds gloss over a matte glaze.

WATRAL PURPLE

INGREDIENTS	AMOUNTS
G-200 Feldspar	40.00
Silica	25.00
Dolomite	10.00
Gillespie Borate	10.00
Talc	10.00
EPK	5.00
Total	**100.00**

Also Add:

Manganese Carbonate	5.00
Cobalt Carbonate	2.00

NOTES:
Chemical Analysis:
Cobalt: 0.05 ppm (max 0.5 ppm)
Manganese: 0.05 ppm (max 0.05 ppm)
A great cone 10 purple, Watral Purple is highlighted with white and pinks specks. It's another glaze that looks great on its own but contributed to some of our most dynamic combinations.

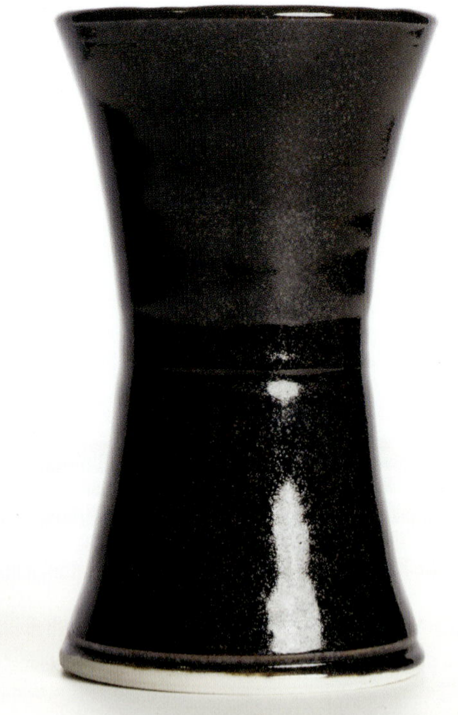

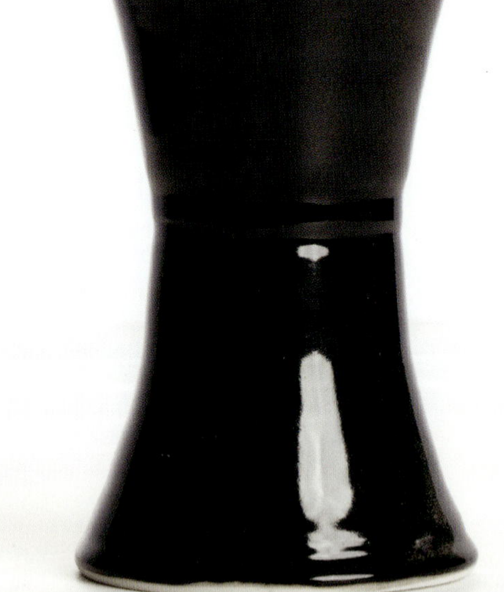

OIL SPOT BLACK

INGREDIENTS	AMOUNTS
G-200 Feldspar	40.00
Silica	30.00
EPK	10.00
Talc	10.00
Whiting	10.00
Total	**100.00**

Also Add:

Red Iron Oxide	10.00
Cobalt Carbonate	1.00

NOTES:

Chemical Analysis:
Cobalt: 0.07 ppm (max 0.5 ppm)
Iron: 0.15 ppm (max 0.2 ppm)
This creates a dark, dark black that will go classic oil spot on horizontal surfaces but still looks great on a vertical surface. Try it on the inside of a bowl. Get as much on there as you can without the glaze cracking. Double dipping is rude at most parties but not this one.

SATINY BLACK

INGREDIENTS	AMOUNTS
G-200 Feldspar	67.00
Silica	17.00
Whiting	6.00
Dolomite	5.00
EPK	5.00
Total	**100.00**

Also Add:

Mason Stain 6600 Best Black	8.00

NOTES:

Chemical Analysis:
Chromium: 0.00 ppm (max 0.05 ppm)
Cobalt: 0.05 ppm (max 0.5 ppm)
Iron: 0.00 ppm (max 0.2 ppm)
Manganese: 0.00 ppm (max 0.05 ppm)
Satiny Black is a smoother alternative to Oil Spot Black that utilizes Mason Stain for its deep color.

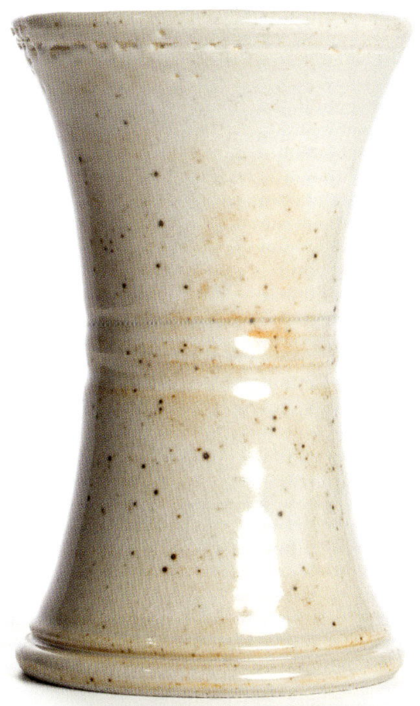

AMERICAN SHINO

INGREDIENTS	AMOUNTS
Nepheline Syenite	50.00
OM4 Ball Clay	25.00
Spodumene	25.00
Total	**100.00**

Also Add:

Soda Ash	2.00

NOTES:
Chemical Analysis:
Lithium: 0.02 ppm (max 0.06 ppm)
This Shino crazed over porcelain and stayed very white, but it excelled and went all awesome Shino orange/white when we tried it on stoneware. There was some crawling, but isn't that what we love about Shinos?

WHY WE OMITTED LOW-FIRE GLAZES FROM THIS BOOK

Our experience of the current landscape of potters suggests that most people who make low-fire ceramics utilize commercially produced underglazes and glazes. Very few folks mix their own low-fire glazes, and the commercially produced products' recipes are closely guarded. If you are a low-fire ceramist, exclusively or otherwise, we recommend that you lab test your fired pieces if you think they might contain any of the ingredients we test for in this book. But your glaze may not contain any objectionable ingredients, and our testing suggests that use of Mason Stains, or underglaze, underneath a food-safe glaze are great ways to add bright colors while keeping your pots safe to use.

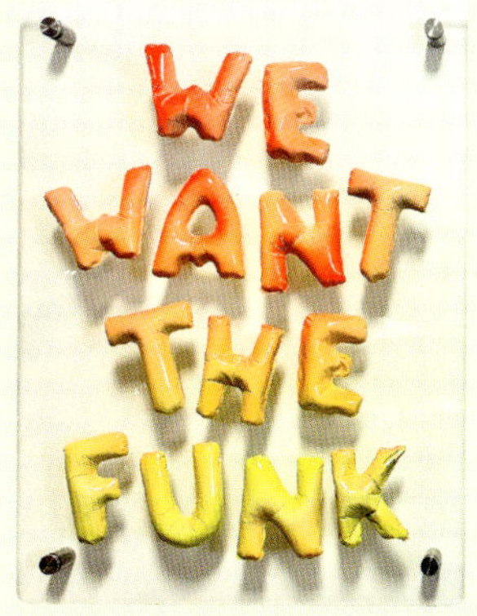

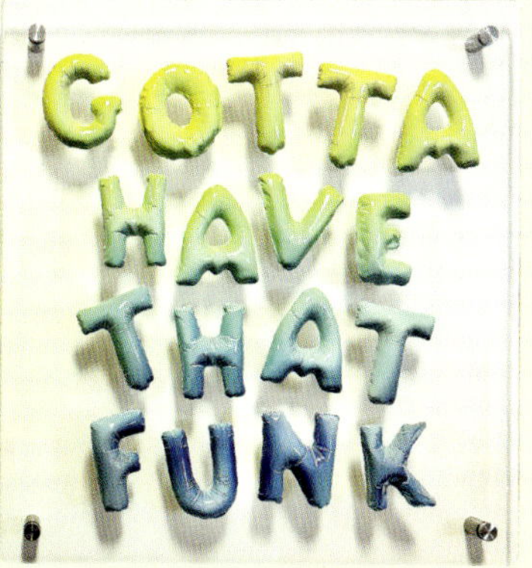

We Want the Funk. Maddison Graybill.
Maddison uses low-fire commercial glazes to tremendous effect on her ceramic balloon letters. Bright and bold.

ULTIMATE PEACE OF MIND
Glazes with Nothing to Test For

NOTE: Rutile contains variable, trace amounts of iron. In the few instances that we have tested glazes specifically for iron leaching from rutile, we find either no leaching, or amounts in exceedingly low quantities. Because of this, we generally consider rutile as a nontoxic additive.

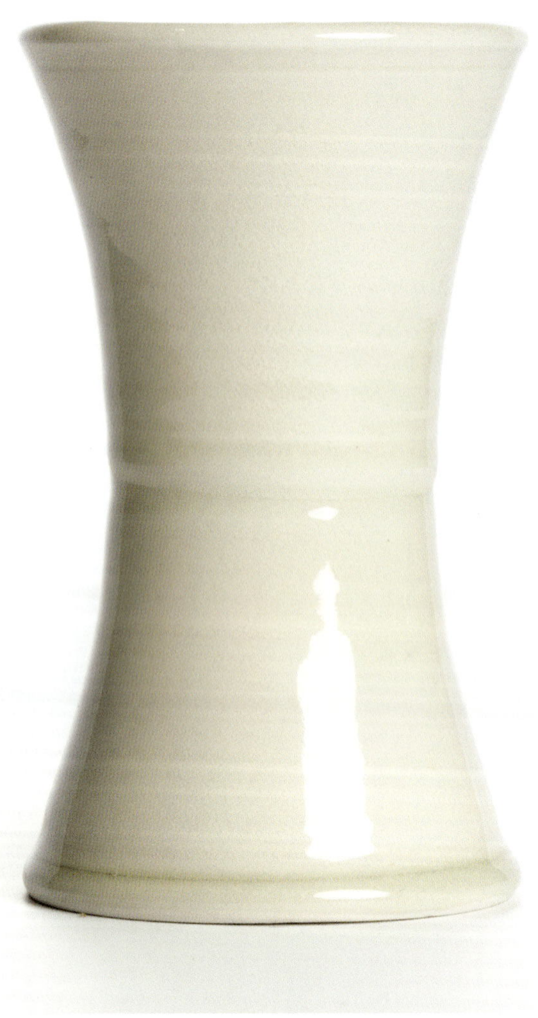

TY'S EZ SATIN CLEAR (CONE 6)

INGREDIENTS	AMOUNTS
Ferro Frit 3124	35.00
EPK	34.00
Wollastonite	26.00
Silica	5.00
Total	**100.00**

NOTES:
This is an agreeable glaze but make sure to apply on the thinner side because it can go cloudy when thick.

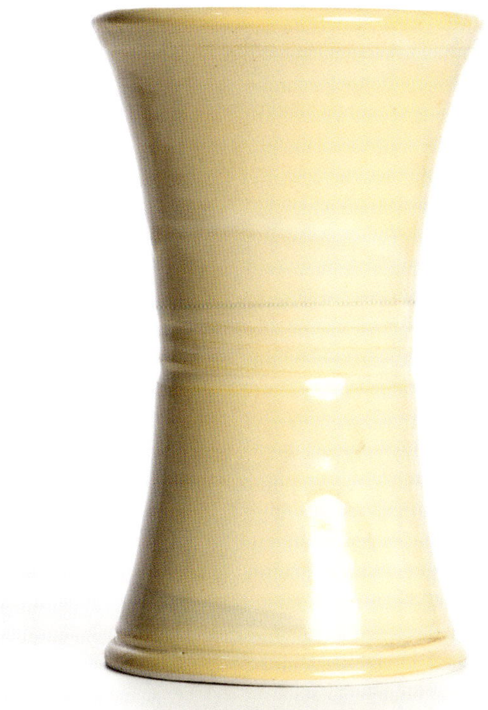

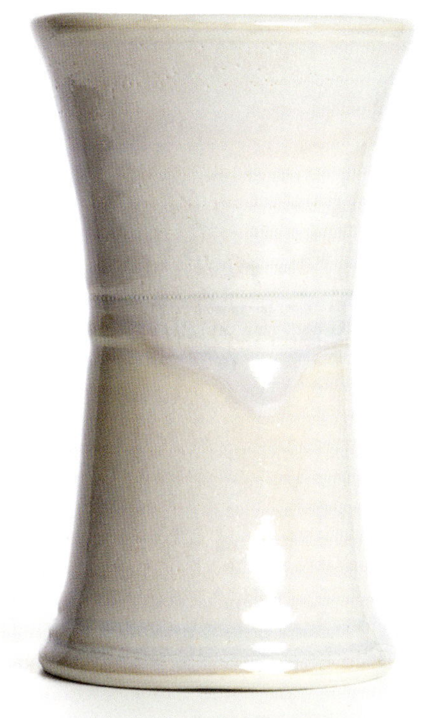

OLD FORGE FIRST FIVE FLOATING RUTILE (CONE 6)

INGREDIENTS	AMOUNTS
Silica	32.50
Ferro Frit 3134	25.00
Nepheline Syenite	20.00
EPK	12.50
Whiting	10.00
Total	**100.00**

Also Add:

Rutile	10.0
Titanium Dioxide	2.50
Bentonite	2.00

NOTES:
This mid-fire yellow worked well in combination with glazes that used iron or rutile as a colorant.

BLEU DE RUTILE (CONE 10)

INGREDIENTS	AMOUNTS
G-200 EU Feldspar	60.00
Dolomite	20.00
Silica	15.00
EPK	5.00
Total	**100.00**

Also Add:

Rutile	5.00

NOTES:
Although it needs red iron oxide–based slip underneath to go "bleu," this is a pretty glaze with iridescent qualities on its own that's also very interesting in combinations.

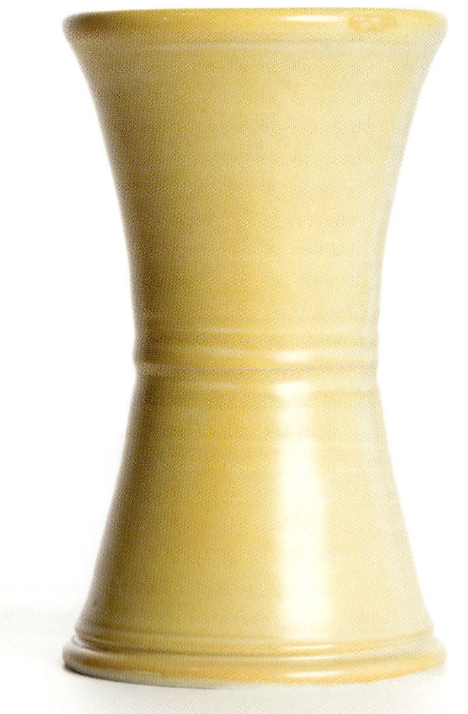

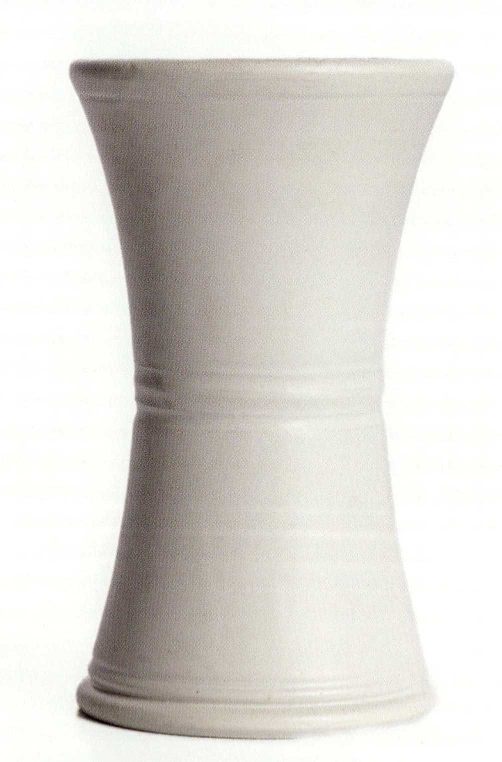

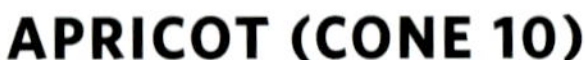

APRICOT (CONE 10)

INGREDIENTS	AMOUNTS
G-200 Feldspar	45.00
Dolomite	22.00
Silica	16.00
Zircopax	11.00
EPK	6.00
Total	**100.00**

Also Add:

Titanium Dioxide	10.00
Rutile	5.00

NOTES:
One of the best "modifier" glazes we tested at cone 10, Apricot is a pleasant glaze on its own, but did really dynamic things when layered over McPherson Blue and Gavin's Purple. We think there are many more cool combinations with Apricot to discover.

SMOOTH MATTE WHITE (CONE 10)

INGREDIENTS	AMOUNTS
G-200 Feldspar	44.90
EPK	19.40
Dolomite	17.40
Zircopax	14.30
Wollastonite	4.00
Total	**100.00**

Also Add:

Tin Oxide	2.50

NOTES:
A nice white without all the gloss, Smooth Matte White likes to hardpan, so use a little Epsom salts to keep it from settling out.

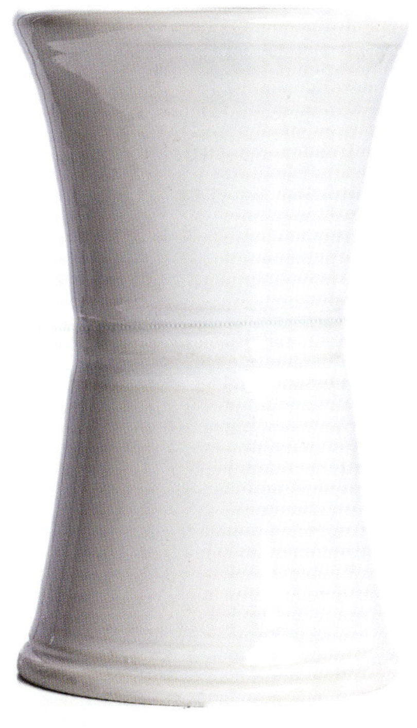

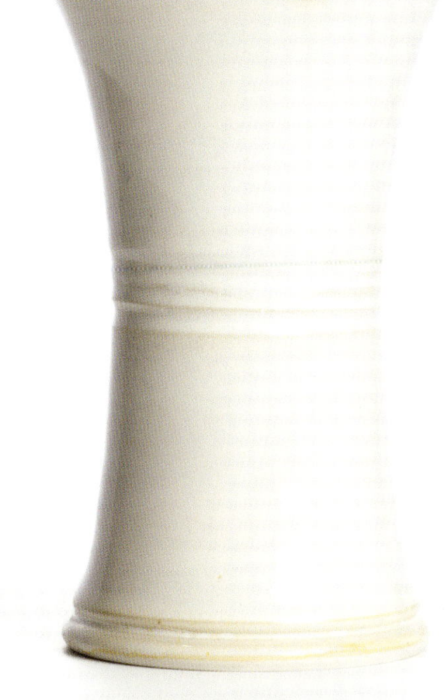

CMW WHITEOUT (CONE 10)

INGREDIENTS	AMOUNTS
Nepheline Syenite	40.00
Silica	30.00
Whiting	20.00
EPK	10.00
Total	**100.00**

NOTES:
From Rose and Matt Katz at Ceramics Materials Workshop, CMW Whiteout is EXTREMELY white, smooth, and glossy. We love it.

HEATH IVORY (CONE 6)

INGREDIENTS	AMOUNTS
Silica	34.50
Gillespie Borate	29.00
Nepheline Syenite	20.00
EPK	6.50
Strontium Carbonate	6.00
Wollastonite	3.00
Dolomite	1.0
Total	100.00

Also Add:

Titanium Dioxide	4.0
Rutile	4.0
Bentonite	2.0

NOTES:
This is a fantastic glaze. A beautiful off-white on its own, but we think it works best in combinations, adding depth and movement to other glazes. We used it in more successful combinations than perhaps any other glaze in the book.

GLAZES FOR MASON STAINS

As previously mentioned, as long as the glaze is properly formulated, stains can be a great way to add color without worrying about leaching. We tested over 30 mason stains in both Marc Egan's Inclusion and Tony Hansen's Clear glaze. For these two glazes, we observed either no leaching or exceedingly low amounts of leaching. In all cases, the amount of leaching was well below the max amount.

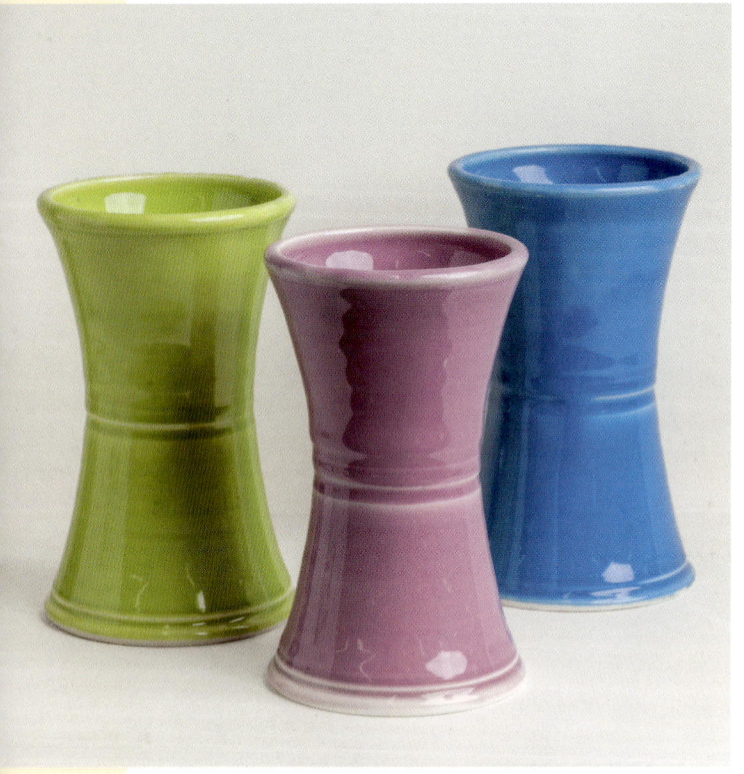

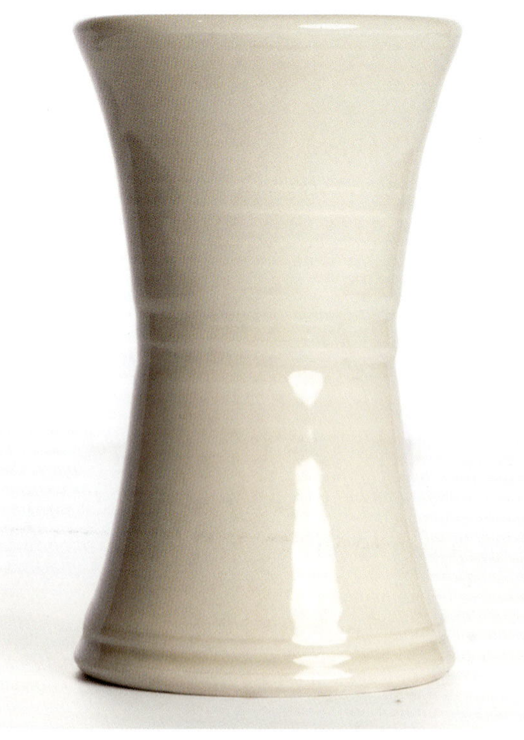

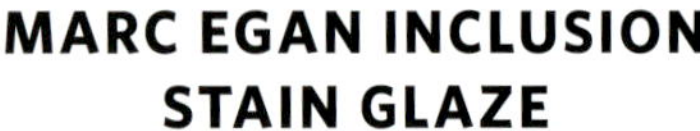

MARC EGAN INCLUSION STAIN GLAZE

INGREDIENTS	AMOUNTS
Minspar 200	34.00
Silica	16.00
EPK	14.00
Ferro Frit 3124	12.00
Wollastonite	12.00
Zinc Oxide	8.00
Dolomite	4.00
Total	**100.00**

Also Add:

Zircopax	3.00

NOTES:
This glaze loves Mason Stains! We added 10 percent Zircon Blue 6314, 10 percent 6304 Violet Chrome Tin, and 10 percent 6236 Chartreuse to create some bright, confident variations.

TONY HANSEN 5X20 CLEAR

INGREDIENTS	AMOUNTS
Custer Feldspar	20.00
Ferro Frit 3134	20.00
EPK	20.00
Wollastonite	20.00
Silica	20.00
Total	**100.00**

NOTES:
We tried a number of different tests with Mason Stains and found a great black with 5 percent Mason Stain 6600 Best Black and a bold red with 10 percent Degussa Stain 279496 Intense Red. If you are experimenting with adding Mason Stains to a base glaze, try intervals of 5 percent, 10 percent, and 15 percent to start and then refine from there.

COMBINATIONS

Here's where things get really exciting! While we weren't able to run an exhaustive set of two and three glaze combinations (a feat which would have required thousands of tests), we did nearly 200 combinations of glazes, and here are the most dynamic.

We tested a number of these combinations and found that leaching stayed within range when using glazes that had already passed as individual glazes. While testing every combination was outside the scope of this book, see Appendix B (page 145) for the results of test combinations we tested. Combinations marked with an asterisk should be used with a liner glaze as one or more of the glazes in the combination failed our tests..

CONE 6 COMBINATIONS

How to read our combinations: For all two and three glaze combinations, the entire tumbler was dipped in the first glaze for two seconds and allowed to dry. Then the tumbler was inverted and dipped a third of the way down from the top in the second glaze listed. If a third glaze was applied, the second glaze was allowed to dry (this can take up to an hour unless a fan is used to speed up the process, which we did) and then the tumbler was inverted again and the third glaze was applied to the top fourth of the pot.

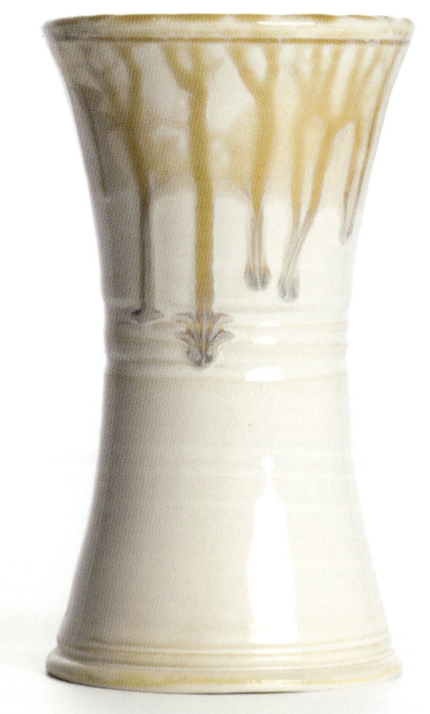

C6 Heath Ivory + Hannah's Fake Ash

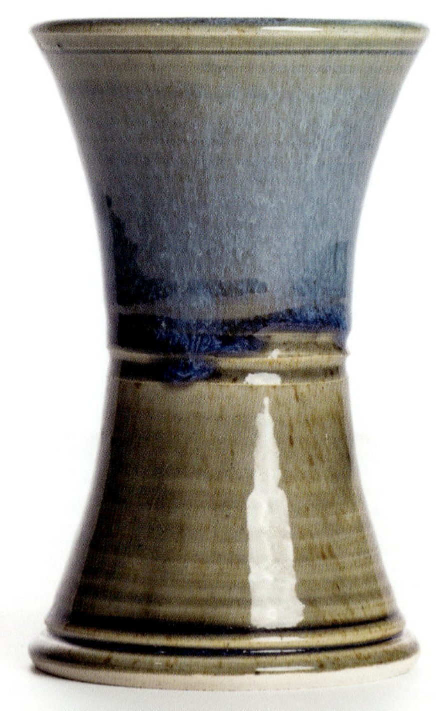

C6 RMC Grey + Val's Turquoise

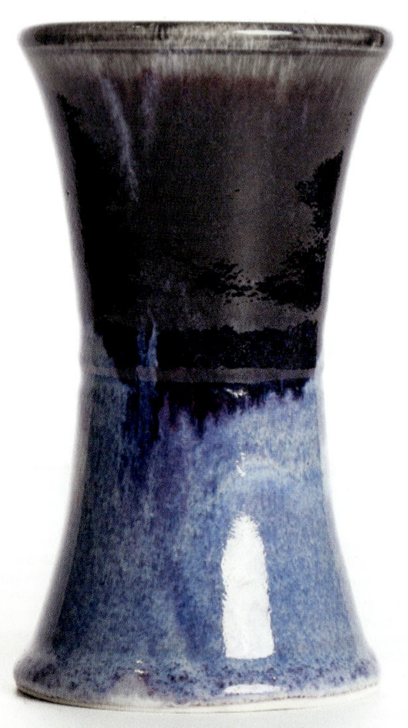

C6 Sic(k) Red + Katz-Burke Matte Black

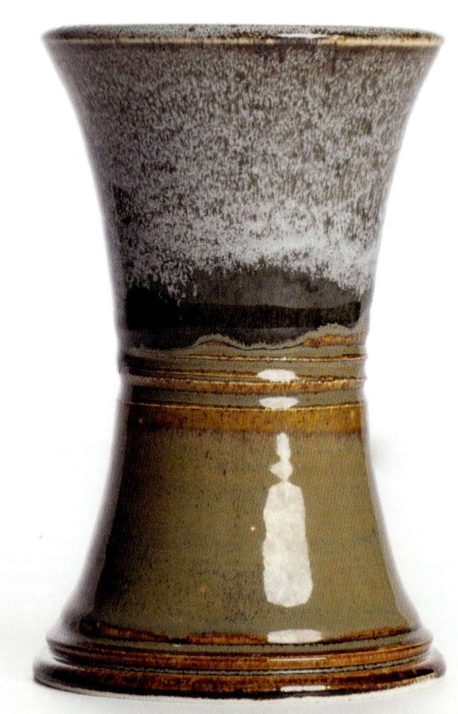

C6 Rust Red + Bluestone + Donte's Lumos

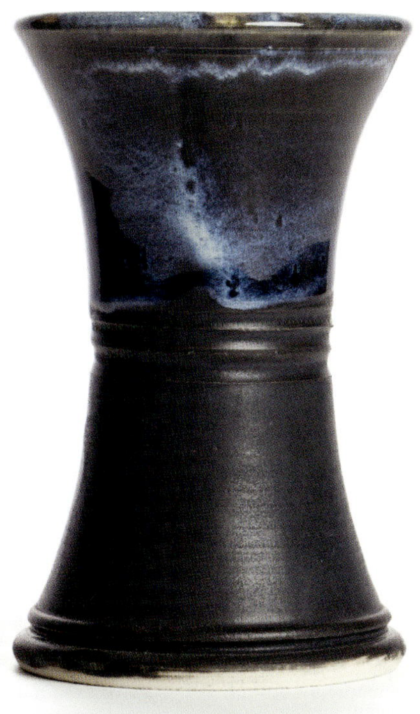

C6 Katz-Burke Matte Black + Heath Ivory

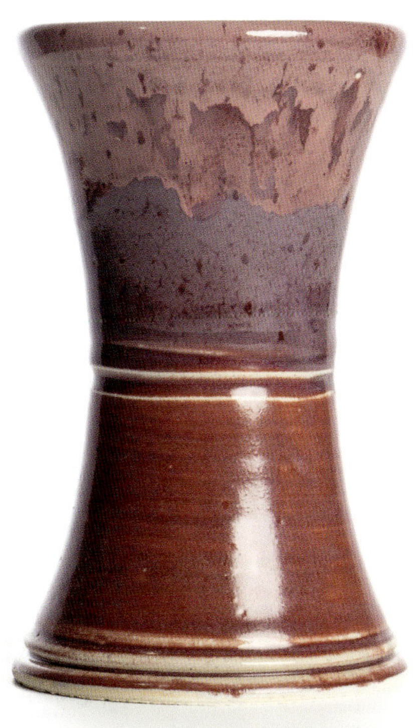

C6 June Perry Red + Old Forge Blurple + Old Forge Floating Pink

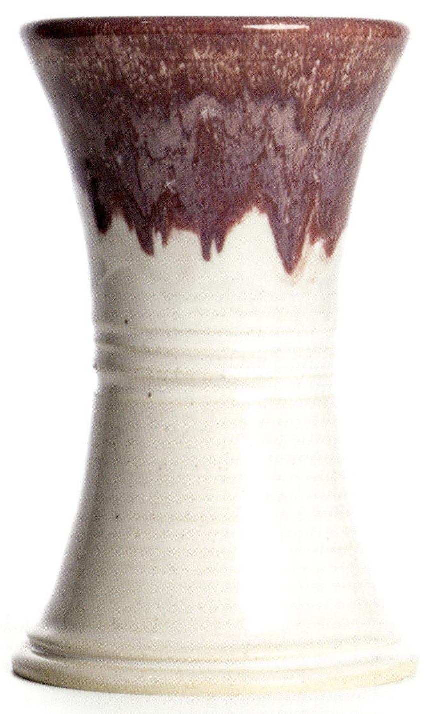

C6 Donte's Lumos + Old Forge Floating Pink + June Perry Red

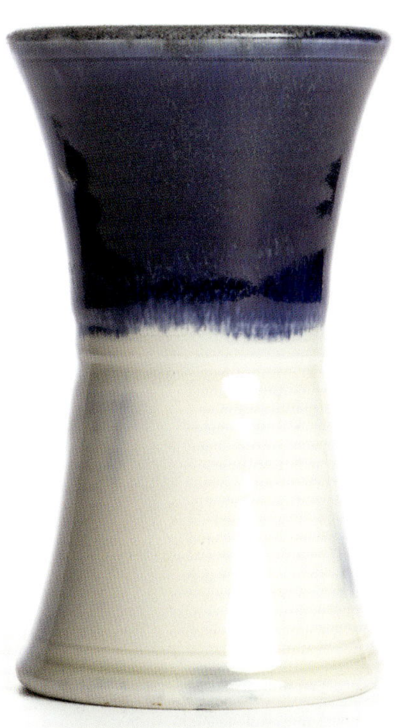

C6 Ty's Ez Satin Clear + Gloss Oil Spot*

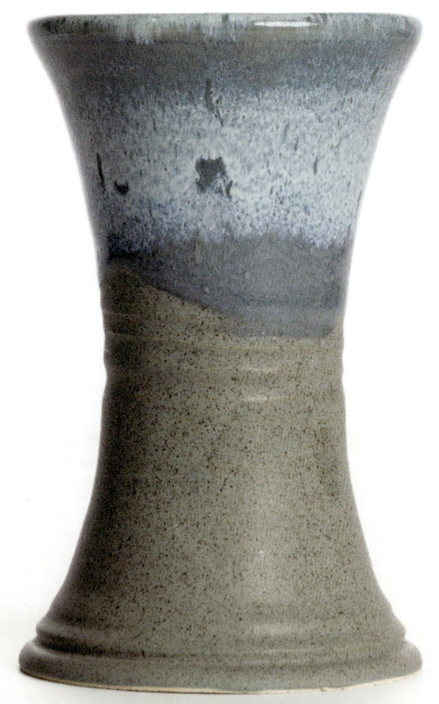

C6 Bluestone + Heath Ivory +
Sweet Minty Turquoise

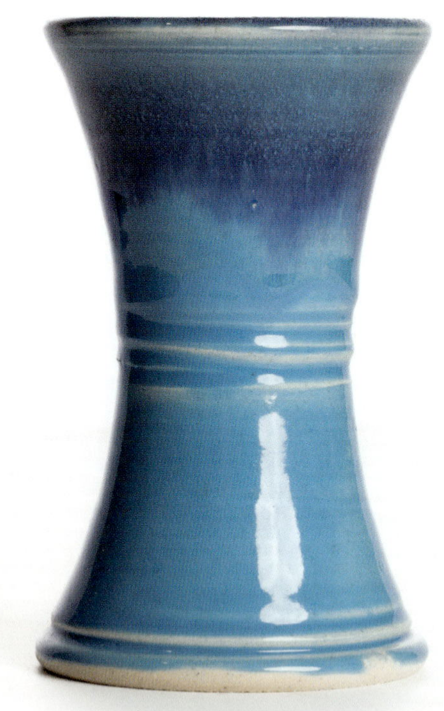

C6 Marc Egan Inclusion (10% Zircon Blue) +
Ty's EZ Satin Clear + Ol' Blue

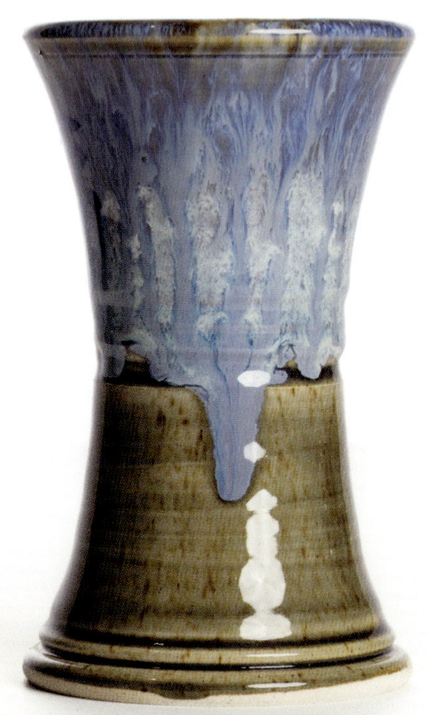

C6 RMC Grey + Heath Ivory + (Ty)Tanic Blue*

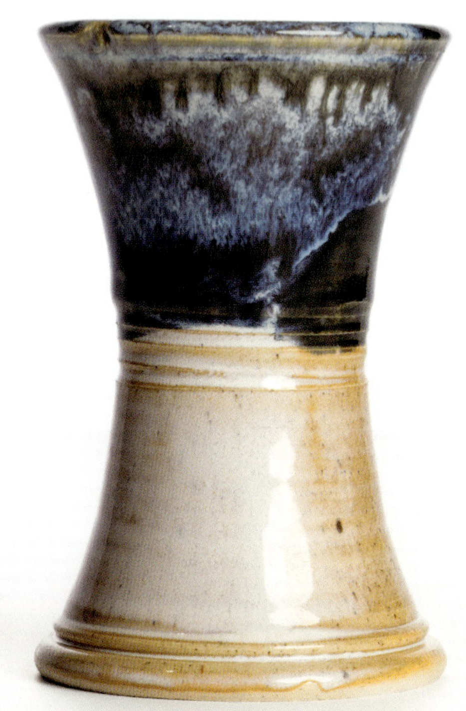

C6 Heath Ivory + Katz-Burke Matte Black +
Heath Ivory

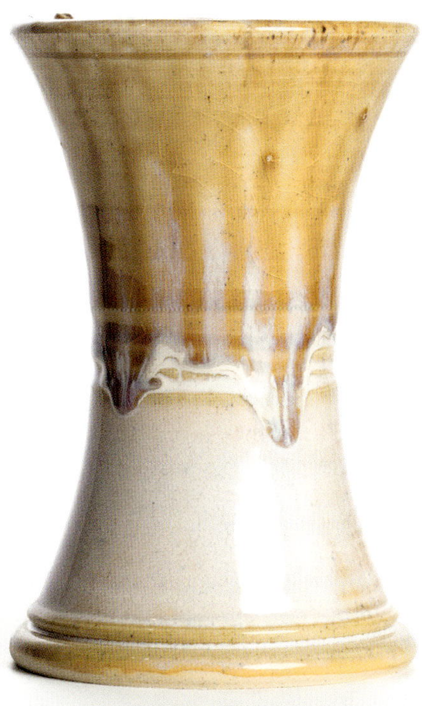

C6 Heath Ivory + Old Forge Sunset + Hannah's Fake Ash

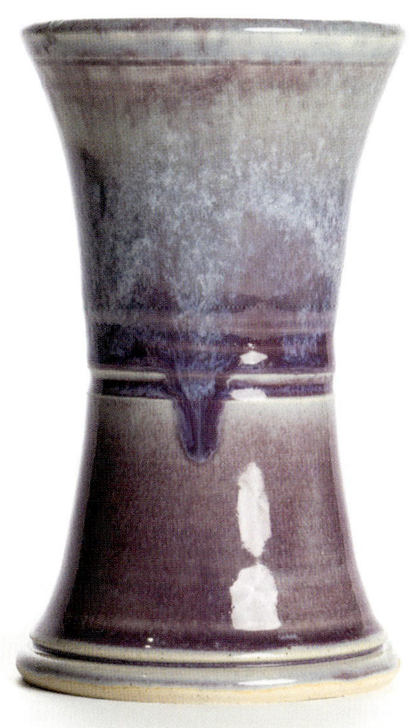

C6 Fancy Pants Purple + Sic(k) Red

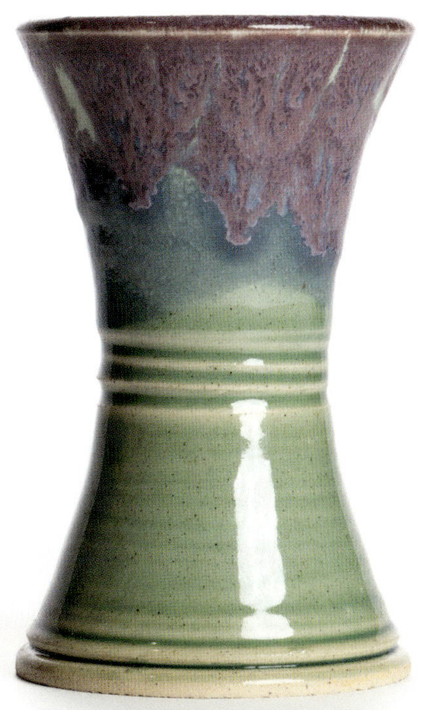

C6 Blue Egg + Old Forge Blurple + June Perry Red

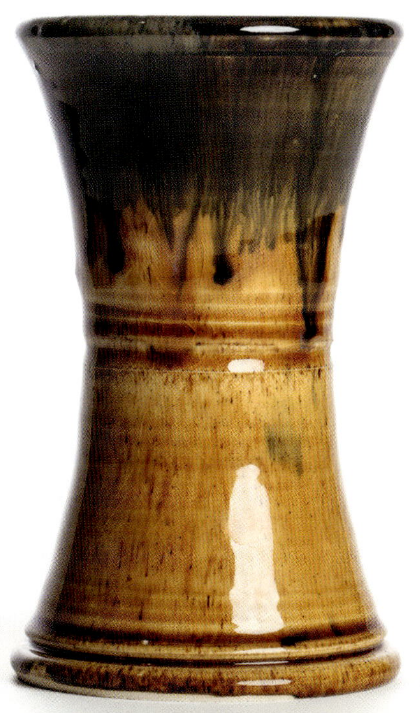

C6 Old Forge Sunset + Britt's Pretty Matte Mustard + Gloss Oil Spot*

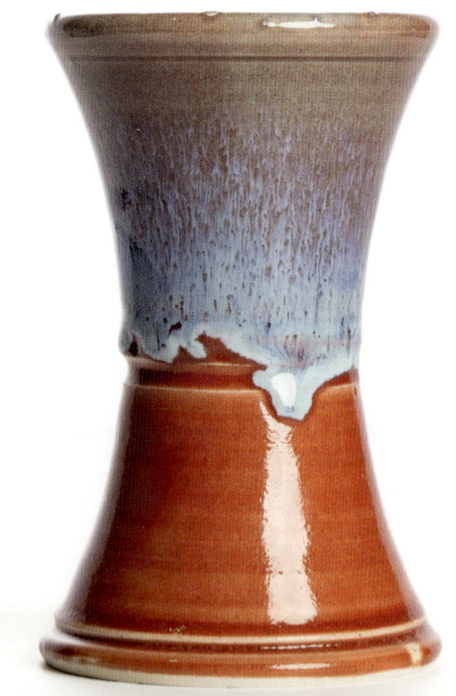

C6 Tony Hansen 5x20 Clear (10% Degussa Stain 279496 Intense Red) + Val's Turquoise + Fancy Pants Purple

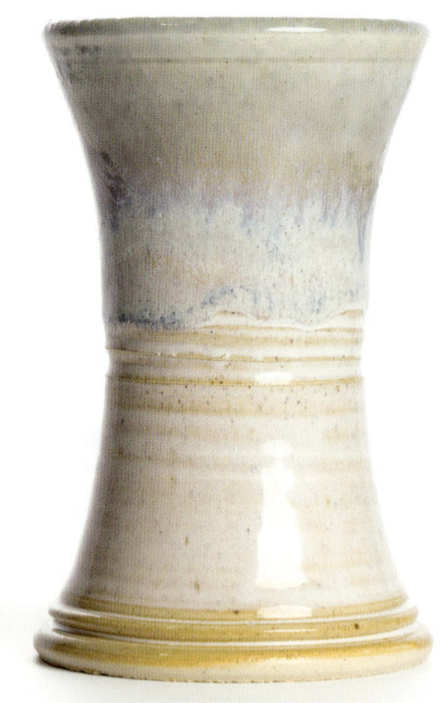

C6 Heath Ivory + Sic(k) Red + Fancy Pants Purple

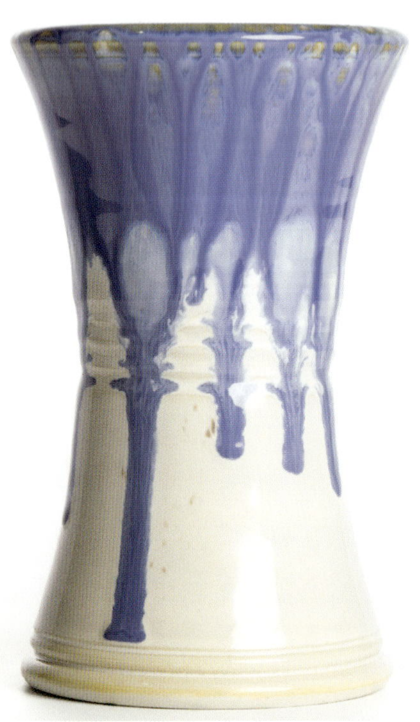

C6 Heath Ivory + (Ty)tanic Blue*

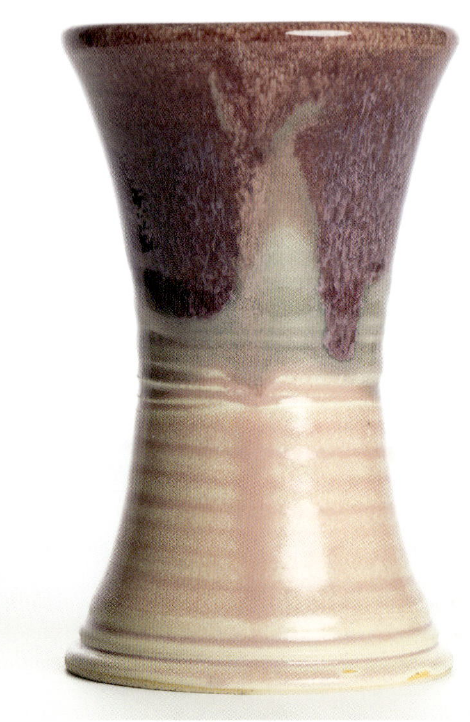

C6 Old Forge Floating Pink + Blue Egg + June Perry Red

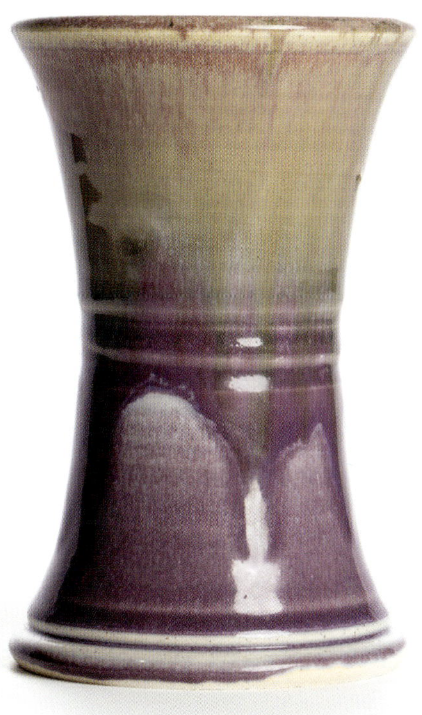

C6 Fancy Pants Purple + Britt's Pretty Matte Mustard

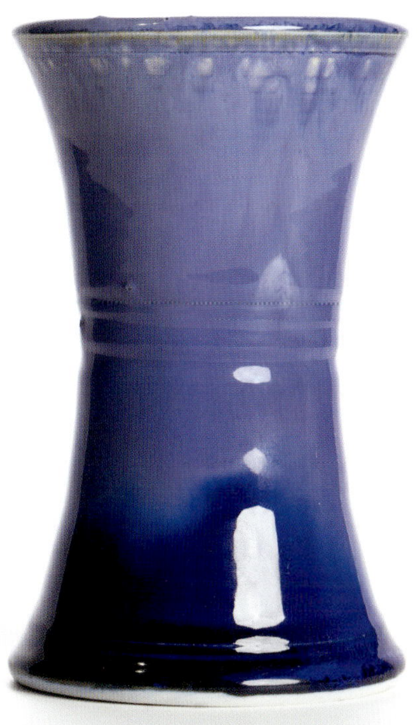

C6 (Ty)tanic Blue + Heath Ivory*

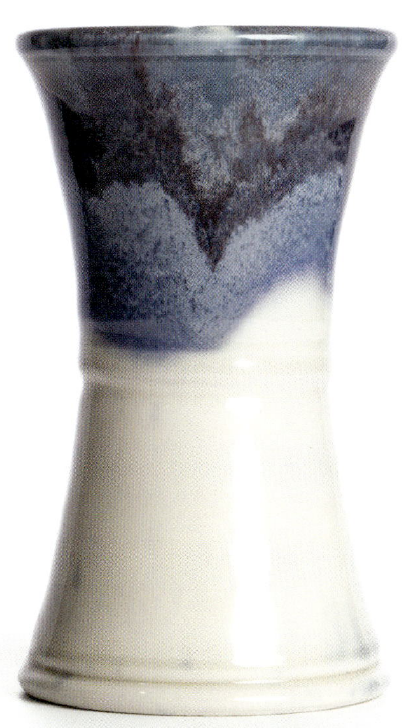

C6 Ty's EZ Satin Clear + Overcast Blue + June Perry Red

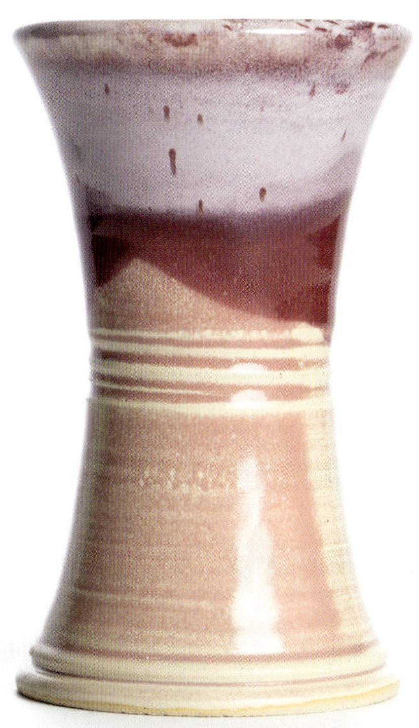

C6 Old Forge Floating Pink + June Perry Red + Donte's Lumos

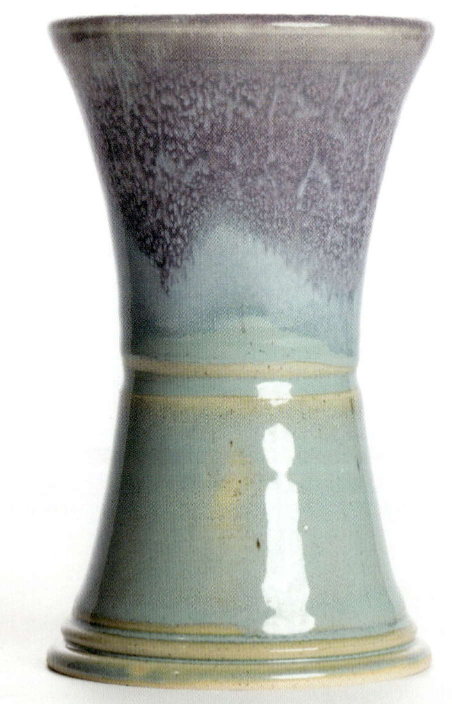

C6 Sweet Minty Turquoise + Donte's Lumos + Old Forge Blurple

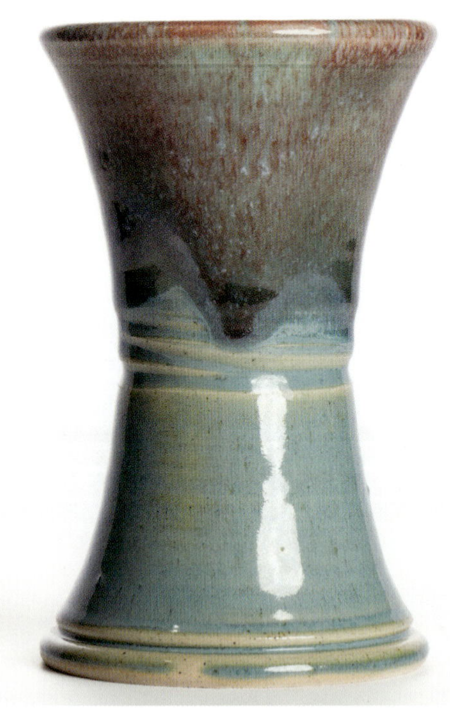

C6 Val's Turquoise + Old Forge Floating Pink + Tony Hansen 5x20 Clear (+10% Degussa Stain 279496 Intense Red)

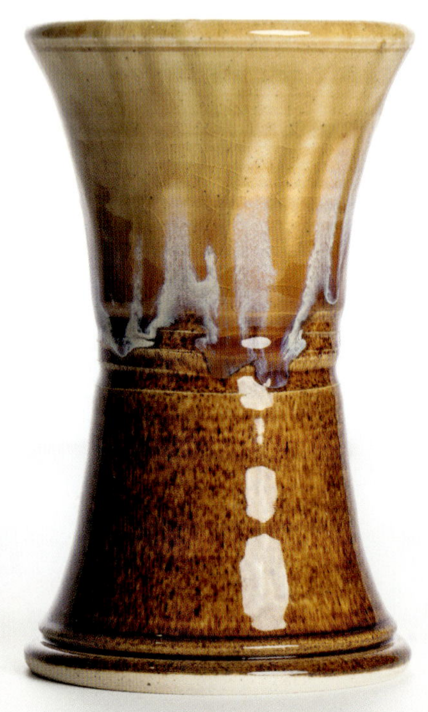

C6 Old Forge Sunset + Heath Ivory + Hannah's Fake Ash

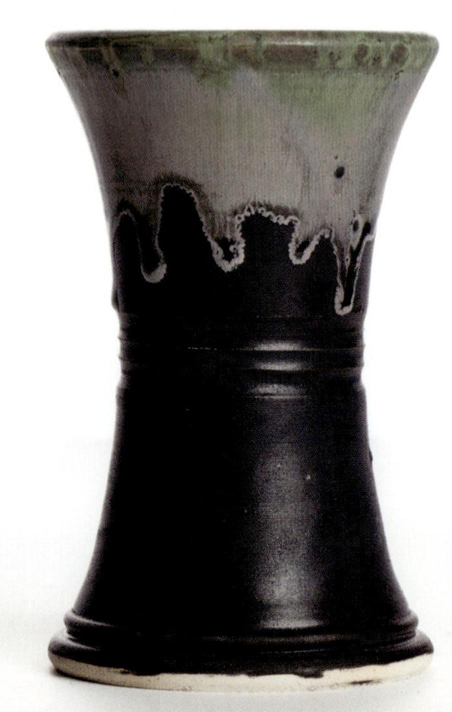

C6 Katz-Burke Matte Black + Britt's Pretty Matte Mustard

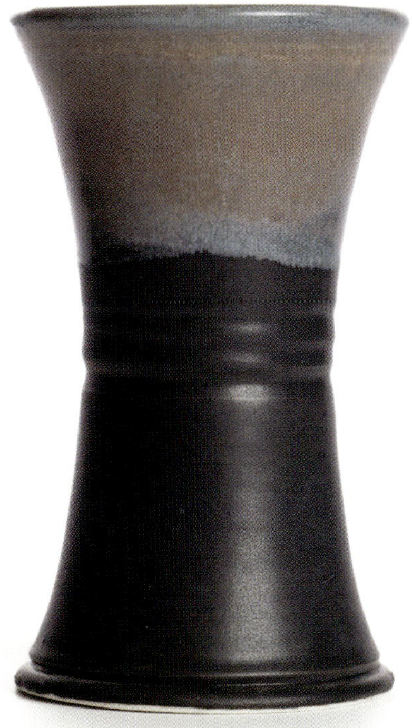

C6 Katz-Burke Matte Black + Old Forge First Five Floating Rutile

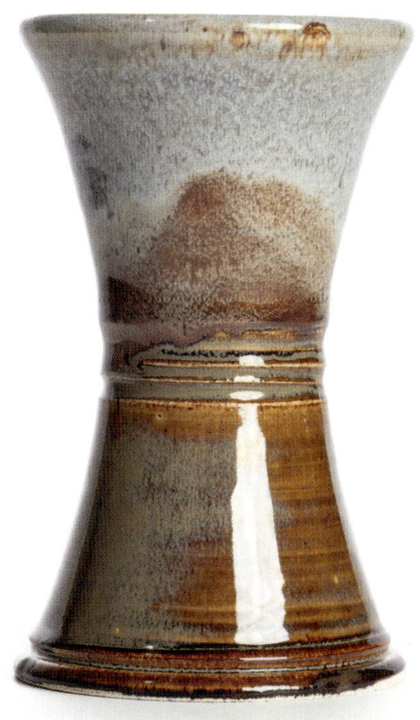

C6 Rust Red + Donte's Lumos + Old Forge Blurple

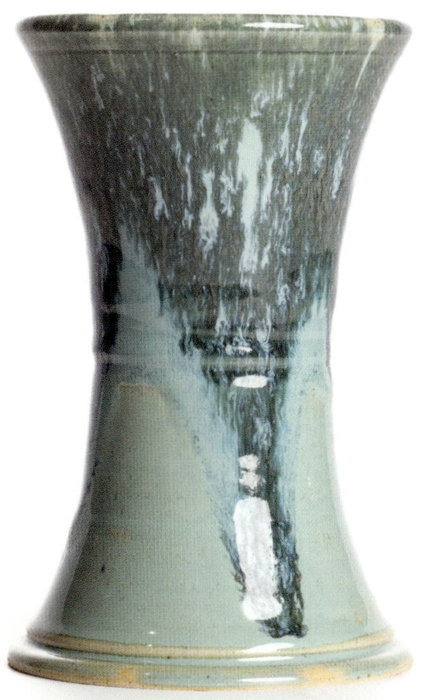

C6 Sweet Minty Turquoise + Blue Egg + Bluestone

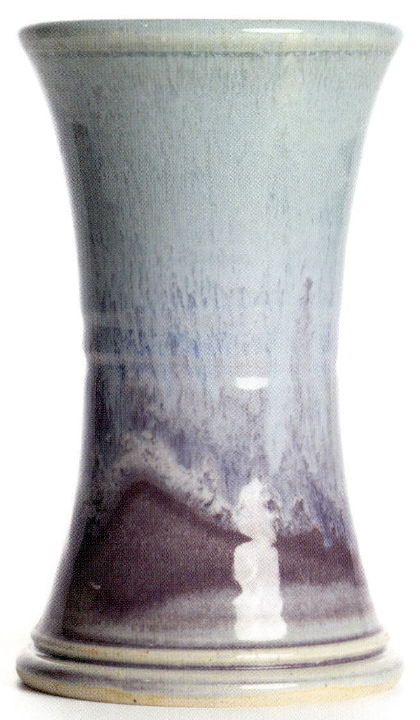

C6 Fancy Pants Purple + Heath Ivory + Val's Turquoise

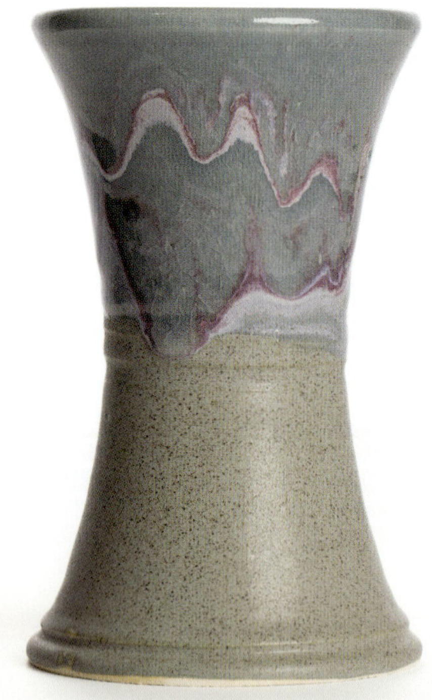

C6 Bluestone + June Perry Red + Heath Ivory

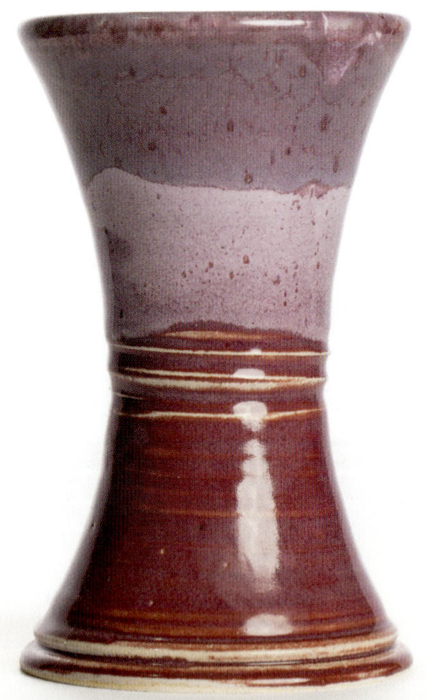

C6 June Perry Red + Donte's Old Forge Lumos + Old Forge Blurple

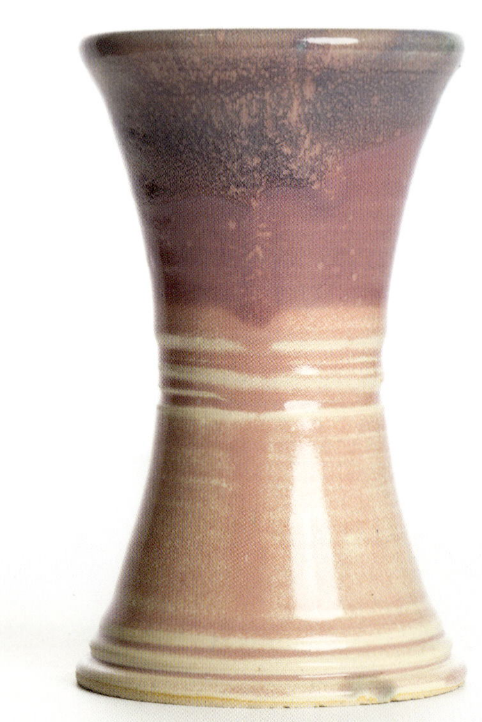

C6 Old Forge Floating Pink + Old Forge Blurple + Blue Egg

CONE 10 COMBINATIONS

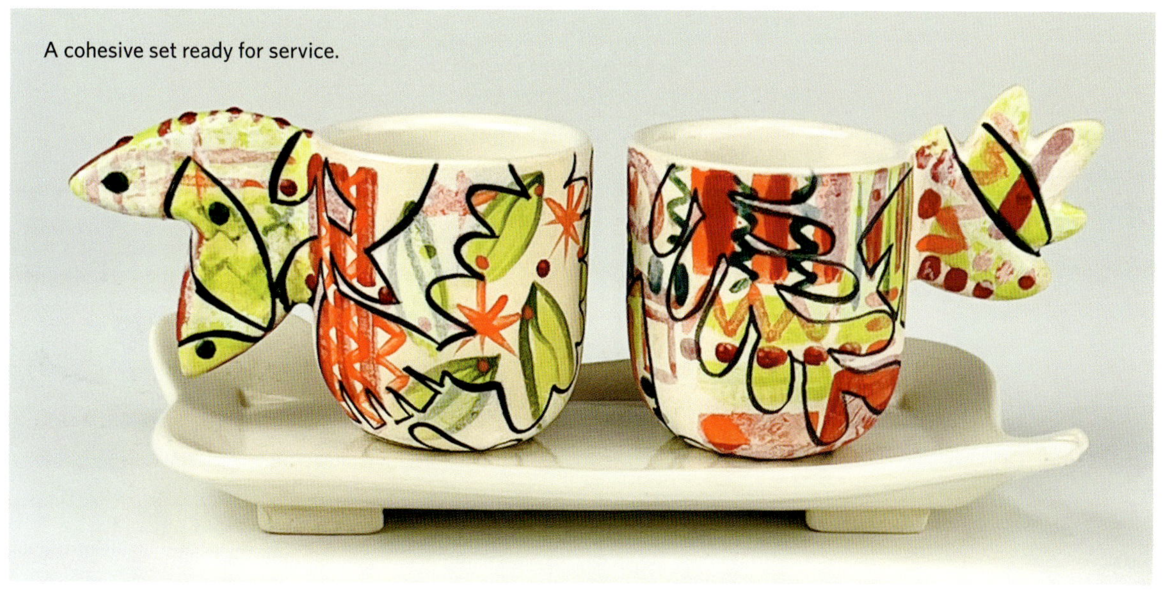
A cohesive set ready for service.

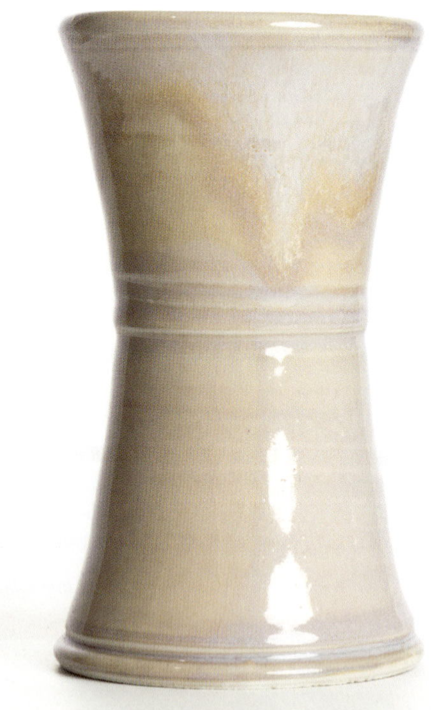

C10 Bleu de Rutile + Smooth Matte White + CMW Whiteout

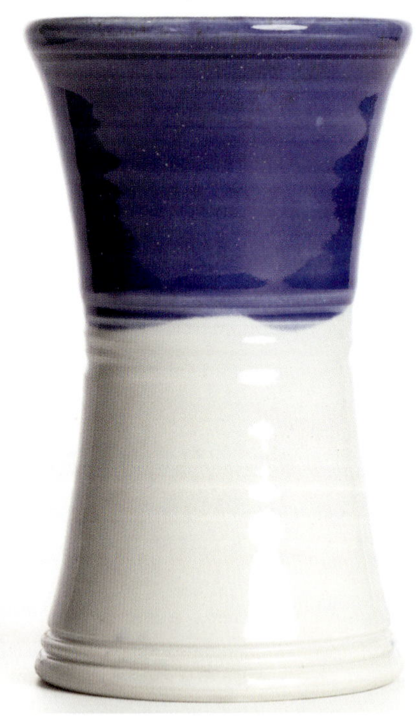

C10 CMW Whiteout + Watral Purple

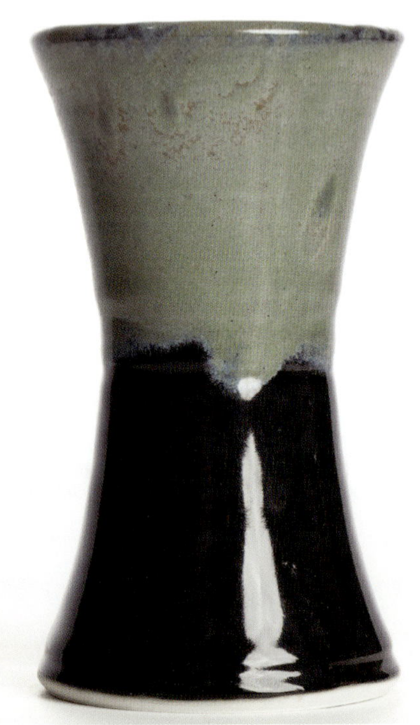

C10 Satiny Black + Apricot

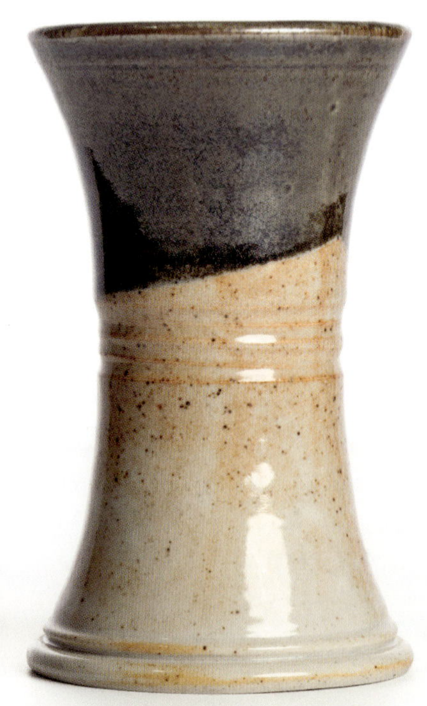

C10 American Shino + Oil Spot Black

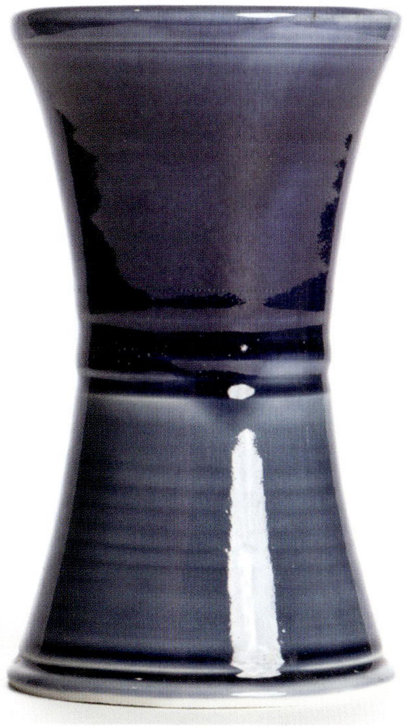

C10 Tin Purple + Watral Purple

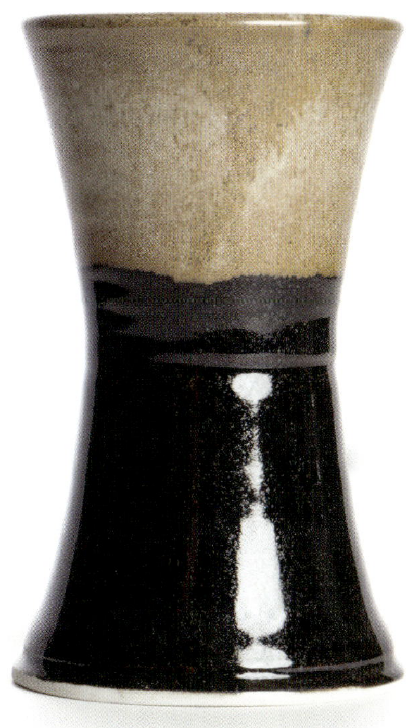

C10 Oil Spot Black + Apricot

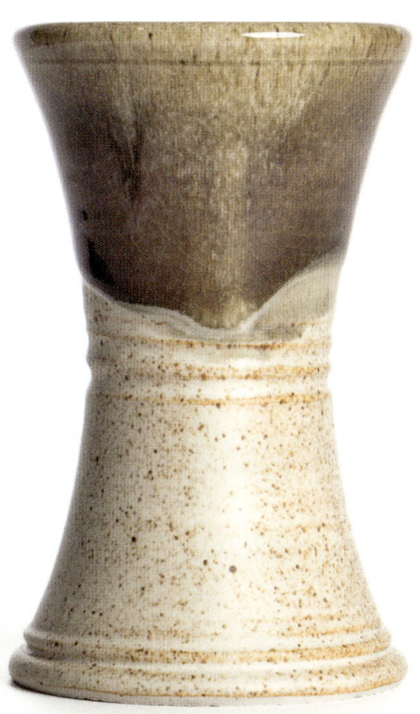

C10 Winokur Yellow + Hamada Rust + Bleu de Rutile

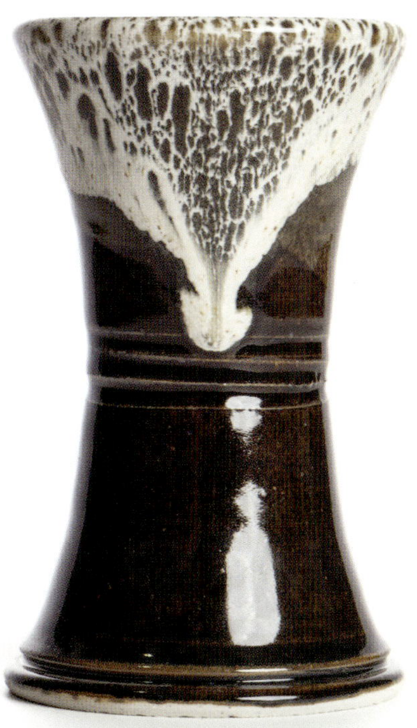

C10 Gavin's Purple + Frasier Celadon + Winokur Yellow

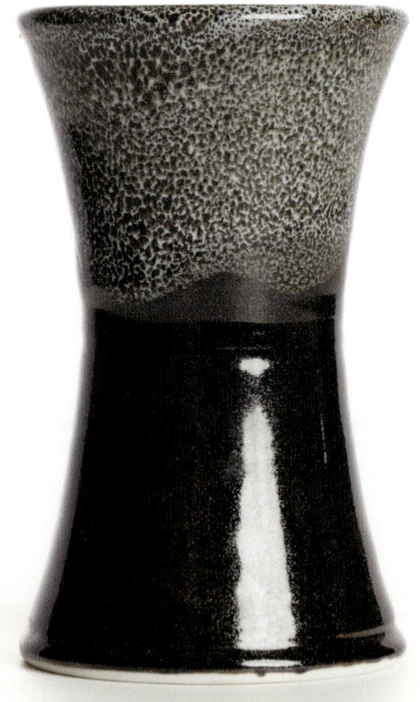
C10 Oil Spot Black + CMW Whiteout

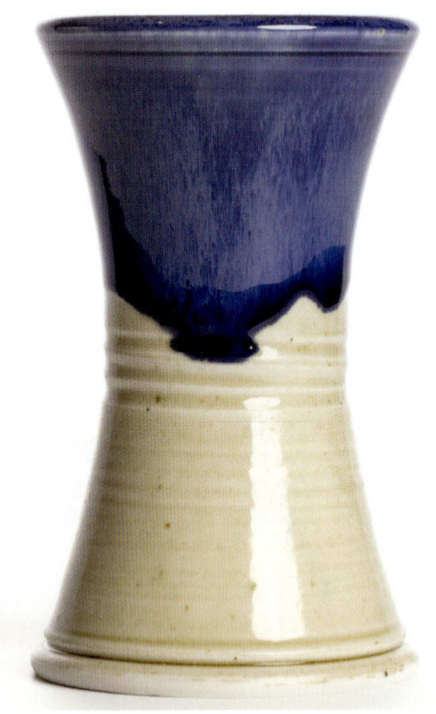
C10 Phil Rogers Ash + McPherson Blue

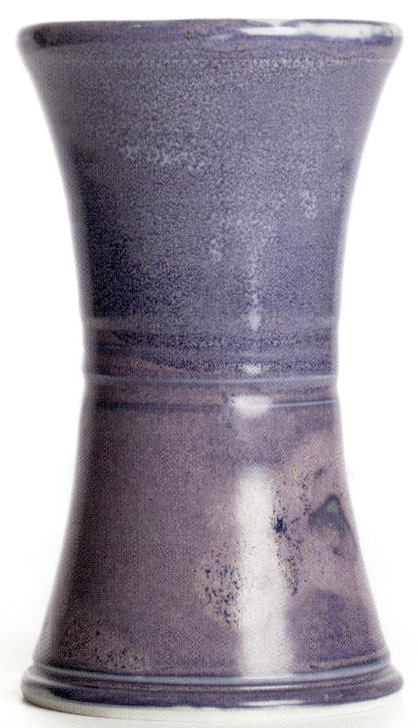
C10 Watral Purple + Smooth Matte White

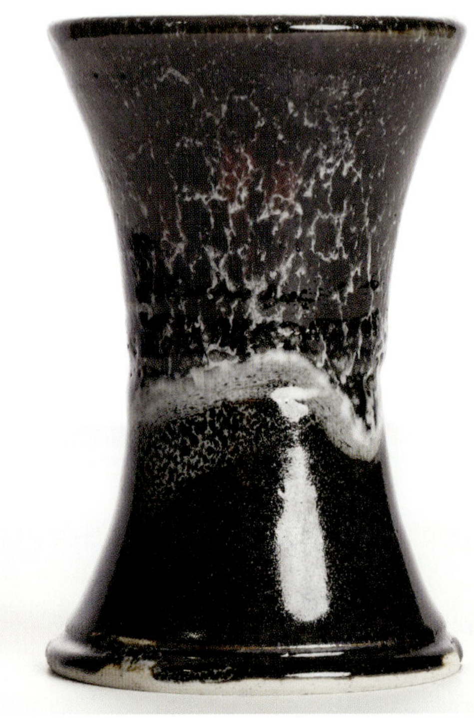
C10 Oil Spot Black + Cranberry + CMW Whiteout

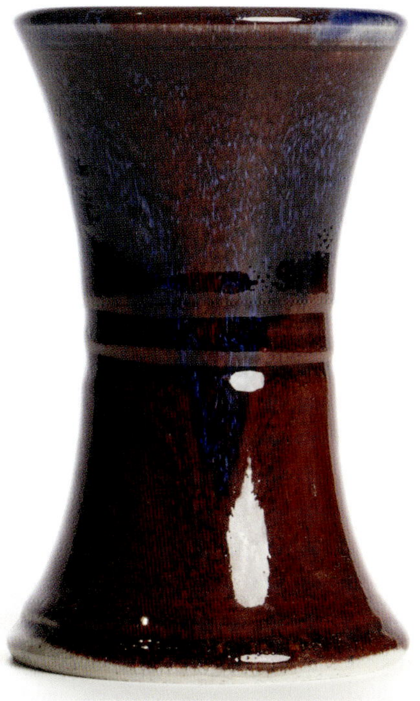

C10 Cranberry + McPherson Blue

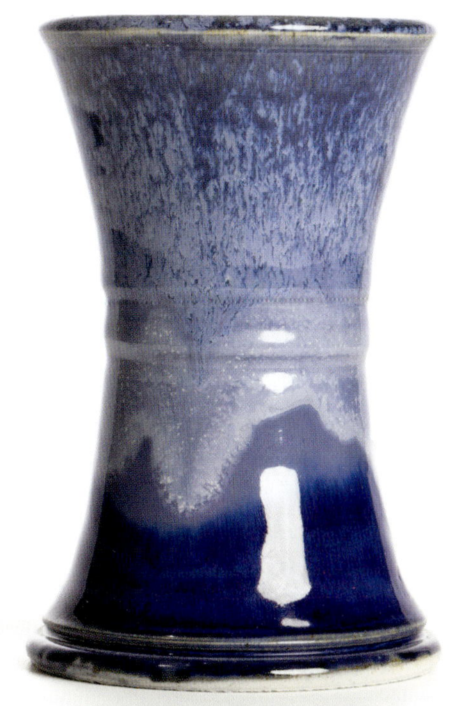

C10 McPherson Blue + Apricot + Frasier Celadon

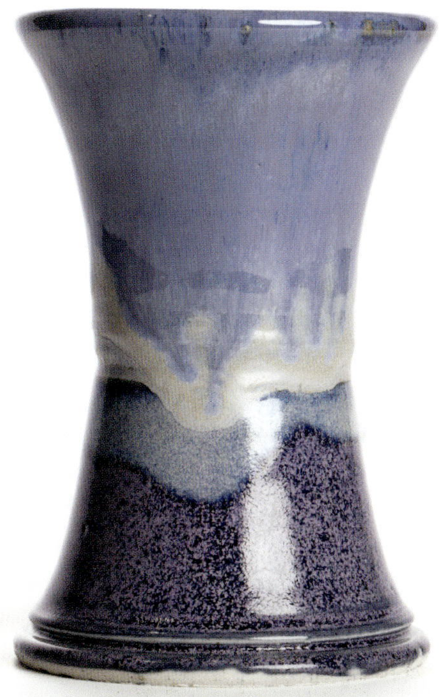

C10 Watral Purple + Apricot + McPherson Blue

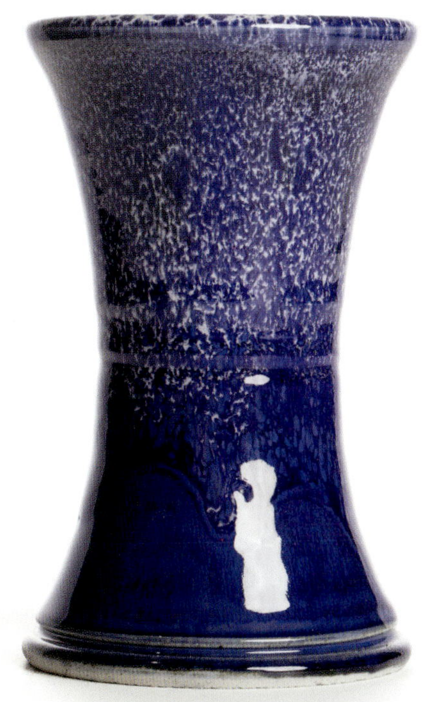

C10 McPherson Blue + Cranberry + CMW Whiteout

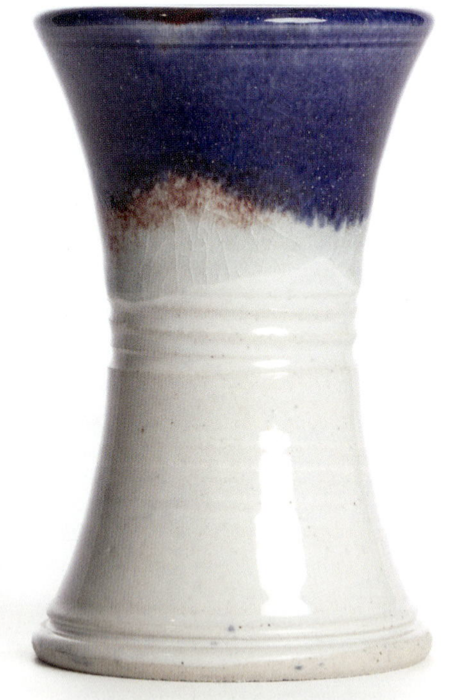

C10 CMW Whiteout + Cranberry + Watral Purple

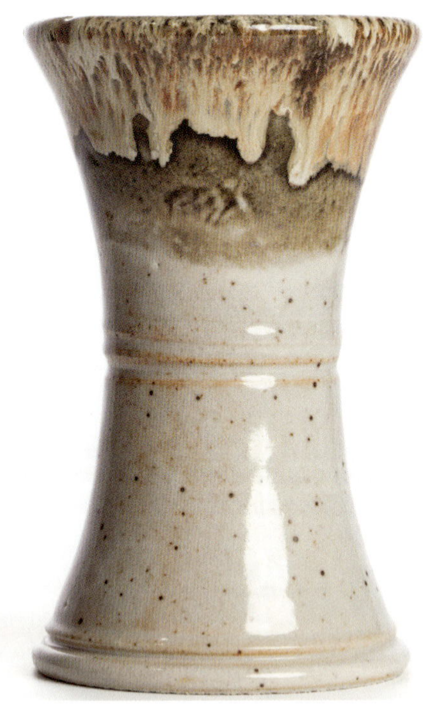

C10 American Shino + Hamada Rust + Winokur Yellow

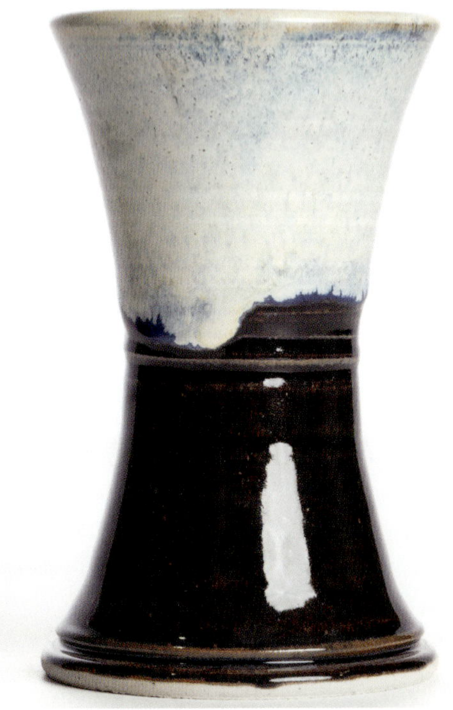

C10 Gavin's Purple + Bleu de Rutile + Apricot

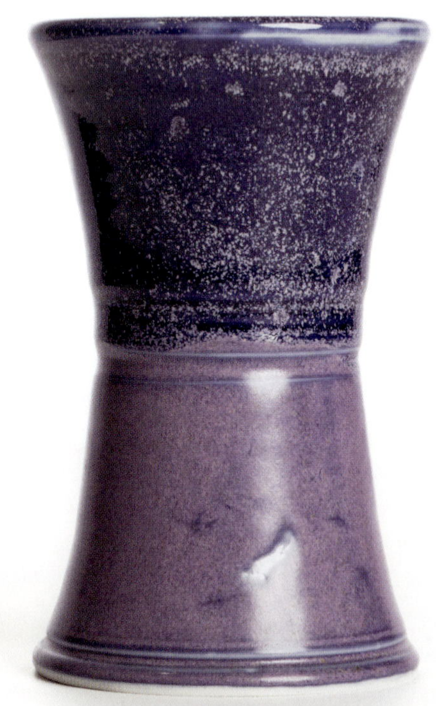

C10 Watral Purple + Tin Purple

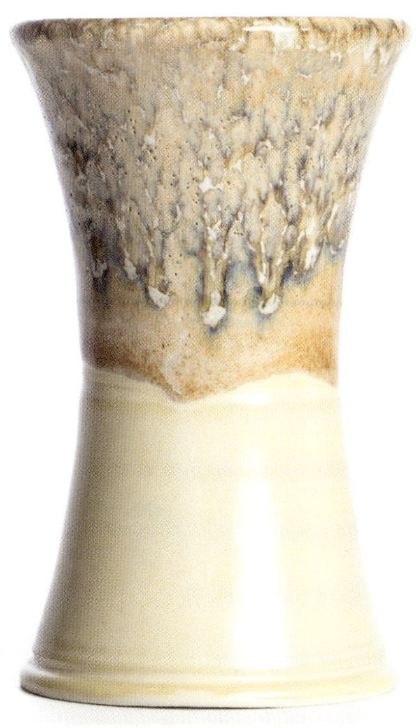
C10 Apricot + Hamada Rust + Winokur Yellow

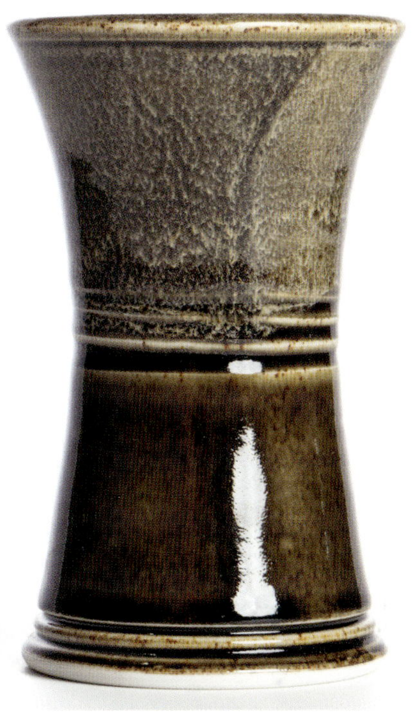
C10 Hamada Rust + Smooth Matte White

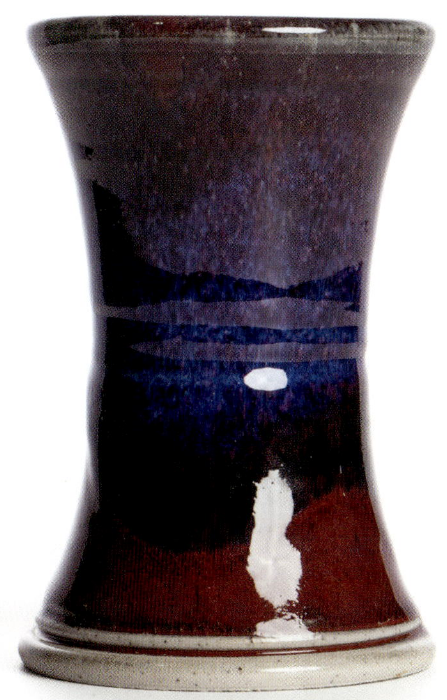
C10 Cranberry + Tin Purple + Bleu de Rutile

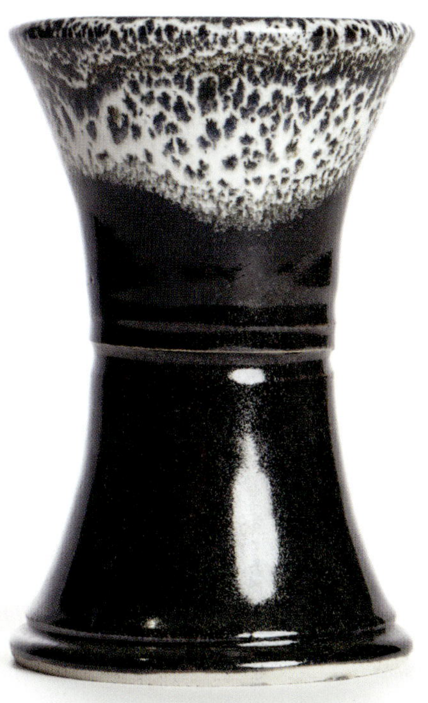
C10 Oil Spot Black + Bleu de Rutile + Smooth Matte White

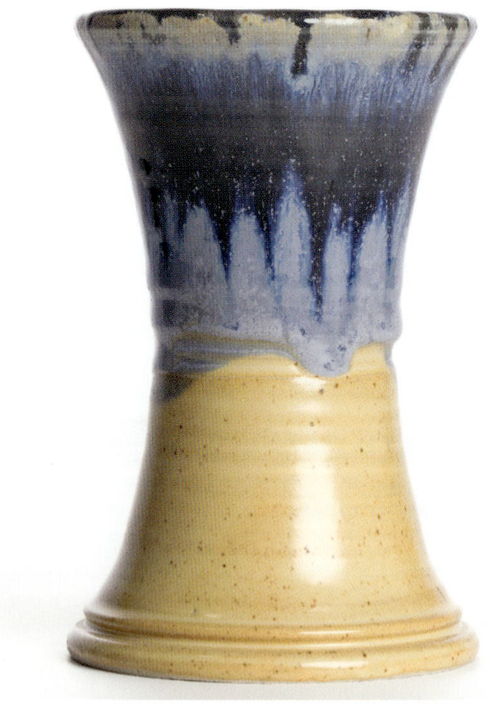

C10 Apricot + McPherson Blue + Phil Rogers Ash

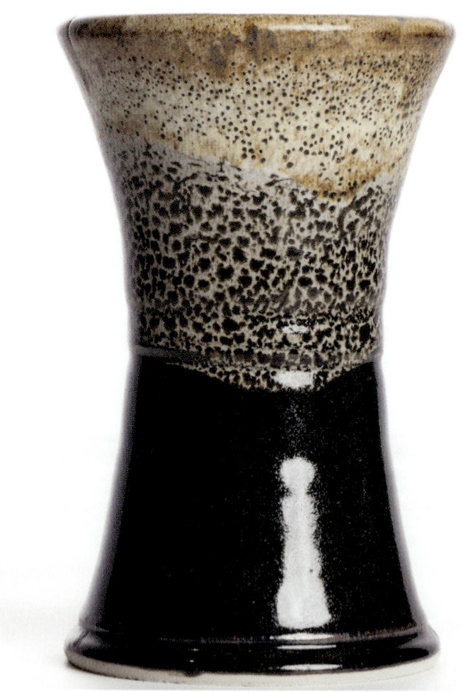

C10 Oil Spot Black + Winokur Yellow + Apricot

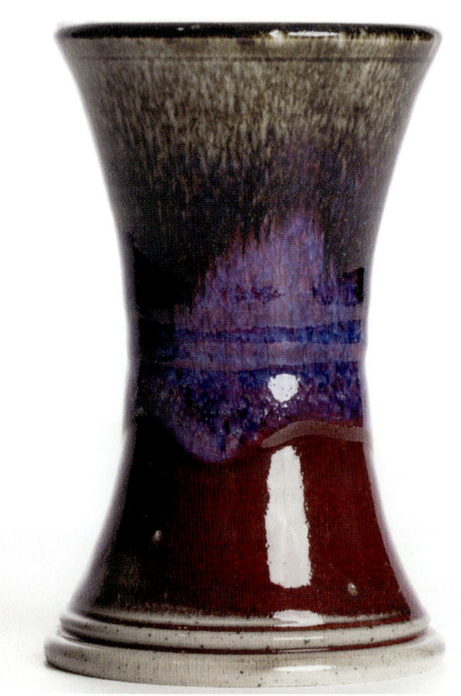

C10 Cranberry + Bleu de Rutile + Satiny Black

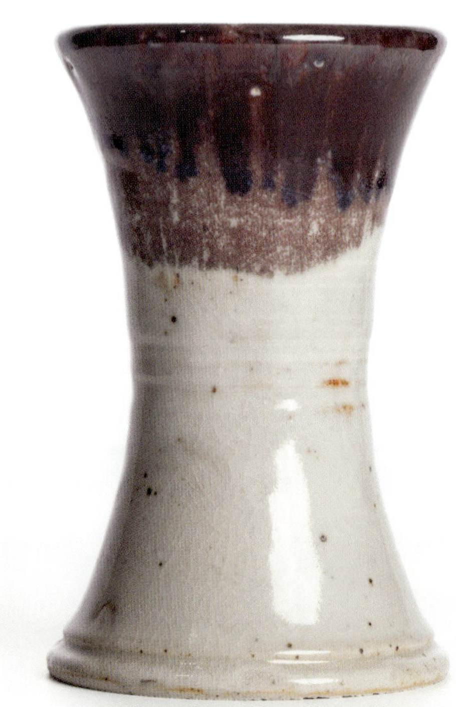

C10 American Shino + Cranberry + Tin Purple

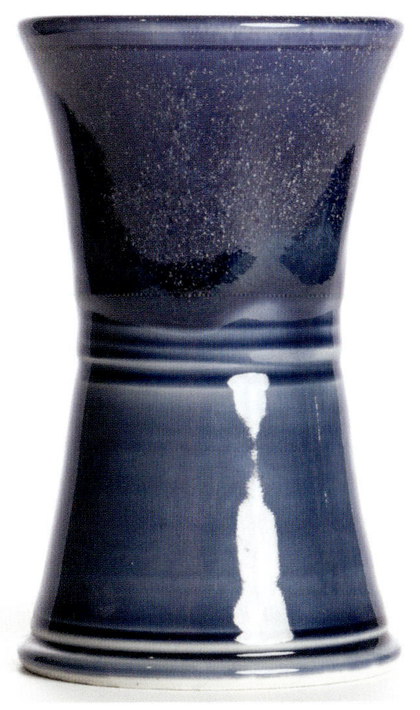

C10 Tin Purple + Cranberry + Watral Purple

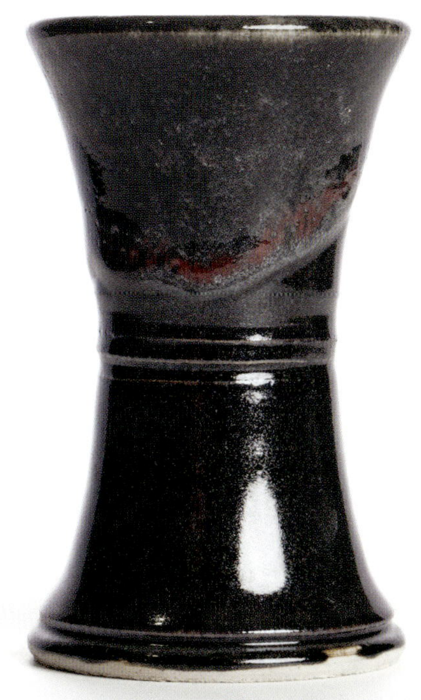

C10 Oil Spot Black + Frasier Celadon + Cranberry

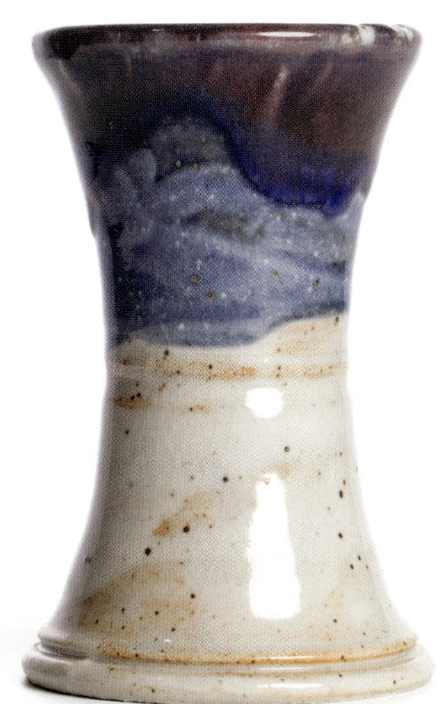

C10 American Shino + McPherson Blue + Cranberry

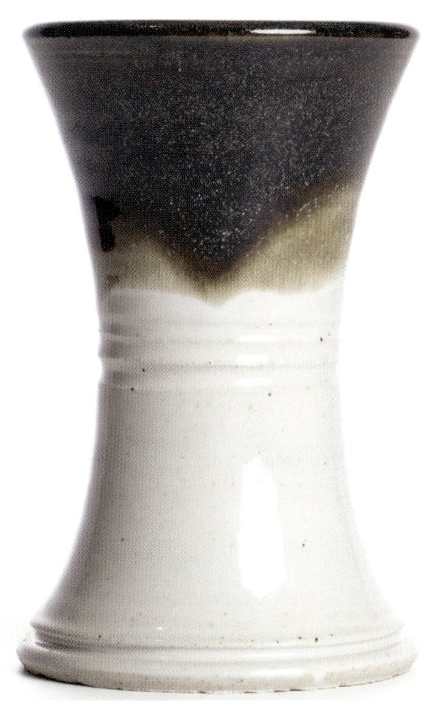

C10 CMW Whiteout + Hamada Rust + Oil Spot Black

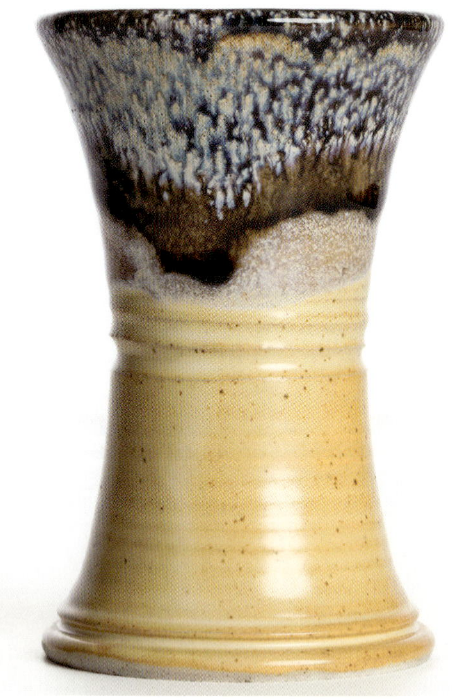

C10 Apricot + Frasier Celadon + Hamada Rust

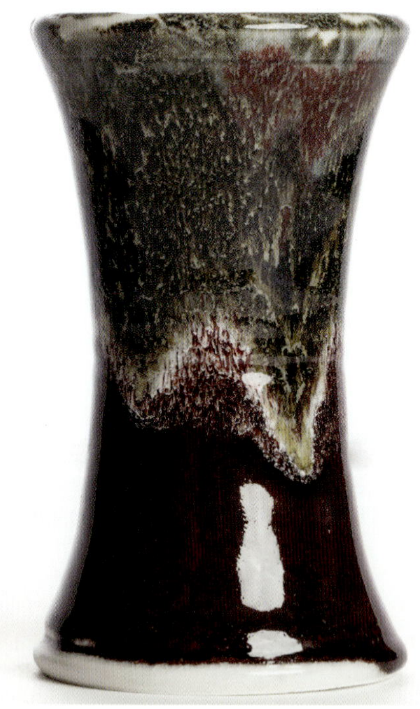

C10 Cranberry + Oil Spot Black +
Smooth Matte White

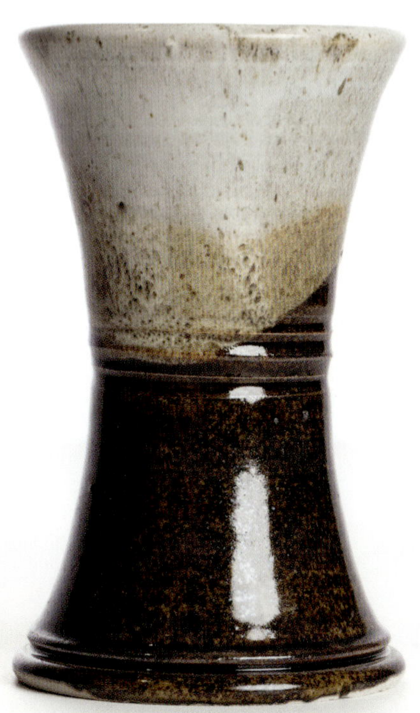

C10 Hamada Rust + Winokur Yellow

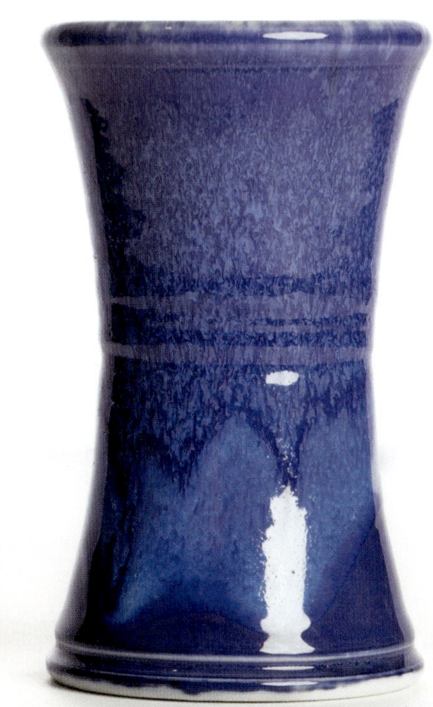

C10 McPherson Blue + Bleu de Rutile + Cranberry

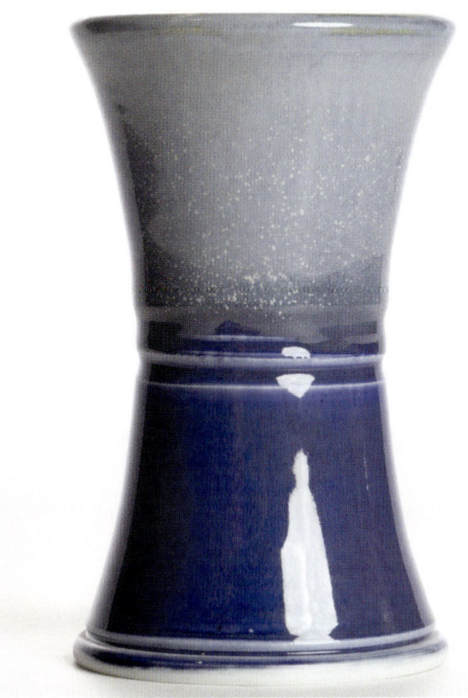

C10 McPherson Blue + Apricot

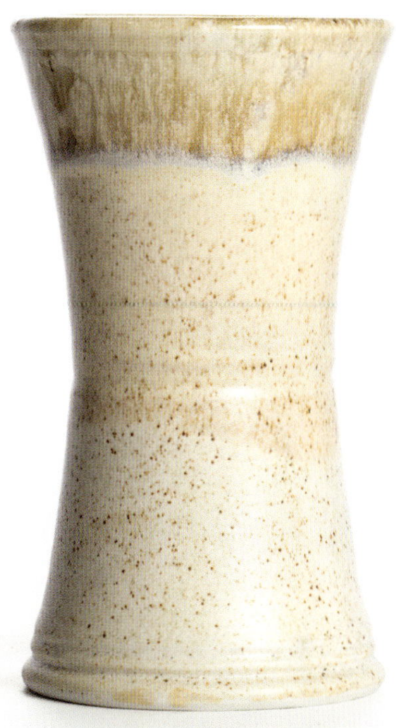

C10 Winokur Yellow + Apricot + Phil Rogers Ash

TESTING UNDERGLAZES

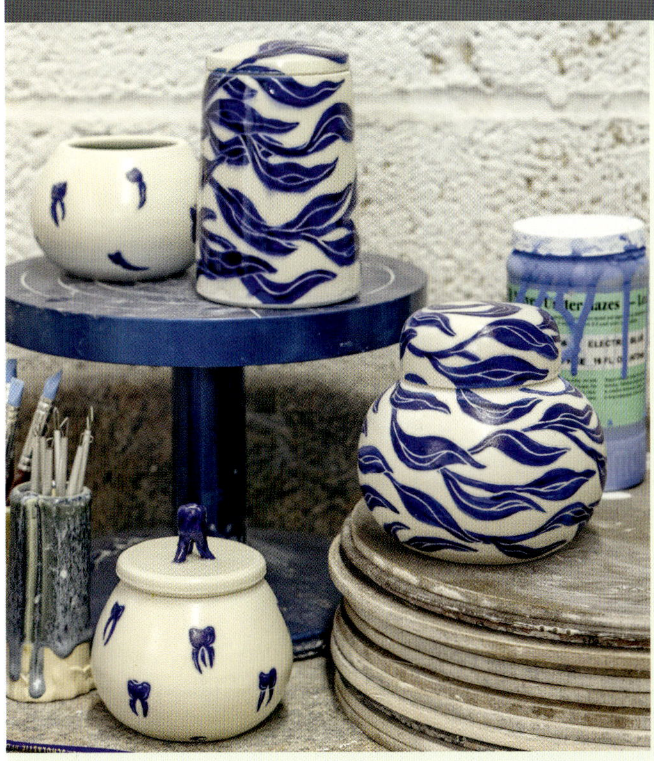

In pottery making, a common way to control bright colors with reliable results is to use commercially produced underglazes underneath a glossy glaze, as shown in the images here. Is this method food safe? We covered a variety of bisque-fired underglaze test tiles with Tony Hansen 5x20 Clear and fired to cone 6. In nearly every example, we observed no leaching. In a few cases, we saw extremely low levels of metals near our instrument's detection limits. In our opinion, completely covering underglazes in a glossy glaze is a great way to ensure food safety. Conversely, when we leach tested a black underglaze without a glossy glaze overcoat, we observed cobalt leaching above the max limit, indicating that underglazes by themselves should not be in contact with food for long periods of time.

Haley Cloyd uses underglazes beneath a clear glaze to create a dynamic food-safe surface.

Joe Thompson

oldforgecreations.co.uk Instagram @oldforgecreations

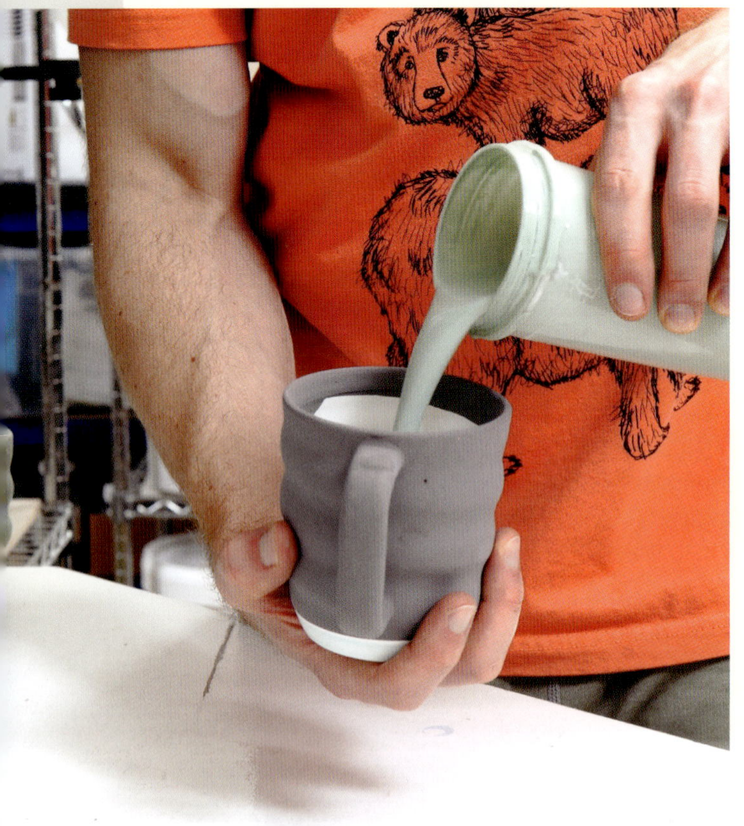

Joe Thompson applying glaze to the inside of a mug. Joe has been hitting the gym!

You'll notice a number of the most dynamic glazes in the book have the name "Old Forge" attached to them. Old Forge Creations is the brainchild of British potter Joe Thompson and the project has several facets including beautiful pottery, handmade tools, and an online community that he inspires with his glazes and research. Check out the timeless elegance of his signature "White Impulse Bowls." These pots feature a stunning snow to ocean effect that lowers our blood pressure just to take them in. What a wonderful effect art can have on our spirit. We are fascinated with Joe's project called "First Five," which he has graciously outlined in this interview.

AMAZING GLAZE FOOD-SAFE RECIPES: *Why is it important for you to teach others ceramic science and glaze chemistry? Why do you share your glaze formulations and discoveries?*

JOE THOMPSON: I'm self-taught in ceramics, and I got started using the free resources on websites such as DigitalFire and Glazy. These were hugely beneficial to me at the beginning as I didn't really have the budget for taking paid classes to learn the basics, and I still feel that gratitude for everyone who made such valuable information available for free. I never intended to produce educational content, as I didn't expect to have anything useful to add to the wealth of info already out there online, but over time I developed processes and glazes that I hadn't seen elsewhere. I was happy to be able to participate in the tradition of sharing information and did my best to put that content out in a way that would help the next generation of beginners.

AGFSR: *Can you talk about the impetus for the development of the "First Five?"*

JOE: The First Five series of glazes are a range of cone 5 to 6 recipes that use a limited selection of five common glaze base ingredients (nepheline syenite, Ferro Frit 3134, whiting, kaolin, and silica). The idea was that someone looking to get started in glaze-making could buy the smallest selection of ingredients possible and use them to make a wide range of glazes. This was partially inspired by feeling overwhelmed as a beginner when looking at the extensive range of glaze ingredients, many of which I purchased to use in a recipe test and never used again, but the real impetus was talking to an art teacher. He wanted to offer his students a range of glazes but didn't have the budget or storage space for any more ingredients than the absolute minimum. I was sure that with the right ingredients and recipes, this wouldn't be too limiting. Since then I've used the same basic ingredients to create dozens of recipes, and they seem to travel well due to those materials being fairly con-

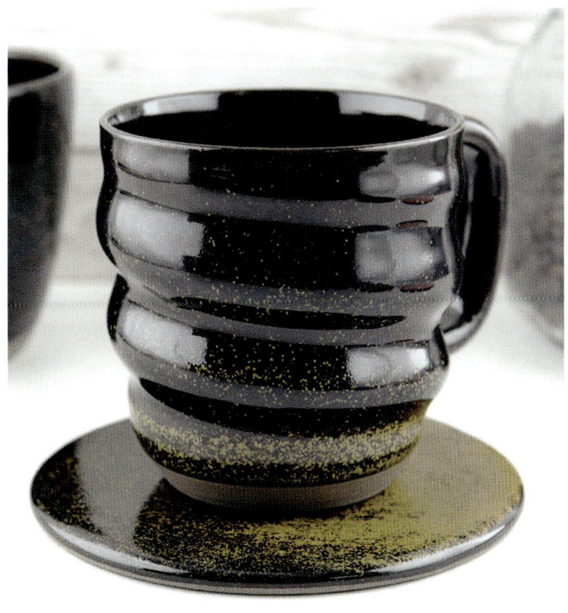

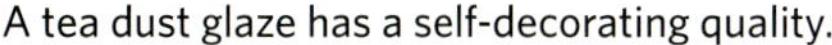

A tea dust glaze has a self-decorating quality.

Slip and glaze interact to create rivulets of color.

sistent across different regions (although availability of 3134 can be an issue). I found that the confusion around purchasing initial ingredients was what put a lot of people off mixing their own glazes; having a simple and clear starting point lowers the barrier and allows many more people to give it a go.

[You can find more about the project here on his website: oldforgecreations.co.uk.]

AGFSR: *Glaze chemistry sits at the intersection of science and art. What are some of the challenges this creates? How do you overcome barriers when it comes to communicating complex, scientific ideas to nonscientists?*

JOE: I feel like a lot of people expect glazes to behave like paints, where colors can be mixed with predictable results. Sometimes this can be the case, but often the resulting color will only make sense with an understanding of the underlying chemistry. Most potters are approaching the subject from the art side of that intersection and have little interest in diving deep into the science side, but just knowing that there is an underlying logic to the results can help them make some sense of glaze combinations through testing.

When I try to communicate the practical implications of more complex ideas, I aim to start the explanation from the most basic point and try to move the reader through a series of small logical steps. I often try to use comparisons to help make it more relatable (e.g., comparing kiln heatwork to cooking pizza, where three minutes in a really hot pizza oven or twenty minutes in a normal oven will result in well-cooked pizzas). While this might not necessarily give the reader the most complete understanding of the underlying complexity, it (hopefully) helps the information click in a way that means they can apply it in their studio.

AGFSR: *In what ways do you think that the ceramic education process (mentoring, apprenticeships, self-taught, university) could be improved?*

JOE: I can't really comment much on the formal education side of ceramics, other than to say that I know a lot of ceramics students graduate without a good understanding of the steps required to become a full-time ceramic artist in the social media era (but that's a topic for another conversation). With regard to the process of becoming self-taught in ceramics, I think we're fortunate to have so many people putting excellent information out for free or within paid

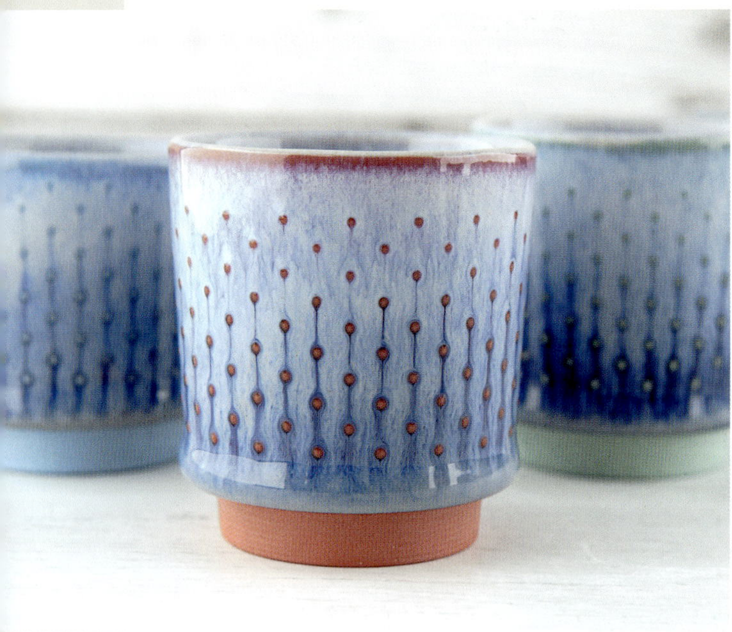

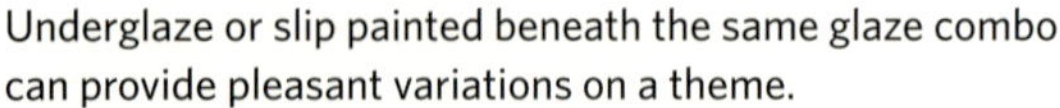

Underglaze or slip painted beneath the same glaze combo can provide pleasant variations on a theme.

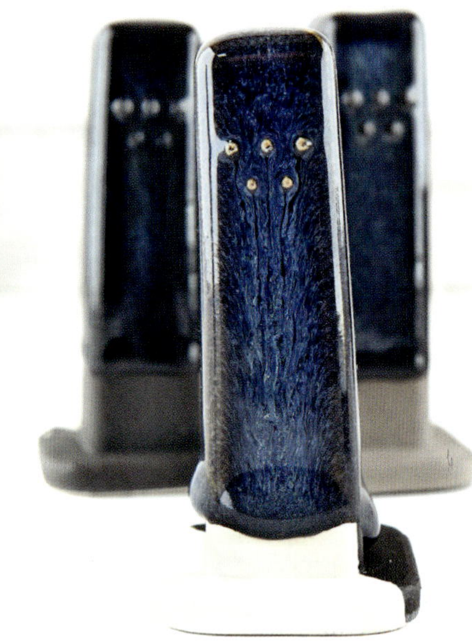

Even Joe's test tiles are works of art, and sometimes available for sale!

online courses. I do worry that the online educational space might become harder to navigate in future though, as there are online course platforms actively saturating other areas with low quality courses . . . Hopefully this won't happen to the ceramics education space!

AGFSR: *As more people learn to develop, take control, and experiment with their glaze chemistry, how will that change our art form and in what ways do you see the ceramic community evolving in the future?*

JOE: For the individual potters learning to make and control their glazes, it will certainly help them find their unique voice and refine their making process. Whether that evolves the overall community, I'm not sure. I do think there will be many more publicly available glaze recipes as more people learn to test and adjust glazes, but I think the cosmetic differences will allow for more individual expression rather than a greater overall change. There are glaze categories that were established hundreds of years ago (if not more) and development within those categories seem to be small cosmetic adjustments (e.g., with Oil Spot glazes, which have been in use for over 1,000 years and remained similar throughout).

One area that I can see evolving is crystalline glazes, although they're not something I have much experience with personally. The shape and pattern of crystal growth is affected quite dramatically by small changes in the kiln temperature. Kiln controllers are becoming more accurate and capable of precisely replicating complex firing schedules, which makes it easier for crystalline potters to build a shared knowledge base and apply that to their own process in a way that wouldn't have been possible in the past.

AGFSR: *Ceramics is becoming more accessible to a greater number of people with commercially available clay, glazes, and programmable electric kilns. As barriers come down and more people get into this field, what opportunities and challenges do you see this creating?*

JOE: As someone who benefited from this increased accessibility when I got started, I think it's great that the barriers to entry are becoming lower. There's less risk of beginners creating work with safety issues when they're able to buy a commercial clay and glaze that should work well together and use a preprogrammed schedule to fire them consistently. And once they're ready to move from premade glazes to mixing their own, there are plenty of good recipes for them to try.

It's extremely hard for beginners to know what glaze recipes are sensible and which are problematic. I would say that over the time I've been making glazes this generally hasn't been a big problem. Most recipes that are posted online have been formulated and tested by someone who has at least some idea of what they are doing, and example pictures of a glaze recipe give a fair indication of what the glaze will do. If a glaze recipe is a failure, it is less likely to be posted. Recently I've seen a few people using artificial intelligence (AI) to generate glaze recipes and pictures, and I feel this might be a bigger issue in future. The AI output will follow the form of a typical glaze recipe (so at a glance it looks like a normal recipe), but something like AI doesn't understand the implication of any individual glaze ingredient and will combine them in nonsensical ways. If you ask it for a glossy cone 6 glaze, it might give you a recipe that would never melt (because three out of five ingredients were a type of kaolin) or a recipe that would be a puddle on the floor (because three out of five ingredients were a source of boron). It doesn't know what the ingredients do, so it can't consistently make sensible selections. If people are going to publicly share AI-generated recipes (especially with generated "result" photos), it's going to become a lot harder for beginners to select safe recipes to make themselves.

AGFSR: *What does food safe mean to you? When developing your own glazes, how does food safety influence your decision making process?*

JOE: Food safety can be quite a polarizing and confusing topic, but I'm glad so many potters are taking it seriously. For me, food safety means: Firstly, avoiding the elements that would need to be tested within defined limits (e.g., cadmium and lead have legal limits in the UK) so there is no possibility of being outside the limit; secondly, paying close attention to the chemistry of any glaze that will be in contact with food to make sure everything is within a sensible range; thirdly, doing the (admittedly quite limited) glaze tests that can be performed at home to check that the glaze doesn't degrade over time; and fourthly, monitoring firings to make sure they are consistent over time and any glaze within that firing should have been correctly fired.

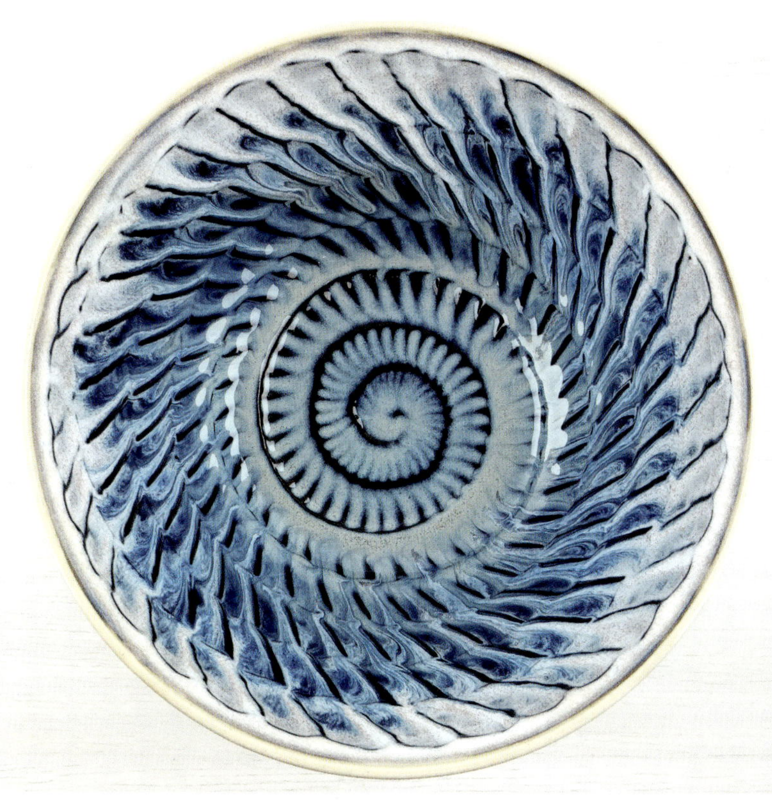

Incredible whirlpool effect using textured slip and glaze.

GALLERY

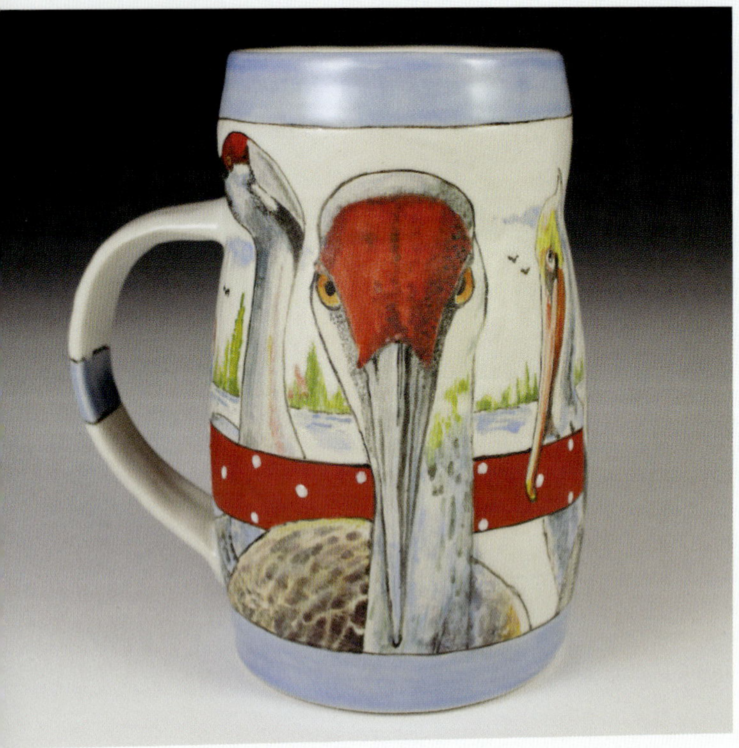

Mug. Ann Ruel.
Excuse me. Are you going eat that? Ann Ruel with a winner!

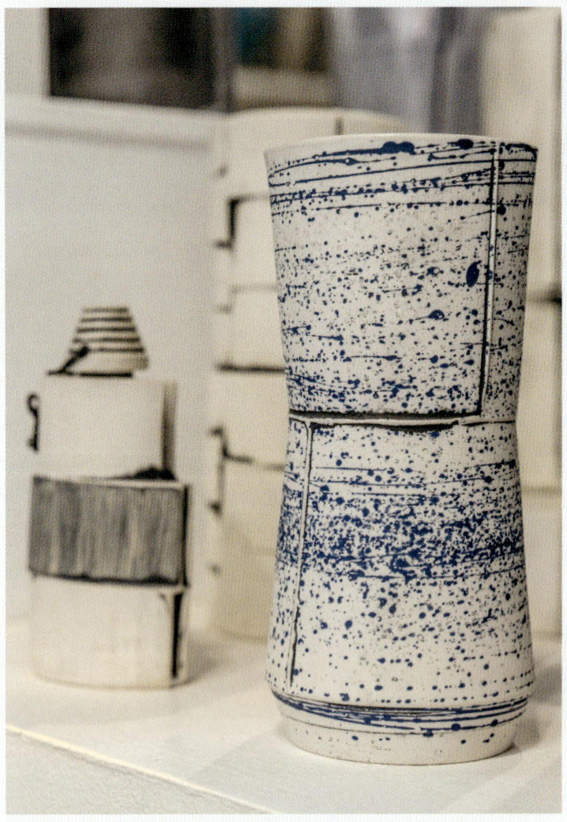

Gallery Grouping. Tyler Anderson.
The exteriors are left stained and unglazed. The interiors of these pieces are glazed, glossy, and smooth.

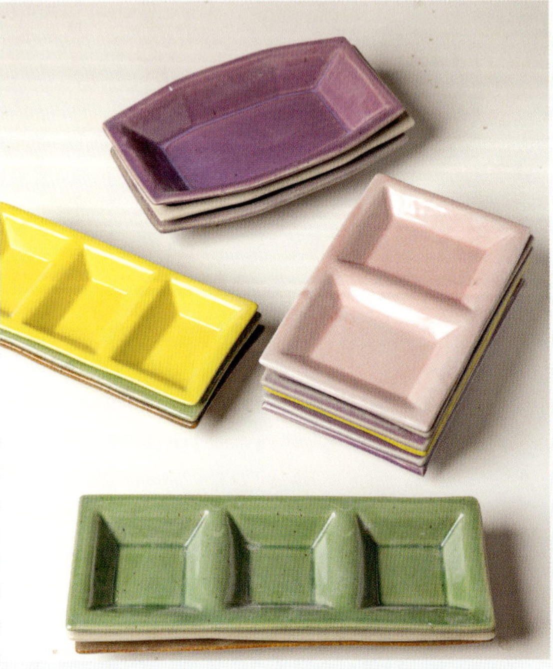

Food-safe glazes on Odyssey ClayWorks's production line.

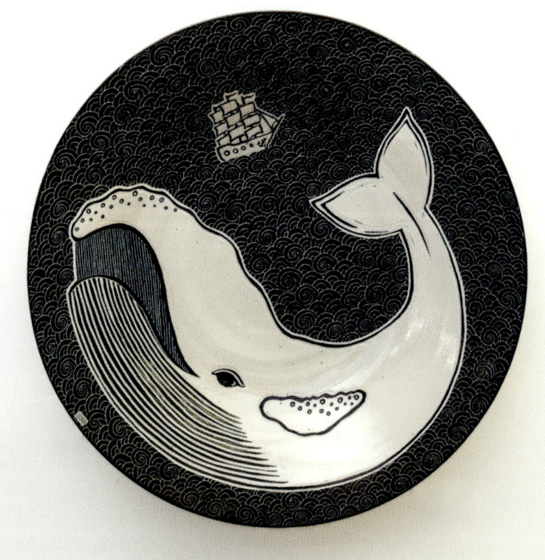

Big Whale, Small Ship. Anja Bartels.
Black underglaze, snow white porcelain, clear glaze, and an exacting hand are all required to execute this piece.

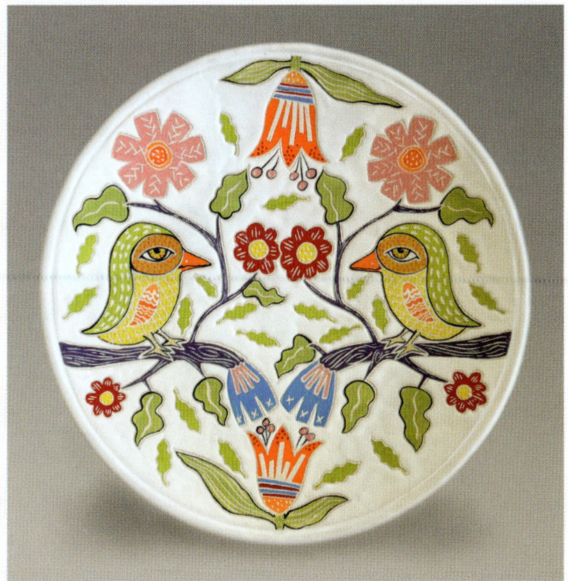

Multi Sgraffito Bowl, Two Birds. Jennifer Rosseter.
As you eat all the teacakes, you reveal two birds making plans.

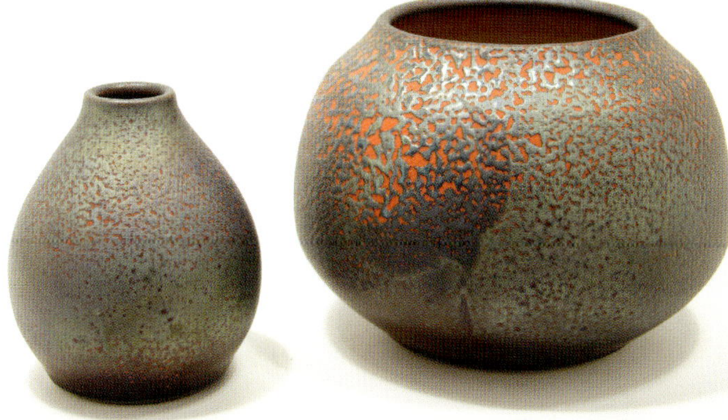

Experimental Glazes. Alex Thullen.
Not all glazes should be used as liners, but it is nice to see the range of possibilities, as in these dynamic pieces produced for Pewabic.

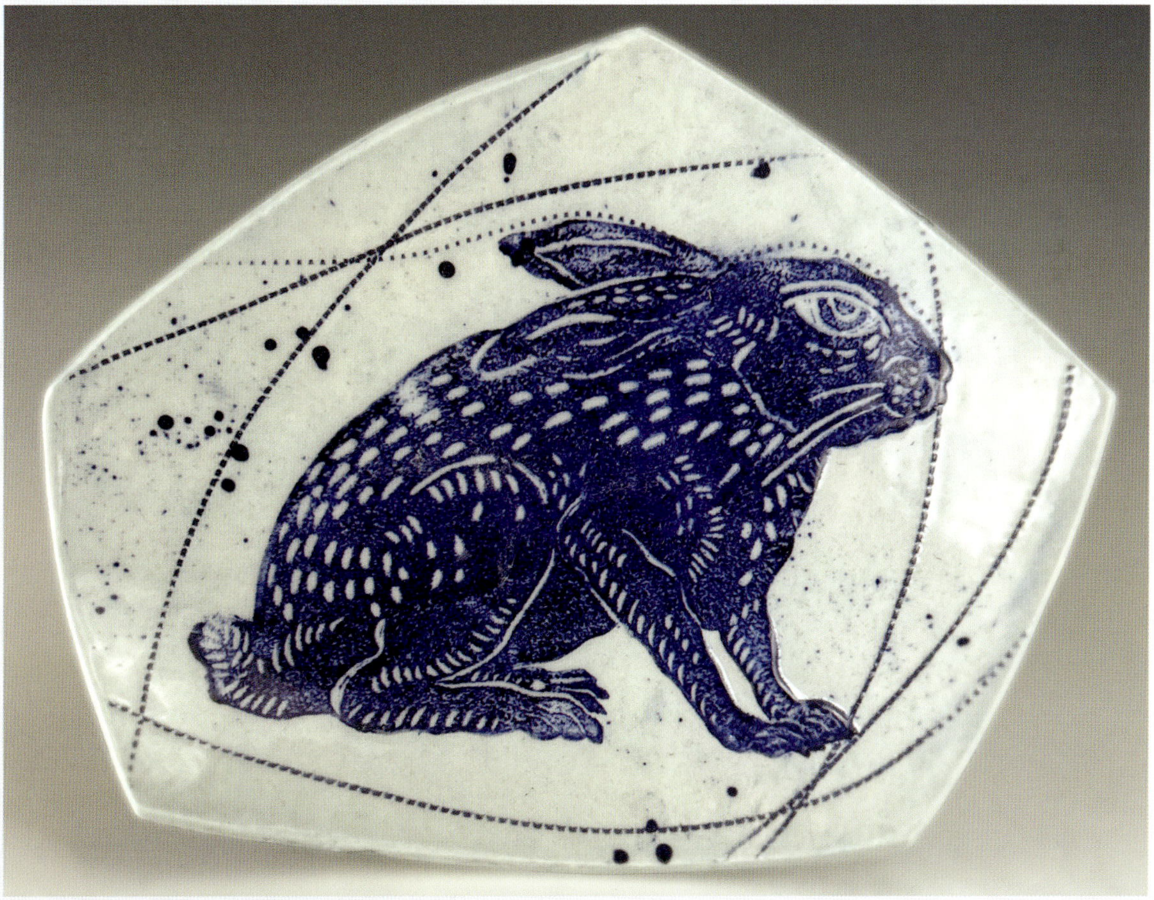

Animal Plates, Sgraffito Rabbit. Jennifer Rosseter.
This hare is simultaneously bound by the form of the plate and looking like it might hop right off it.

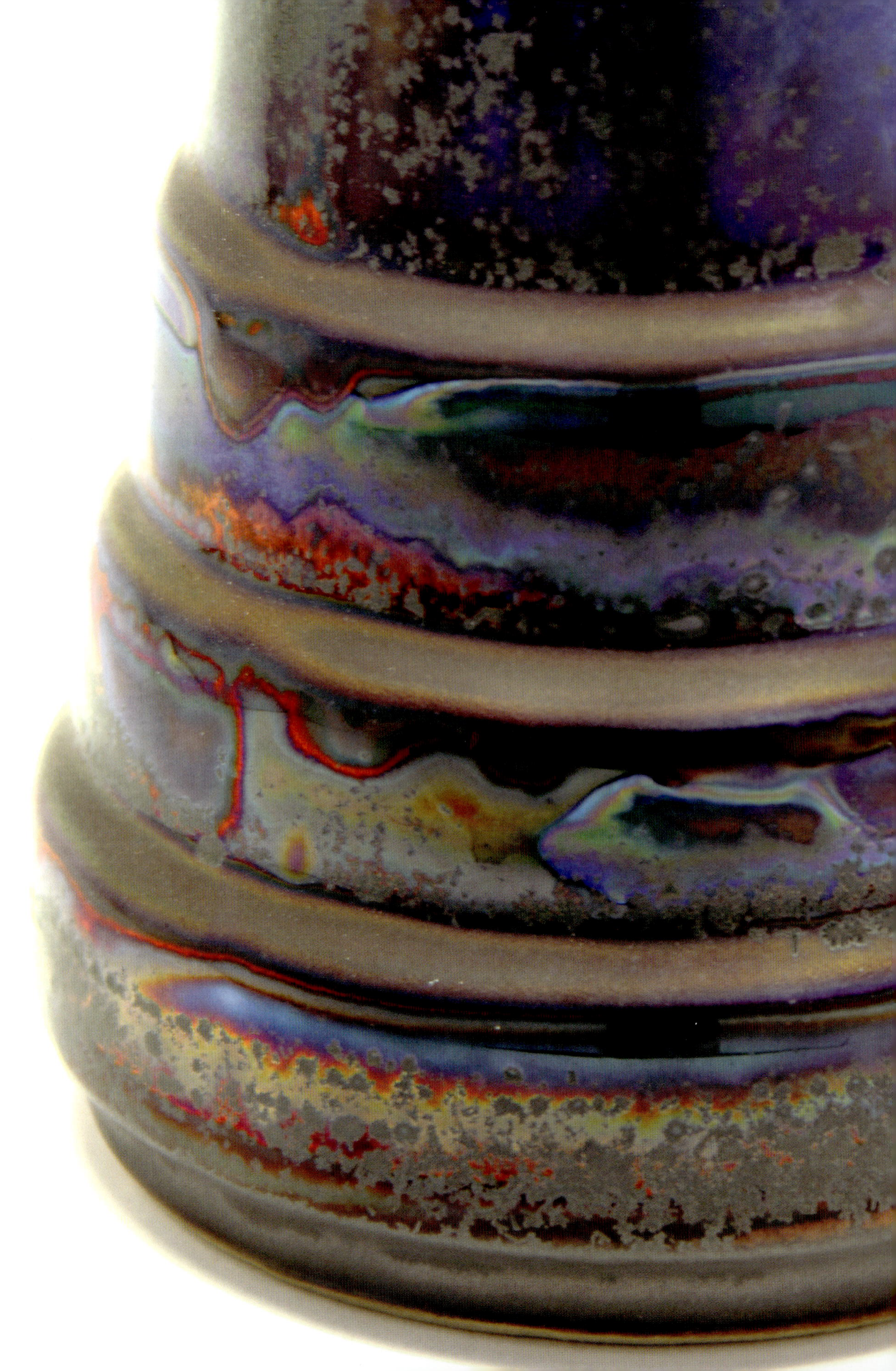

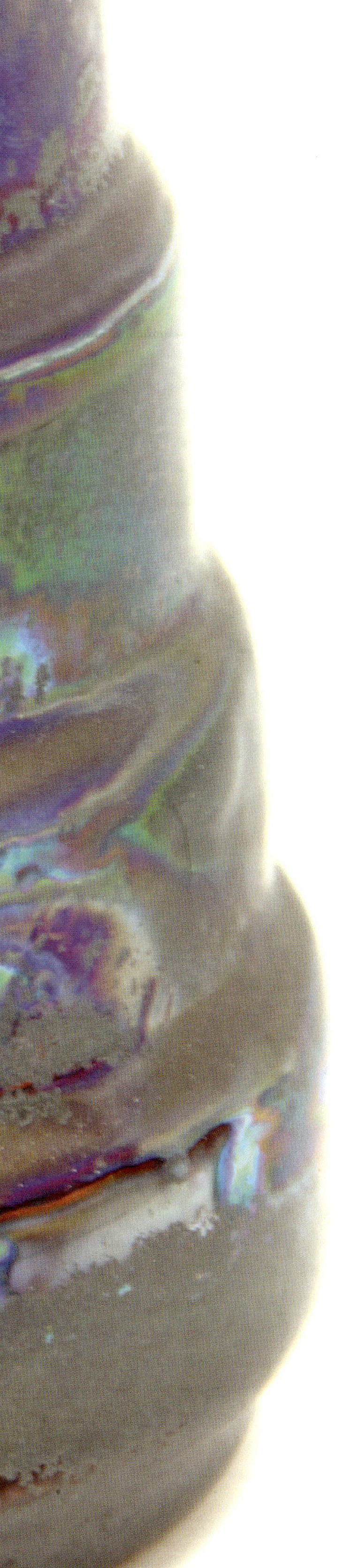

5

Firing for Durability

POTTERY AND GLAZES must undergo an intense trial by fire! Both bisque firing and glaze firing transform ceramic materials in meaningful ways. Let's make sure we are engaging best practices to ensure great results.

Detail, Experimental Glaze. Alex Thullen.
Iridescence is challenging to achieve in glazes, but brilliantly formulated and applied here by Alex.

HEATWORK: CONES AND TEMPCHEKS

Consider the similarities between cooking food and fully melting a glaze. When you are baking something in the kitchen, you have to think about three interconnected pieces: what you are making, how hot to set the oven, and how long to bake. For the novice cook, getting any one of these slightly wrong can change a potential culinary masterpiece into an undercooked disaster. As we also know, each of these variables influences the others. A deep-dish pizza will take longer than melting cheese on a thin-crust pizza. As Joe Thompson stated in his interview (see page 110), time and temperature are also related: you can fully cook a pizza quickly at a high temperature or slowly at lower temperatures. We must also consider what's in the recipe, the temperature, and the time it takes to fully melt a glaze.

Looking at recipes, we can see that they are largely grouped into three categories: high-fire (typically cone 10), mid-fire (around cone 6), and low-fire (cone 1 and below). It is important to recognize that besides cone 10, these temperature groupings are largely arbitrary. Indeed, in countries outside of the United States, mid-fire can mean cone 7 or even cone 8. So, what is the point of mid- or low-fire glazes? These glazes require lower peak-temperatures and are inherently more energy efficient. For electric kilns they also put less wear and tear on the heating elements. One counterpoint, however, is that these glazes have intrinsically more complex recipes and require the mining and transport of additional resources, which is energy intensive and can have a negative environmental toll.

Cone 10 (2,345°F to 2,381°F [1,285°C to 1,305°C]) is significant because it represents the lowest temperature at which silica and alumina can be fully melted using only fluxes. Below cone 10, additional additives such as boron, lead, or other specialty fluxes are required to help the melting process. Oftentimes, mid-fire glazes possess combinations of fluxes and boron that allow for complete melting around cone 6 (2,232°F to 2,269°F [1,222°C to 1243°C]). As you get to low-fire glazes, boron is required in such large amounts that the boron source is often the primary component.

At this point, you might be noticing that the melting temperatures are given in ranges. This is because, like the pizza analogy, a glaze will fully melt at a lower temperature if it is cooked slowly, for longer. This is why the term *heatwork* (a combination of time and temperature) is used to describe what is required for complete melting, in lieu of a specific melting temperature.

From a chemistry perspective, very little happens to a glaze in a kiln until roughly the last 212°F (100°C). Some carbonates are converted to oxides at lower temperatures, but if a glaze is formulated properly, then only in the last bit of the firing do the components actually begin to melt, rearrange, and combine to form a glass lattice. This is often why many firing schedules have a quick climb up to approximately 2,010°F (1,100°C) and then a slower approach to the target cone. This is also why some ceramicists insert temp holds right before or after peak temperature to manipulate how long the glaze remains melted.

FIRING SCHEDULES AND BEST PRACTICES

So, what happens when you have a cone 6 glaze and you heat it up to cone 8? As one would expect, if your glaze is designed to completely melt at 2,228°F to 2,246°F (1,220°C to 1,230°C) and you heat it 86°F (30°C) hotter to 2,300°F to 2,318°F (1,260°C to 1,270°C), it will probably fully liquify and possibly run off the sides of your pot. Conversely, If you have a cone 6 glaze and you intentionally modify its chemistry by adding more boron to the mix, then it will probably flow more at cone 6, and may even get drippy.

What is more concerning is the opposite issue: underfired pots. These are glazes that are formulated to melt at a higher cone than they are actually fired to. The most common result is a rough texture that can feel and look like a matte glaze. In fact, this is a partially fused matrix of glaze material—a.k.a. partially melted rocks on the surface of your pot. Throughout hundreds of metal leach tests, in no other area have we observed more leaching occur than underfired glazes. In one particularly memorable example, an underfired black glaze leached an incredible 72 ppm of cobalt (max 0.5 ppm) and actually turned the leach solution a pink-purple color.

To illustrate this point, we ran an experiment testing leaching of the same glaze when fired to cone 3, 4, 5, 6, and 7. We ran cone 6 Jade Green on different tiles at these cones to show the surface going from underfired to smooth and glossy. The copper leach results are noted for each.

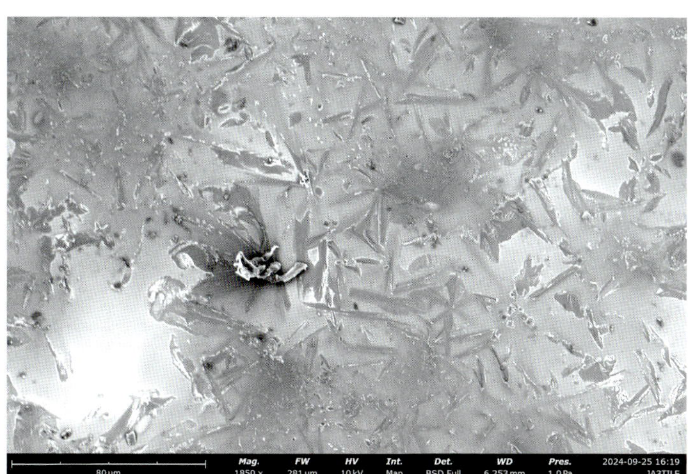

SEM image (80 micrometer scale): Unmelted material covers the surface of the cone 3 fired glaze.

Copper leach results: 2.8 ppm (fail).

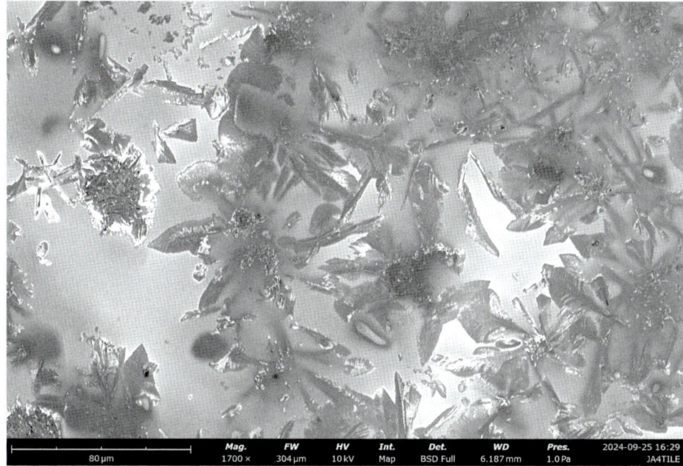

Still considerable unfused material at cone 4.

Copper leach results: 2.4 ppm (fail).

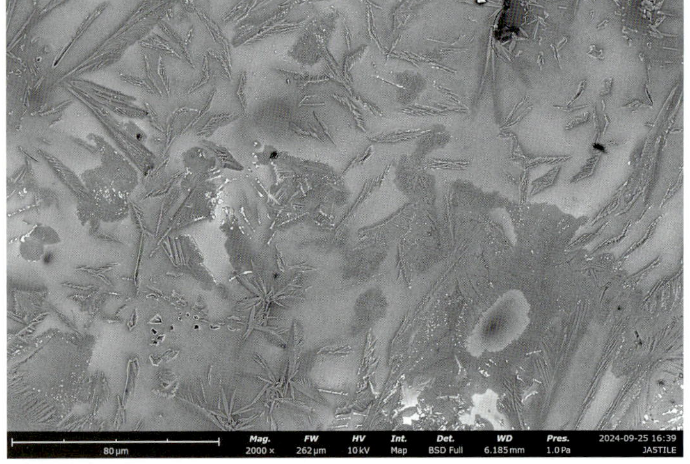

Melting begins in earnest at cone 5, but unmelted material can still be seen.

Copper leach results: 1.7 ppm (fail).

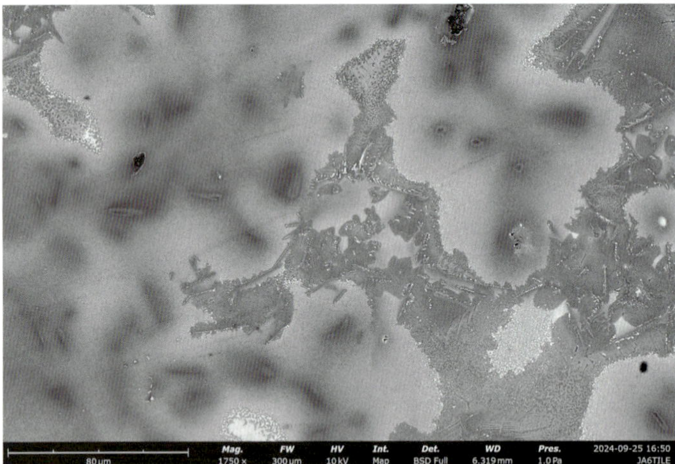

Nearly all of the surface is melted at cone 6.

Copper leach results: 1.3 ppm (note: 1.3 ppm is our copper limit; this just barely passes).

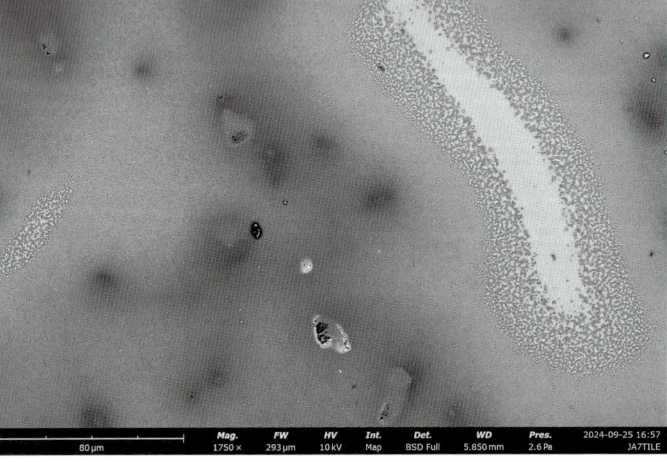

The surface is completely glossy at cone 7.

Copper leach results: 0.9 ppm.

How can you tell the difference between a matte glaze and an underfired glaze? If you are unsure about a glaze, the simplest test is to refire at a higher cone. Underfired glazes will often turn glossy as they completely melt at the correct temperature. As mentioned in chapter 3, matte glazes result from their chemistry and will be matte at any temperature. Therefore, if your glaze is actually a matte, it will still be a matte at higher cones, although it might begin to run off the pot.

Undeniably, underfired glazes leach more than "mature" ones. But, on the other hand, if we are careful in the way we fire our work, we can produce (and reproduce) consistent and reliable results over time. This is our goal! Let's go over the best practices for firing our work to ensure we get the results we want.

WHY BISQUE FIRE?

You don't absolutely have to (see the section on once-firing, page 124), but most potters bisque fire their work because it creates a stronger piece of pottery to glaze, one more resistant to chipping. This means you can handle the pieces (a bit) more aggressively. Smaller pieces can even be picked up with a set of metal tongs, which is nearly impossible with a piece of glazed greenware.

Do make sure that you fire your work to the same cone every time. We recommend cone 04 on a preprogrammed "slow" schedule. This gives the organic materials in the clay the greatest amount of time to burn out and can reduce problems like pinholing. If you are inputting your schedule manually or have an older "kiln sitter" kiln, you can follow this schedule. Never bisque fire anything other than slow unless you like vacuuming shards out of your elements.

The preprogrammed "slow" schedule on most kilns looks like this schedule. Converting rate of climb from Fahrenheit degrees per hour to Celsius degrees per hour is not as simple as converting Fahrenheit to Celsius and requires a little extra math. Bullseye Glass has a great online temperature and rate calculator (bullseyeglass.com/temperature-and-rate-conversion/). We used it to convert our rate of climb from Fahrenheit degrees per hour to Celsius degrees per hour.

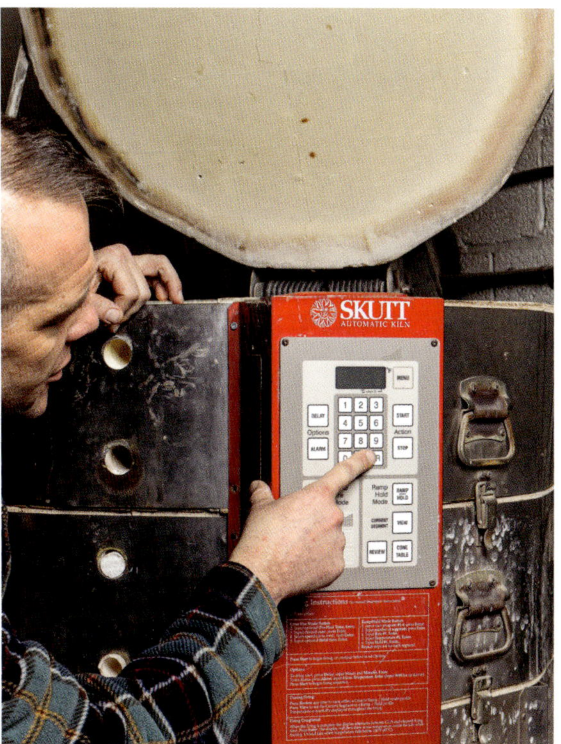

Programming an electric kiln.

Segment 1	80°F (44°C)/hour to 250°F (121°C)
Segment 2	200°F (111°C) /hour to 1,000°F (538°C)
Segment 3	100°F (56°C)/hour to 1,100°F (593°C) (suggested by kiln manufacturers, but optional. Some people choose to stay at the 200°F [111°C]/hour rate of climb from Segment 2)
Segment 4	180°F (100°C)/hour to 1,500°F (816°C)
Segment 5	108°F (60°C)/hour to 1,946°F (1,063°C)

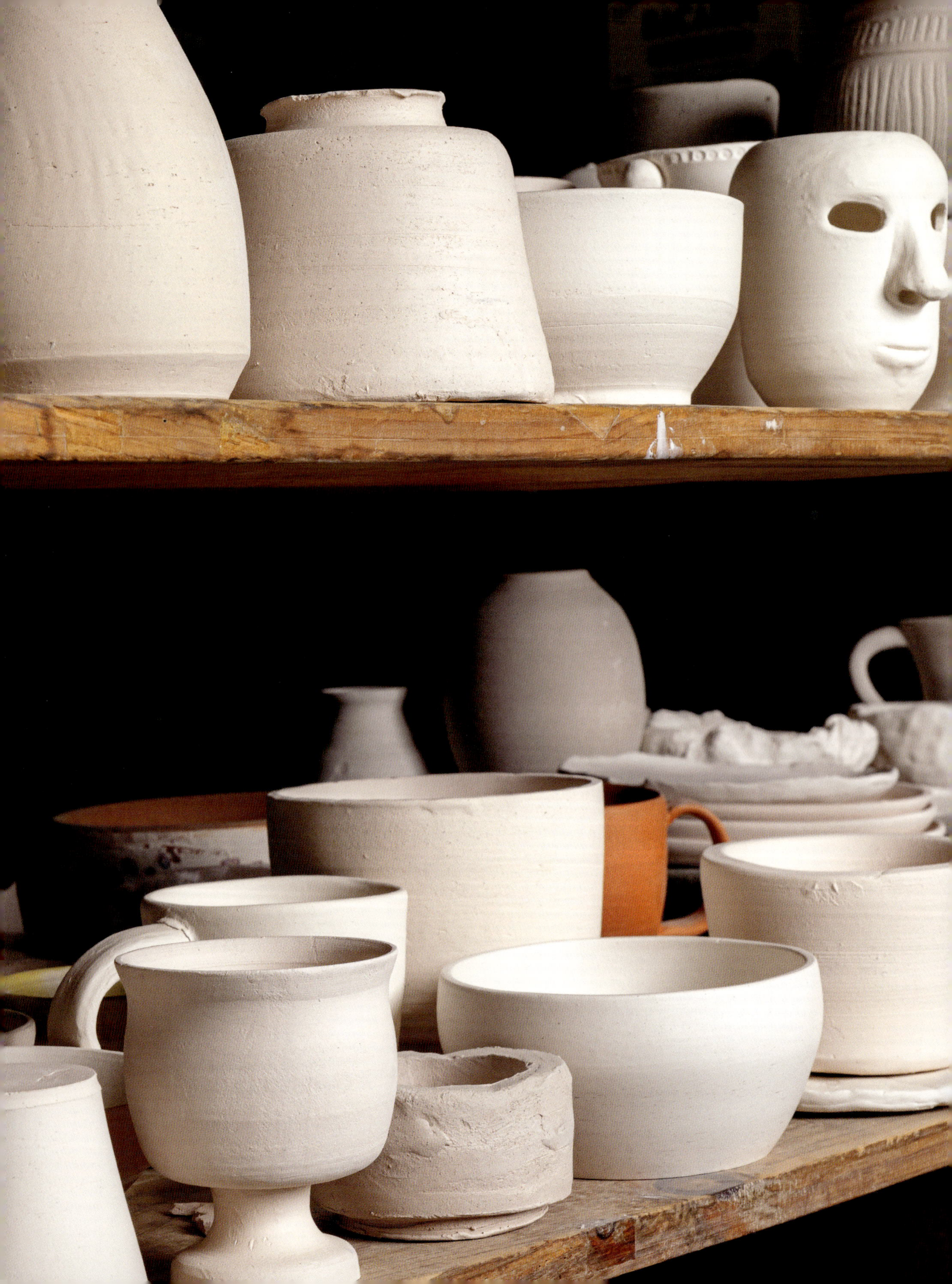

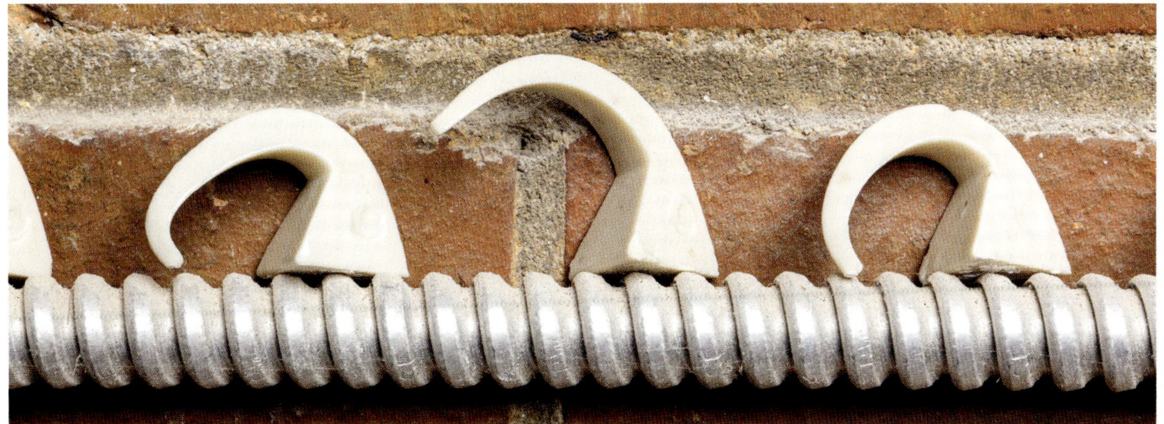

Which cone is closest to cone 6? The middle! The other two are overfired. Many people think a large self-supporting cone is mature when the tip touches the ground, but it is actually when the tip is at the same level as the top of the pyramid.

Note that your kiln's thermocouple may or may not be perfectly calibrated with the inside temperature of your kiln. Additionally, that temperature does not necessarily indicate that the appropriate amount of heatwork has been accomplished, which is really what we are after. That is, reaching a certain cone is different than reaching a certain temperature, though the two are related. For this reason, we want to rely on **witness cones** or **TempCheks** rather than the thermocouple reading on the computer. Also, you want to put several witness cones or TempCheks throughout the kiln in case there are cool spots. This could be due to elements or relays wearing out, or poor circulation in the kiln. A downdraft vent on an electric kiln can generally create a more uniform atmosphere.

John Britt told us, "Kilns don't overfire, people do." This means that you could have been there at the top of the firing, looking through the spyhole and turning the kiln off manually when the cone melts just the right amount, thus preventing the theoretical overfire. Conversely, one can avoid underfiring by being there at the top of the firing, and if the kiln shuts off before the cone melts, you can turn the kiln back on, programming it one cone hotter, then turn the kiln off as soon as the witness cone is melted. Truth? Almost nobody does this, but if you are really serious about getting the best results, then you should!

For larger pots and sculptures, or work that is thick in some places and thin in others, you may want to use an even slower schedule as follows:

Segment 1	75°F (42°C)/hour to 180°F (82°C) (a few degrees below the boiling point of water). Hold at this temperature for 2 to 8 hours, depending on the size or thickness of the piece.
Segment 2	150°F (83°C)/hour to 1,100°F (593°C)
Segment 3	108°F (60°C)/hour to 1,946°F (1,063°C)

This schedule will feel like it takes forever, sometimes lasting a full day or more plus cooling time, but it's better than going too quickly and having to remake the piece! And the larger or heavier the piece, the slower you will need to go. Jun Kaneko, who makes some of the largest ceramic sculptures we've ever seen, has a bisque program that lasts 6 weeks (!) and certain segments heat or cool at a rate of 1 degree per hour.

Wait until the kiln has cooled to kitchen oven temperatures to unload if using gloves.

(*opposite*) Student bisqueware awaiting glaze.

THE CASE FOR ONCE-FIRING

Producing ceramics is a resource-intensive endeavor. Unless we dig our own clay and refine it by hand, it is likely that at some point fossil fuels are being used to mine, transport, blend, and package the materials we use. And similarly, more fuel will be used to heat it up and melt glaze. On this note, a good way to make this connection is to see where your electricity comes from. An electric kiln should be considered a coal-fired kiln if the electricity supplied to your outlets comes from a coal power plant. Additionally, a power plant can lose between 60 to 85 percent of its energy in the transmission of electricity to your house.

In some ways, ceramists are the original industrialists. It's important to acknowledge this as we produce and fire our work. At Odyssey we say that it doesn't have to be "good," but it should have meaning to the person who created it if we are going to fire it to a permanent state.

Many wood fire potters once-fire as the slow heating of the kiln provides time for the work to thoroughly dry. But it's also possible to once-fire in an electric or gas kiln, and if you decide to do so, here are some guidelines and a firing schedule specifically designed for glazed greenware.

First, make sure that the work is **good and dry**. We are going to fire slowly, but the greatest risk with once-firing is that a piece will explode and the shards will land on other pieces. When the glaze melts, these shards will be permanently fused to the other work in the kiln. For this reason alone, many community studios decide to separate bisque and glaze firing to avoid this risk.

Unlike a bisque firing, in which you can tumble stack pieces, you should not stack work unless you want it to fuse together.

If you are okay with these parameters, once-firing does reduce the number of firings by 50 percent, which saves both energy (fossil fuels) and wear and tear on the elements and relays. This reduces the impact on the environment and your wallet!

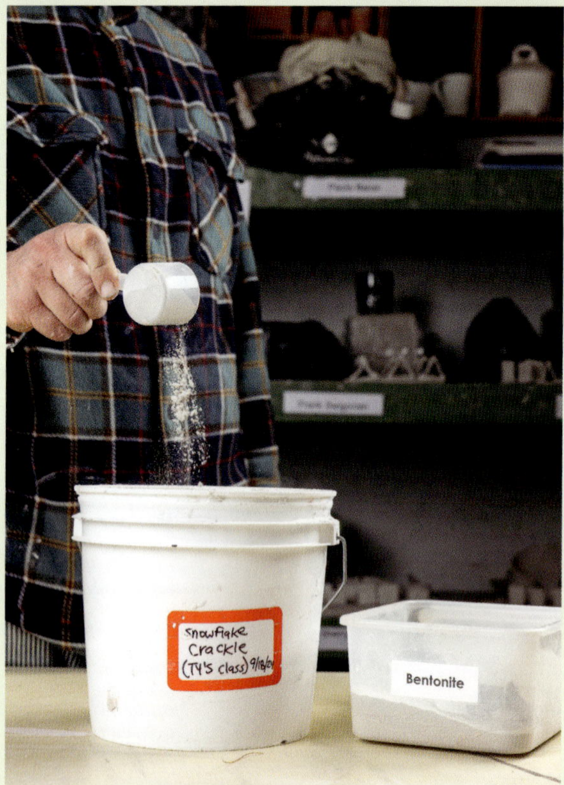

Adding bentonite to the glaze mixture for better adherence.

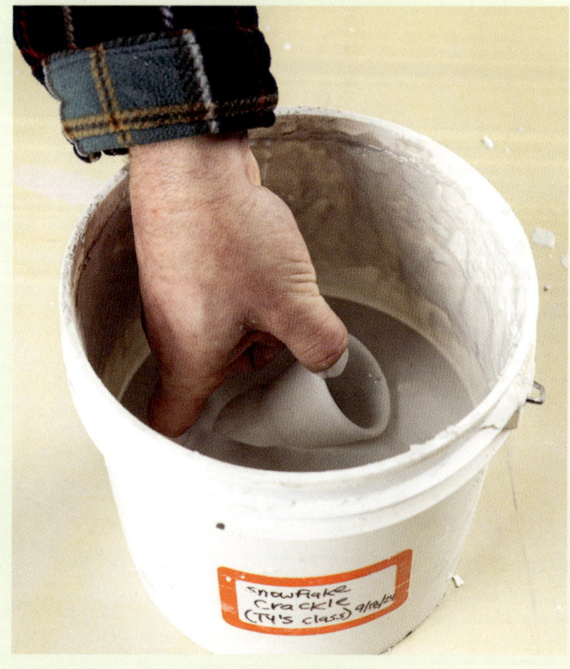

Dipping a piece of greenware in glaze.

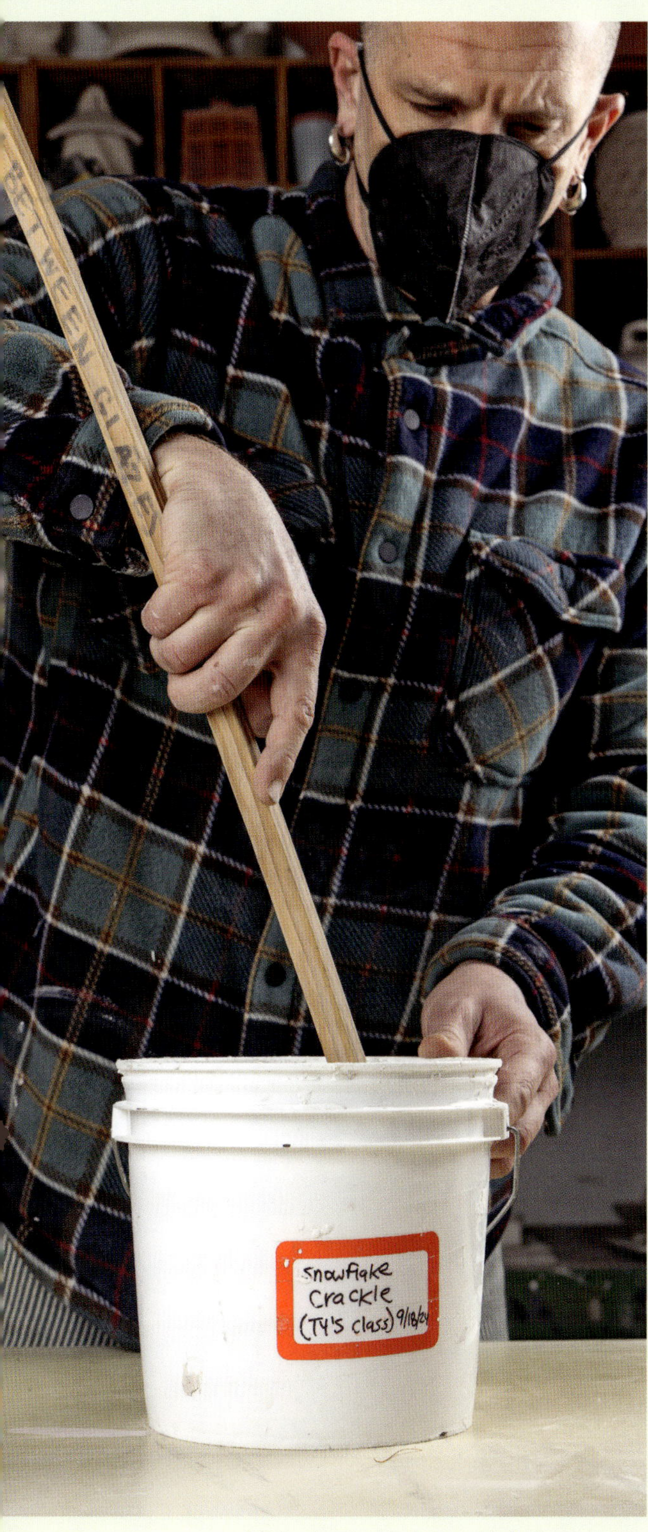

Mixing bentonite thoroughly before glazing.

At Odyssey, Tyler Anderson developed the following once-fire schedule for kids' work using commercial once-fire glazes to cone 05:

Segment 1	75°F (42°C)/hour to 180°F (82°C) hold for 6 hours
Segment 2	150°F (83°C)/hour to 900°F (482°C)
Segment 3	75°F (42°C)/hour to 1,200°F (649°C)
Segment 4	150°F (83°C)/hour to 1,800°F (982°C)
Segment 5	108°F (60°C)/hour to 1,900°F (1,038°C)

Note that this schedule could be adjusted to any cone by first changing the top temperature (in the 5th segment). You should then also change the set value of the 4th segment to 100°F (38°C) below the top temperature. The first three segments can remain the same.

You can try out your current glazes and see how they perform. Glazes with a higher clay content (15 percent or more) generally adhere better to greenware than glazes with less clay in them. Adding a small amount of bentonite (2 to 4 percent) or CMC gum (0.5 percent) to the recipe can help a glaze adhere to a green pot.

GLAZE FIRING

The final major step in the process is now before us: Glaze Firing. Let's do it right. Give your glazed pieces as much time as you can after glazing and before loading. Ideally wait overnight. But if you cannot, at least try to avoid putting glazed work that is still visibly wet into the kiln to make sure that the glaze doesn't flake off during the drying process.

In general, you can fire much more quickly when you glaze fire, as all the chemically bonded water has already evaporated during the bisque fire, and the risk of cracking is much lower.

For programmable kilns, you can use the medium or fast settings to glaze fire. Most of the important changes in a glaze fire (including melting) happen in the last 212°F (100°C) of the firing so you can more or less blast off to within approximately 200°F (approximately 100°C) of the target temperature and then slow the rate of climb for the last part of the firing. Some people choose to *downfire* after the kiln has reached temperature. The goal of downfiring is to promote crystal growth in the glazes, and the same glaze can have a very different look when controlled cooling is used.

STANDARD (MEDIUM) GLAZE FIRE PROFILE

Segment 1	200°F (111°C)/hour to 250°F (121°C)
Segment 2	400°F (222°C)/hour to 1,000°F (538°C)
Segment 3	300°F (167°C)/hour to 1,694°F (923°C)
Segment 4	108°F (60°C)/hour until the kiln reaches temperature.

FAST FIRE PROFILE FROM ROSE AND MATT KATZ

This profile really rips. Blasting off at 540°F (300°C)/hour and then slowing to 108°F (60°C)/hour for the last 180°F (82°C), this profile can be adjusted to suit many different firing temperatures.

Segment 1	540°F (300°C)/hour to 2,052°F (1,122°C) (for cone 6) or 2,165°F (1,185°C) (for cone 10)
Segment 2	108°F (60°C)/hour to 2,232°F (1,222°C) (cone 6) or 2,345°F (1,285°C) (for cone 10)

DOWN FIRE PROFILE

Segment 1	100°F (56°C)/hour to 200°F (93°C)
Segment 2	450°F (250°C)/hour to 1,900°F (1,038°C)
Segment 3	108°F (60°C)/hour to 2,196°F (1,202°C) (for cone 6) or 2,350°F (1,288°C) (for cone 10)
Segment 4	150°C (83°C)/hour to 1,700°F (927°C)

REDUCTION FIRING

So far, our schedules have indicated only temperature rise and heatwork without any mention of atmosphere. You'll hear the words *oxidation* and *reduction* often in ceramics. Let's take a look at how those two terms differ and the effect they will have on our glazes, including a test to see if kiln atmosphere affects leaching.

An **oxidizing atmosphere** refers to one in which there is ample oxygen inside of the kiln. An electric kiln is designed to create an oxidizing atmosphere. A gas kiln with plenty of air flow (the damper should be wide open) can also produce an oxidizing atmosphere. A **reducing atmosphere** is one in which the amount of oxygen is "reduced" either by pushing the damper in to reduce air flow or by turning the gas up to change the ratio of gas to oxygen in the kiln. When starved of oxygen, a gas flame will search for oxygen molecules in the clay and glaze to keep combusting. The flame will break the chemical bonds of the oxygen molecules with their oxides. This results in a different chemical composition of the glaze on the pot and in turn can radically change the appearance of the glaze.

NOTE: People have experimented with adding silicon carbide to their glazes to create localized pockets of reduction in electric kilns. Cone 6 Sic(k) Red (page 76) is a great example.

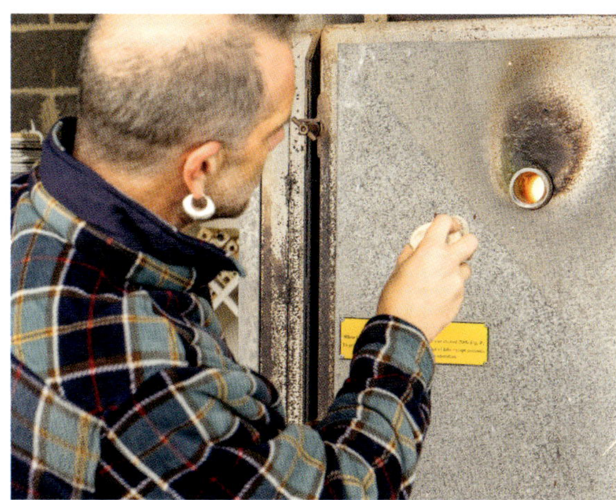

Checking reduction.

REDUCTION GLAZE FIRE PROFILE

Segment 1	Leaving damper open 2½ inches (6.3 cm), climb 100°F (56°C)/hour to 200°F (93°C)
Segment 2	Leaving damper open 2½ inches (6.3 cm), climb 400°F (222°C)/hour to 1,582°F (861°C) (cone 012)
Segment 3	Push damper in until the rate of climb is 60°F to 80°F (33°C to 44°C)/hour to 1,946°F (1,063°C) (cone 04)
Segment 4	Pull damper out until the rate of climb is approximately 100°F (56°C)/hour to 2,350°F (1,288°C) (cone 10). Turn the gas off and push the damper the whole way in to allow for a slow cooling.

Heavier or lighter reduction can be achieved by adjusting the damper during the firing. Push the damper in for more reduction, out for less. We like to reduce really heavily at the start of reduction at cone 012, pushing the damper in so far that the temperature inside the kiln actually decreases for roughly 5 minutes. This ensures that we establish the reduction part of the cycle with authority.

Then we gently inch the damper out until we achieve the climbing reduction indicated in Segment 3. You may find that certain glazes prefer more reduction, such as Carbon Trap Shino, and some look great with less—copper reds have a tendency to burn out with too much reduction. And the aesthetics of glazes are subjective. One artist may prefer a certain glaze with light reduction, while another likes the look better with heavier reduction.

GLAZE DEFECTS AND TROUBLESHOOTING

CRAZING

Crazing is one of the most common glaze defects, and it results from an incompatibility between the clay body and the glaze covering. When most ceramics are heated up, either in a kiln or in a microwave, they expand. As they cool back down, they contract ever so slightly. The degree to which they expand/contract is called *the coefficient of thermal expansion*, and it is specific to both clay bodies and glazes. If there is a significant mismatch, wherein the glaze contracts more than the clay body, then considerable tension is put on the glass, resulting in fine cracks in the glaze called *crazing*. This is akin to a bodybuilder putting on a shirt that has shrunk in the wash. As the person flexes (expands), the shirt must stretch accordingly or suffer torn seams.

A common misconception about crazing is that it has to do with the rate of cooling after a glaze firing. Many people believe that crazing will occur if you take a piece out of a kiln too quickly. Unfortunately, this is not true. The coefficient of thermal expansion of a glaze is based on its chemistry. The most common solution to combating crazing issues is to increase silica content by 5 to 10 percent in your glaze. This is because silica as a glass former has a relatively low coefficient of thermal expansion.

Sometimes we will seek out this effect as decorative, but in terms of functional ware, this flaw is to be avoided as bacteria/mold can get into the cracks. Undoubtedly, crazing can be beautiful and is sometimes sought after in snowflake and Chun glazes, but crazing should be thought of as a challenge to food safety.

DUNTING/SHIVERING

Shivering is a glaze defect in ceramics where small sections or flakes of glaze pop off the clay body, leaving bare patches. Shivering typically happens due to an excessively low thermal expansion in the glaze relative to the clay body. This means that the glaze does not contract as much as the clay does when cooling, and as a result, the tension forces the glaze to separate from the clay surface, especially at edges or lips of pieces where the stress is concentrated. This is the opposite of crazing. Usually reducing silica and alumina content can help raise the thermal expansion of the glaze potentially, making it more compatible with a clay body.

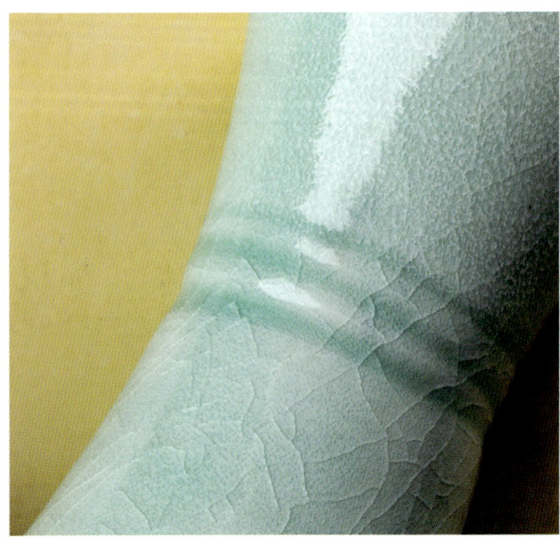

Crazing over porcelain.

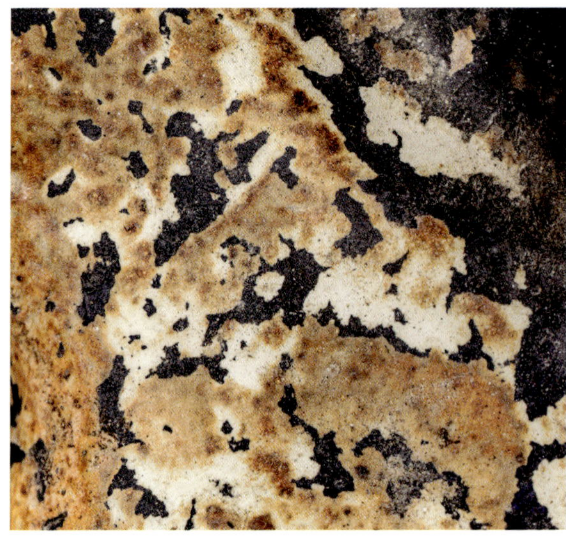

Shivering: When glaze flakes off the surface of the work. Careful—these flakes can be sharp!

Dunting appears as larger, deeper cracks or even fractures in a ceramic piece, often extending through both the glaze and clay body. Dunt cracks are typically clean and straight, unlike the intricate webbing of crazing. Also unlike crazing, dunting results from the thermal shock created by rapid cooling after firing.

There are several strategies to prevent dunting. First and foremost, slowing the cooling rate helps reduce internal stress in the ceramic. Second, some clay bodies are more prone to dunting than others. Stoneware and porcelains, which are more vitrified and denser, are often more susceptible than more porous, grogged, or open bodies like earthenware. Adding additional materials with low thermal expansion such as grog (prefired, crushed clay) or mullite can enhance the clay body's resistance to thermal shock. Finally, overfiring beyond the maximum maturity point of a clay body/glaze can potentially create points of weakness in the ceramic, which can create higher stresses when it cools.

CRAWLING

Crawling is a glaze defect where the glaze pulls away from certain areas of the clay surface during firing, leaving bare spots. This defect results from poor adhesion between the glaze and clay body, often due to a combination of chemical and physical factors. Specifically, when a glaze begins to melt, its surface tension increases, causing it to bead up and pull away from areas where it doesn't bond well with the clay. Glazes with high amounts of clay can shrink significantly when drying and can lead to cracks in the glaze layer even before firing, and as it melts, it can exaggerate the tendency to pull away.

From a physical standpoint, dust, oil, or other contaminants on bisque-fired clay can create a barrier that reduces the bond between the glaze and the clay body, causing the glaze to pull away during melting. Finally, an overly thick glaze application can increase the chance of crawling because the weight of the glaze layer can cause it to slide or crack before it fully fuses.

Methods to prevent crawling include ensuring the bisque surface is free from dust, oil, or other contaminants before glazing, lowering clay content or reducing high-expansion fluxes, and using thinner and more even applications of glaze to decrease the likelihood of it pulling away during firing.

Like crazing, though, crawling can be attractive and a sought-after effect. This Shino below showcases beautiful crawling glaze but probably should not be used for food and drink.

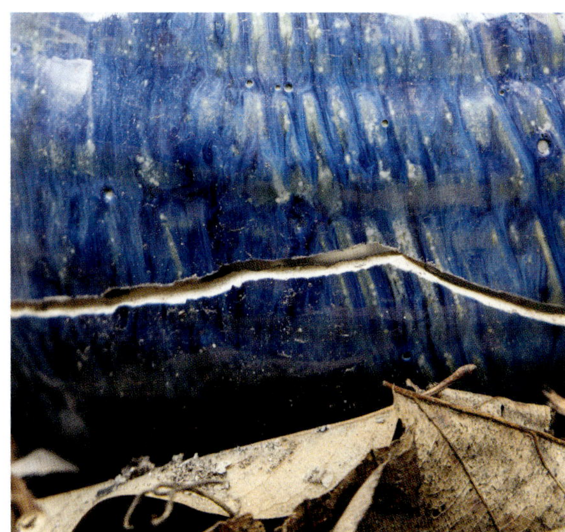

Dunting can happen even after the pot has come out of the kiln.

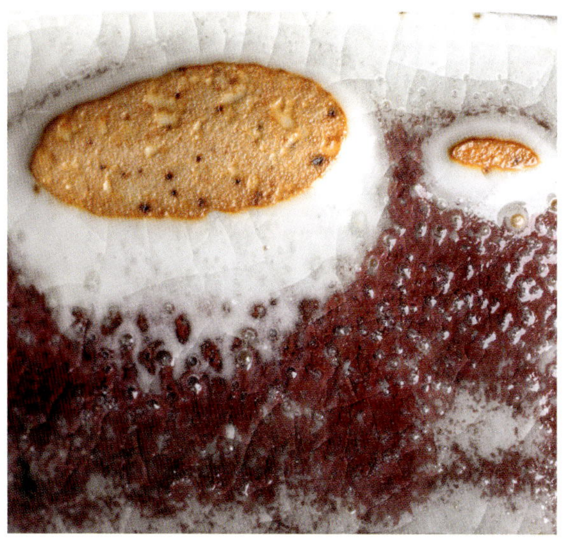

Crawling can leave the clay body exposed.

PINHOLING

Pinholing is a common glaze defect that is characterized by small, craterlike holes on the glaze surface after firing. The exact cause of this phenomena is still not completely understood, but it's probably a combination of microbubbles being generated at peak temperatures in the kiln with a high-viscosity glaze. Viscosity refers to the ability of a liquid to flow, in this case when molten above 2,000°F (1,093°C) in the kiln. Viscous glazes can sometimes struggle to heal over the bubbles. Where are the gasses coming from? The obvious candidates are the metal carbonates that release carbon dioxide to form metal oxides. However, this breakdown process happens much earlier in the firing and probably cannot account for bubbles when the glaze is molten. Another possibility is an incomplete burnout of impurities in the clay body. These organic residues (carbon, sulfur compounds) could potentially become gasses during the second firing and get trapped in the molten glaze. At Odyssey, we switched from bisque firing at cone 06 to cone 04 and noticed fewer pinholes in our glazes overall. A higher bisque firing does require more energy to get to temperature, but we feel like the improvement in success rate of our glazes was worth it.

Preventing pinholing is often accomplished by helping the glaze heal itself. Slowing down the glaze firing cycle in the last approximately 200°F (100°C), when melting is occurring, can allow the gasses to escape fully. A soaking period of a few minutes at peak temperature can also help. Finally, lowering the viscosity of the glaze by increasing the flux ratio will allow the molten glaze to flow more easily. You can also try refiring a piece that has pinholes. In our experience, it will solve the problem about half of the time, and the other half it will get worse, but it's worth a shot.

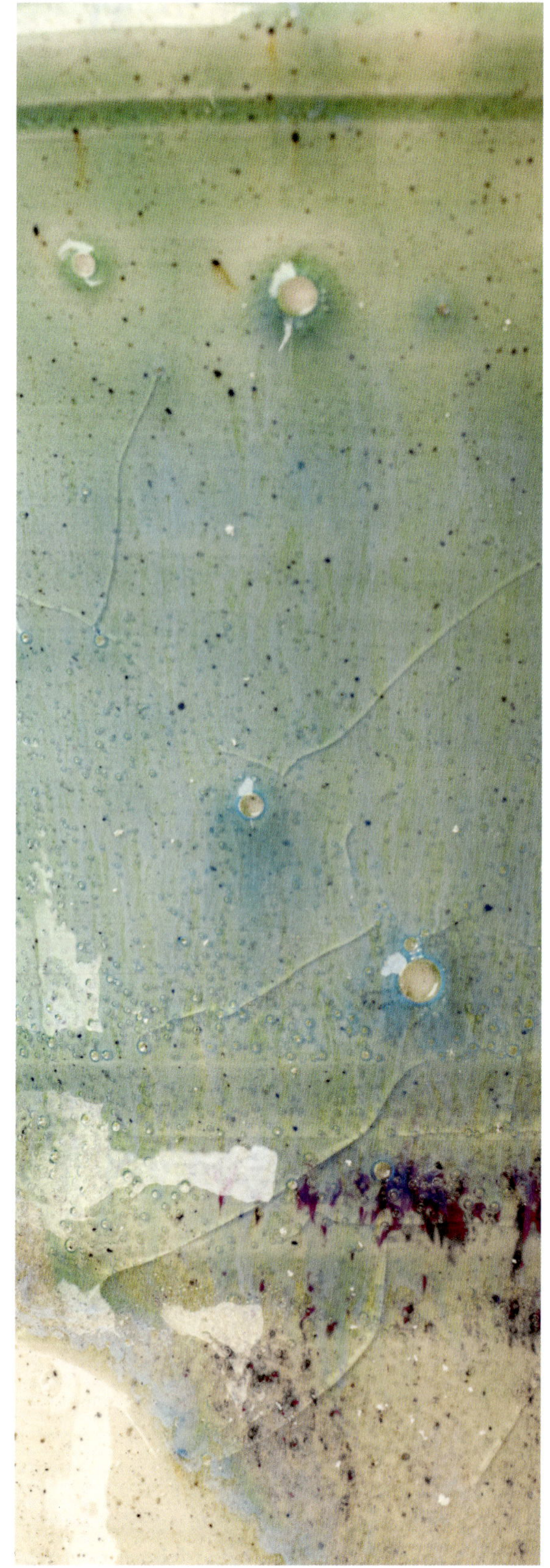

Unlike crazing and crawling, pinholing is always ugly.

FINISHING AND REFIRING

Once you've unloaded the glaze kiln, take some time to assess your pots. A good idea is to wait a couple of days. Sometimes when a piece doesn't turn out the way we've envisioned, we feel disappointed. That disappointment can prevent us from seeing that the piece is actually a stunner. If we come back to it a couple of days after unloading with fresh eyes, we'll perceive it anew. Hopefully, we nailed it like a one-take wonder.

But if we feel that the piece doesn't represent us, all is not lost. Refire! Many a piece have been improved by a second, or even third firing. Cracking is a higher risk when you refire, but if you didn't like the piece it's worth a shot to refire it to get results you like. The piece can be refired as is, great for underfired pieces, or it may need the application of more glaze if the glaze effects are minimal or the clay body is exposed through unwanted crawling or pinholing.

The challenge in reglazing is getting the glaze to stick to the fired piece, which is now vitrified and coated in glaze. A hot pot fresh out of the kiln can be dipped in glaze and the heat will cause the water in the glaze to evaporate out quickly. Similarly, you can heat pots up in the kiln to 250°F (121°C) and then reglaze them. Both of these methods require insulated gloves, and this makes the process somewhat clumsy.

We've found that APT II Enhancer is an excellent product for reglazing. Take a small amount of your glaze, just enough to cover the area you need, and add 3 to 4 drops of APT II per fluid ounce (30 ml) of glaze. Stir until the glaze increases in volume. It should start to stand up like shaving cream. It can then be applied to a glossy surface or vitrified clay and will stick without running. It will take this glaze a longer time to dry, but it will go on thicker than if you dipped a hot pot in glaze. A similar effect can be achieved by adding a small amount (0.25 percent to start) of Epsom Salts to a glaze. We think this is the superior way to reglaze. Allow the glaze to dry, then pop it back into the kiln. Twice baked potatoes are delicious!

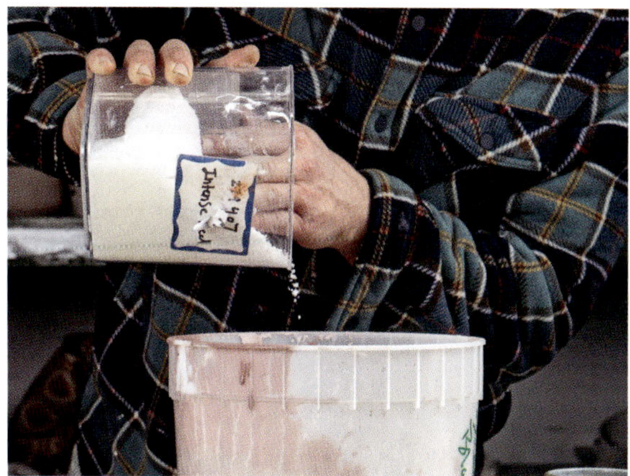

Adding Epsom salts to help the glaze adhere.

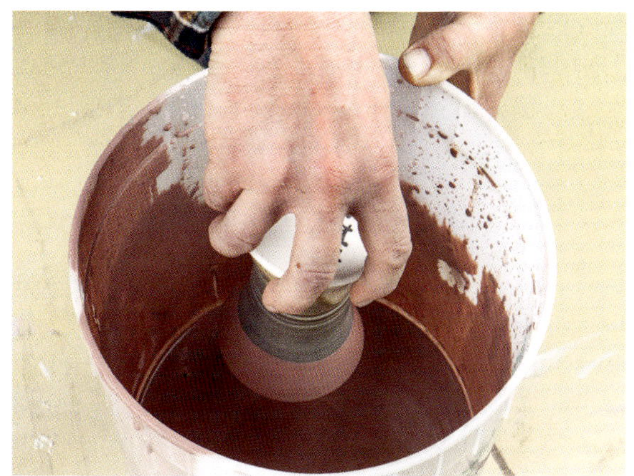

Dipping an already fired piece in glaze.

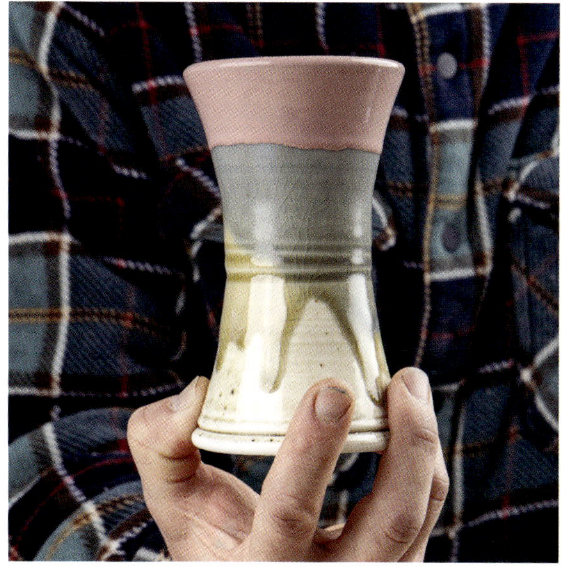

The glaze will stick to the glossy surface without running.

TEMPCHEK AND WITNESS CONES

Historically, ceramicists would look through peep holes and observe the interior color of their kiln to determine if they had arrived at cone 10. This is because flames change colors from reds to oranges to yellows to white as they get hotter. Understandably, staring into a peephole for long periods is not practiced today, as the infrared radiation at these temperatures can permanently damage the eyes. Instead, we add little cones of glaze into our kilns and wait until they begin to melt and slump over.

This ingenious method was developed in the late nineteenth century by Hermann Seger. In effect, a pyramid-shaped (pyrometric) cone made up of glaze is placed inside the kiln. This cone is formulated to completely melt at several cones higher than the actual desired final temperature. For example, a cone 10 pyramid will actually completely melt at around cone 16. This means that the cone doesn't completely liquify with your pots, but instead just begins to slightly melt. This causes the cone to bend and is a signal for the ceramicist that the ideal temperature has been met and to stop the firing. This cone system is especially important because it accounts not just for the kiln's peak temperature, but also for how long the kiln stays at that temperature, making it a way to gauge heatwork in a kiln.

One challenge with pyrometric cones is that there can be uncertainty in interpreting how much a cone bends and whether a desired temperature has actually been reached. A complementary tool to the pyrometric cone is a TempChek. These small ceramic discs can be placed throughout the kiln. They are composed of a material that contracts slightly at different temperatures. If you measure the disc diameter before and after firing, you can determine the peak temperature with high accuracy. The drawback of this tool is that you cannot use them during a firing to know when you need to stop. For that, you need either cones, or a more modern invention: the thermocouple.

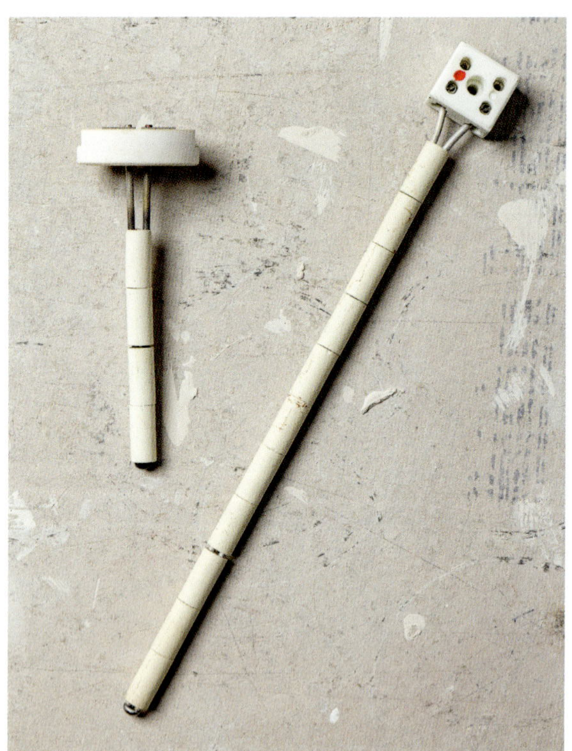

Two styles of K type thermocouples.

THERMOCOUPLES: S vs. K TYPE THERMOCOUPLES

A thermocouple consists of two different metal wires joined at one end ("the junction"). When the junction is heated or cooled, it generates a small electrical voltage based on a phenomenon called the *Seebeck effect*. This voltage is an electrical signal that can then be read by a temperature sensor to give a fairly precise temperature reading.

In kilns there are two options for thermocouples: K type and S type. K type thermocouples are made of nickel-chromium/nickel-aluminum, are inexpensive, tend to oxidize and degrade, and are accurate from room temperature to 2,300°F (1,260°C) (approximately cone 7). S type are composed of platinum and rhodium, are more expensive, do not corrode, and are accurate up to 2,912°F (1,600°C) (way beyond cone 10). In US kilns, most come with the less expensive K type installed. In fact, over time you might have already seen some of the decomposed black nickel-chromium bits at the bottom of your kiln.

One particular problem with the more common K type thermocouples is that although they have fairly good accuracy at cone 6 and below, they are not intended to be accurate for high-fire. It is highly recommended that if your kiln relies on a K type thermocouple and you go above cone 6, that you should also use witness cones or TempCheks. For ceramicists who are looking for the highest level of temperature accuracy, you might consider installing the more expensive S type thermocouple.

OXIDATION VERSUS REDUCTION

Is there a difference in leaching between cone 10 oxidation and reduction? This is a tricky question, as some of the observed chemical changes in the glaze make it harder to analyze. As an example, copper glazes undergo a fairly dynamic green to red change going from copper (II) in oxidation to copper (I) in reduction. These red copper nanoparticles are especially challenging to observe with our instrumentation. Are they still leaching? Probably. But they are difficult to quantify.

For a different experiment, we did look at the glaze Hamada Rust in both cone 10 oxidation and reduction and saw little change in how much iron leached out of the glaze.

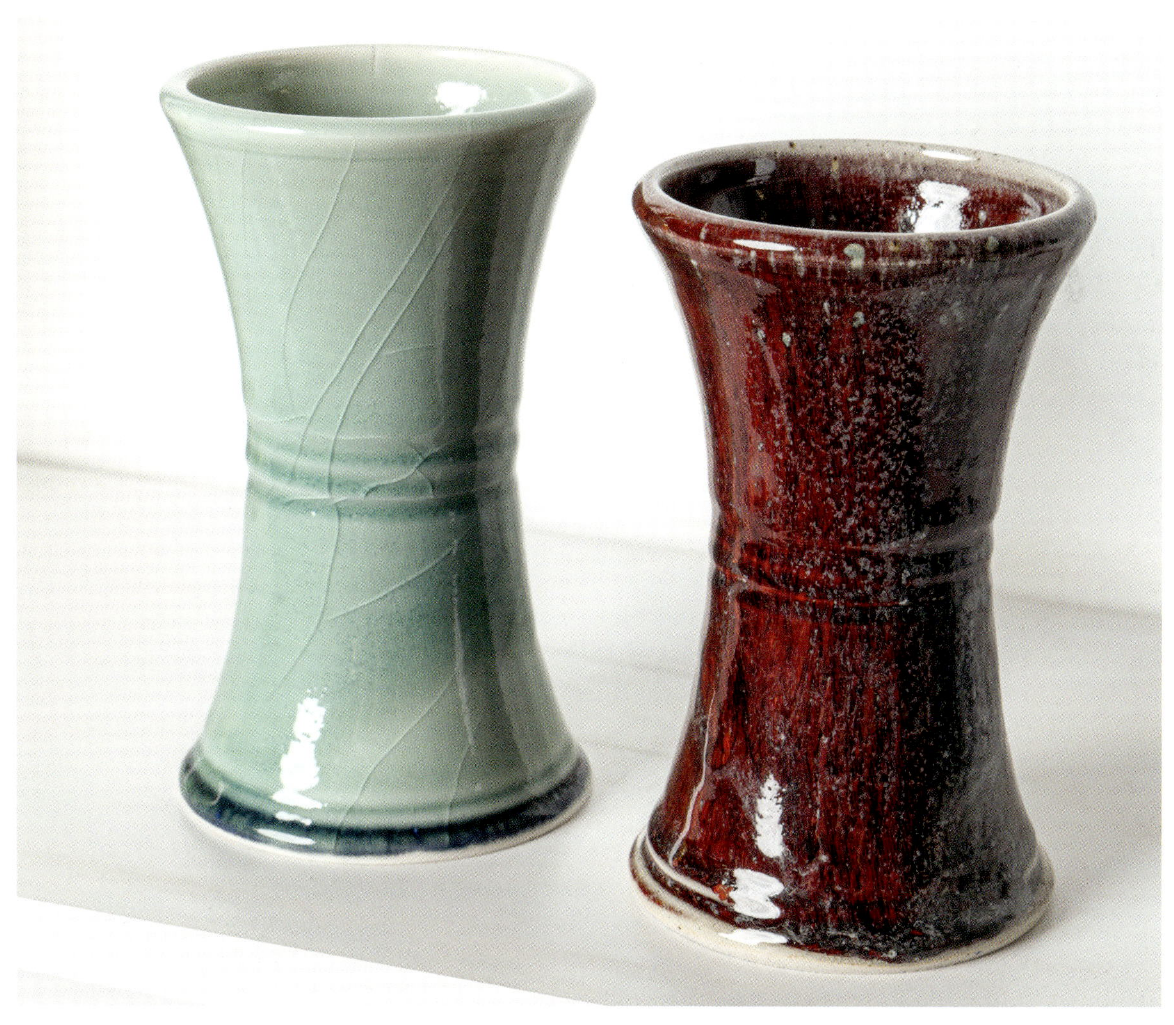

Can you believe this is the same glaze? Cone 10 Cranberry in oxidation (green) and reduction (red).

Alex Thullen

alexthullenceramics.com Instagram @alexthullen

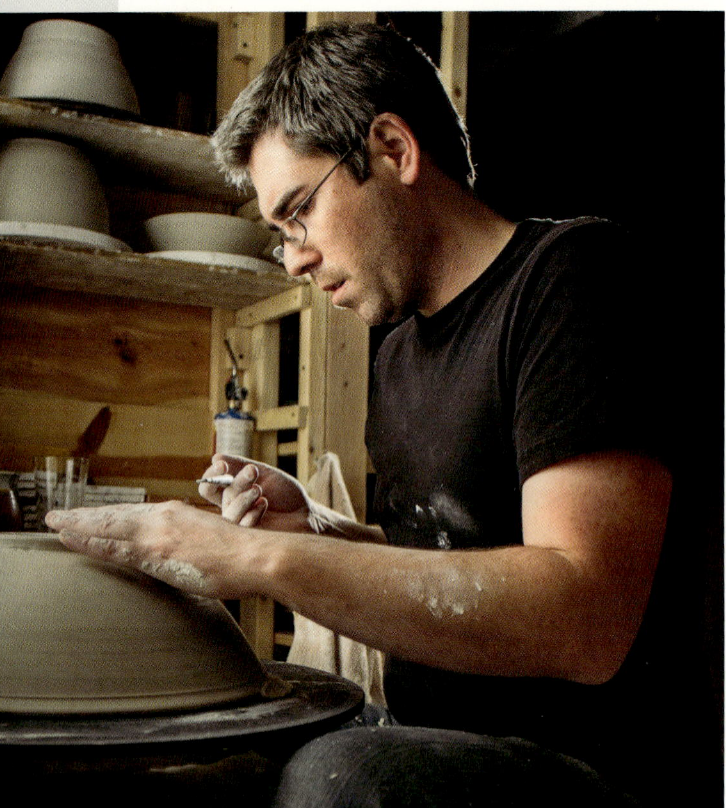

Alex Thullen at work in his studio.

Alex Thullen provides an interesting perspective considering his years of technical work at Pewabic Pottery in a pottery setting where the human hand is still valued. Located in a historic building in Detroit, Michigan, Pewabic holds a special place in ceramic art history in the United States. Nestled between industry and art, between the consumer and the craft, the glazes at Pewabic uniquely enhance the work, referencing the history of the Arts and Crafts movement while updating the palette for today's sensibilities. Alex's work at the factory has focused on modifying recipes to accommodate the changing availability of materials while maintaining a cohesive look. While the glaze recipes are proprietary, Alex's knowledge is not. He has generously shared his insights gained from decades of work within the field with us here.

AMAZING GLAZE FOOD-SAFE RECIPES: *How do you think that glaze design differs between studio potters and commercial pottery production?*

ALEX THULLEN: The most fundamental difference is that as an individual artist, aside from your customers, you are ultimately the only one that you need to please. Within a larger manufacturing business, you can have quite a broad spectrum of input into the direction that the work takes. Manufacturers, particularly of larger scale, will also quite often have an established "visual vocabulary" that any new product will need to conform to, or at the very least reference or use as a jumping-off point. Additionally, if a manufacturer focuses primarily on custom or commission work, the tastes and choices of individual clients will ultimately be the defining factors in the creative direction.

An established business will generally have access to a far wider range of resources, both physical and financial. Theoretically, more resources lead to far greater possibilities in terms of exploration, but this can be a double-edged sword. Larger businesses work at a scale and with a structure that can often be far more resistant to risk-taking or pushing boundaries, as opposed to individuals that generally have less structure and therefore more freedom to explore at less risk to their bottom line.

You also have to consider that in a larger business, tasks are distributed differently as opposed to a single maker who might handle the entire process from start to finish. A glaze designer for a manufacturer will likely not be the same person who mixes or even applies the glaze to the ware or loads it into the kilns. It's essential to always be considering the next user when working within a collaborative process. The focus has to be on the entire process from start to finish and not simply the results.

AGFSR: *In what ways does formulation, application, and firing differ in a large-scale production? Are there safety issues that are unique to working for a commercial pottery production?*

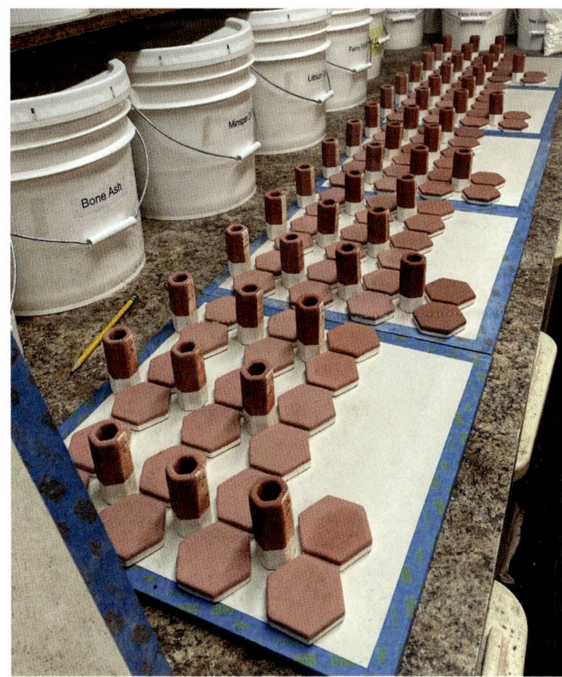

A series of tessellated tiles and extruded cylinders shows how glaze tests perform on both horizontal and vertical surfaces.

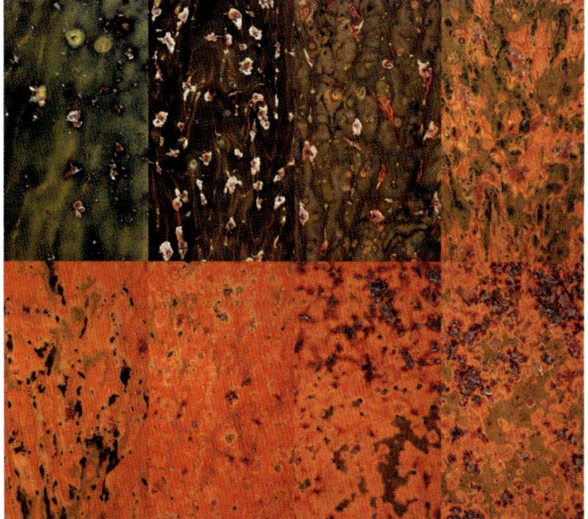

A series of tests using iron oxide.

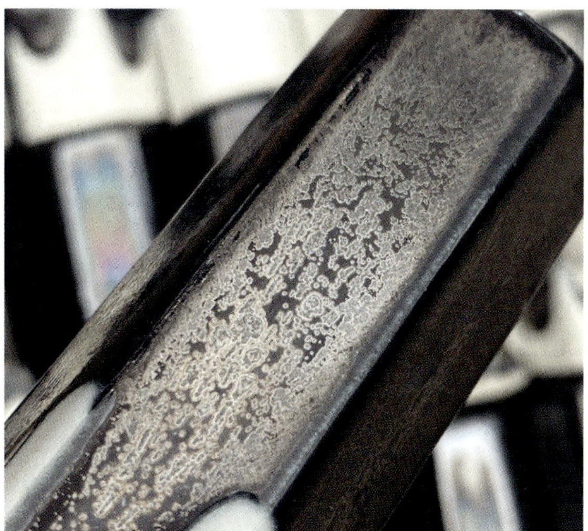

A test tile with facets showcases glazes that break.

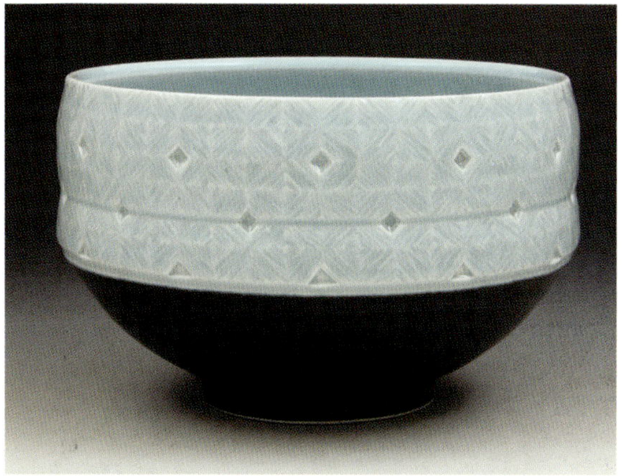

Celadon is an excellent choice over texture, and the flat black beneath it gives the piece a serious tone.

ALEX: Larger-scale manufacturing allows for (and often necessitates) the use of vastly different technology and equipment. These can include mixers, glaze application tools, presses, filters, kilns, and a multitude of other types of equipment. As a rule, production at scale also leads to more hands-off processes, whether these be machine-aided or entirely automated. Glaze design and formulation must take these considerations into account. The working properties of a glaze in the studio can dramatically affect the final outcome by altering its application and firing processes or influencing how it interacts with differing types of machinery and equipment.

Large-scale operations inevitably require a much larger physical footprint, facilitating the need for storage and more importantly movement of resources, along with greater logistical considerations that smaller operations aren't generally troubled by. The larger an operation, the more complex and multi-faceted it must necessarily become, and the more needs to be considered at every stage of the process to take into account how all these various components fit together and what they all require of each other.

AGFSR: *In what ways do you think that the ceramic education process (mentoring, apprenticeships, self-taught, university) could be improved?*

ALEX: I have to believe that there is both space for, and also a profound but unexplored use for, a more holistic approach to the study of the wider "field" of ceramics within the university setting. A major part of this challenge for me is that ceramics is taught as an artistic discipline alongside sculpture, painting, printmaking, et cetera, but is a means to so many ends in a way that other art media simply aren't. We paint with paints, we draw with ink and charcoal, but clay can be used not only to make pottery, sculpture, and design objects, but an array of industrially manufactured products and components used in a vast array of fields outside the artistic disciplines. It is simultaneously a medium for the arts, the crafts, and the design fields, but also for industry, technology, and engineering.

My dream scenario would be to experience a degree program that encompassed the various aspects of ceramics as an art medium but melded with a comprehensive science and engineering foundation that would allow for a wider range of further exploration of the material and its potential applications; one that could be used as a launchpad for advanced studies in any number of fields.

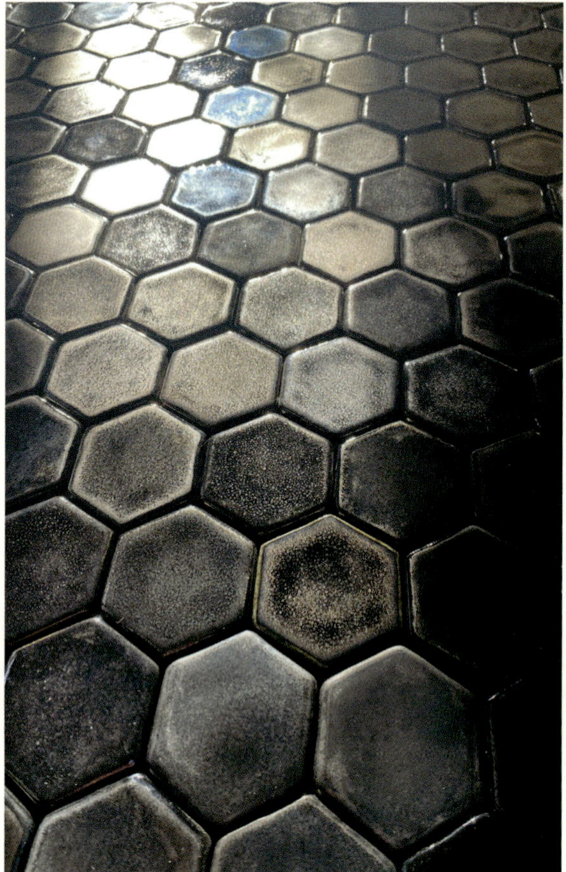

Tesselated tiles, grouted and installed.

AGFSR: *As more people learn to develop, take control, and experiment with their glaze chemistry, how will that change our art form and in what ways do you see the ceramic community evolving in the future?*

ALEX: It's undeniable that the current near-universal access to good technical foundations is like nothing that existed even when I went to school. The access to this information, brought about largely by the internet and the emergence of online learning, has changed everything. In terms of a tangible change to the art form itself, it's an unbelievably empowering tool for those who have the enthusiasm for it. We can only hope that it will enable current and future generations of makers to produce ceramics that are more beautiful, more technically sound, and more in line with their vision of what they're trying to achieve.

AGFSR: *Ceramics is becoming more accessible to a greater number of people with commercially available clay, glazes, and programmable electric kilns. As barriers come down and more people get into this field, what opportunities and challenges do you see this creating?*

ALEX: It's hard to overstate the transformative impact these advances have already made, but the rise of digital communication and the way that it's changed the landscape of how we interact and experience the work of other artists can't be overlooked either. Virtually overnight, social media broke down the barriers of accessibility and exclusivity imposed by the gallery structure that had dominated the field for so long. The flip side of this has been that it did so for everyone equally, leading to more egalitarian opportunities for visibility, but also an oversaturation of the market, which can often overwhelm the consumer.

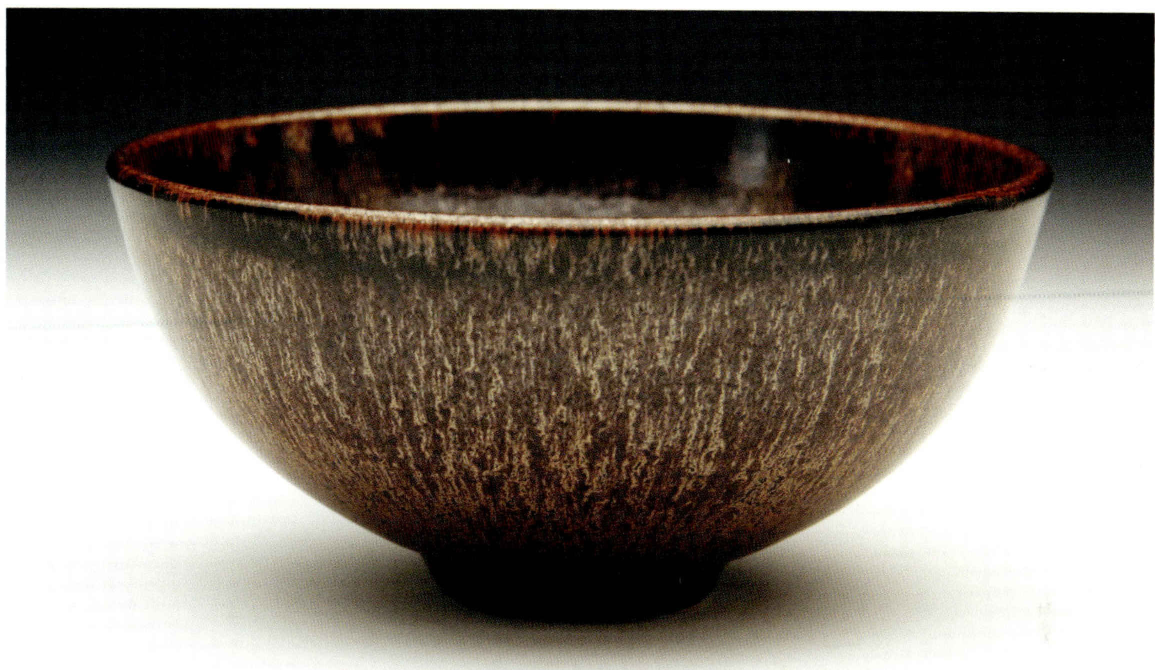

A beautiful example of what iron can do in a glaze.

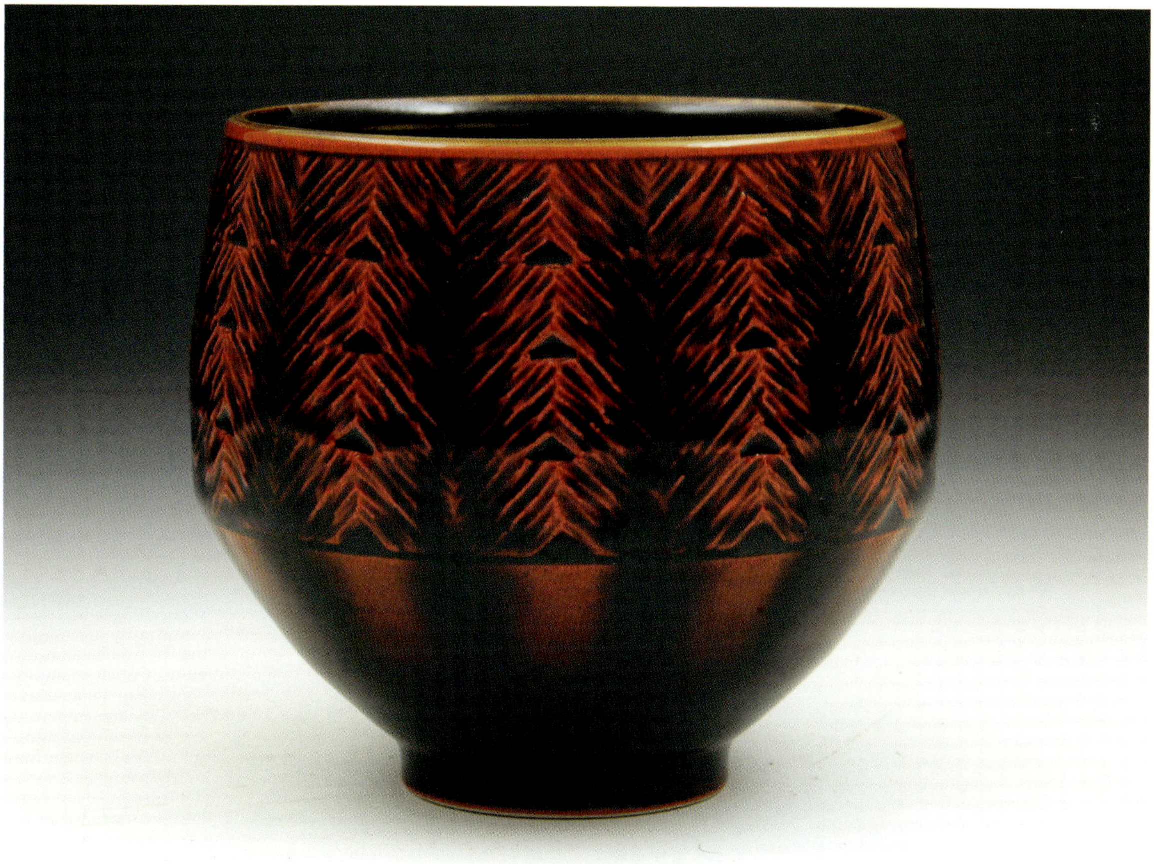

Red highlights break through a dark black glaze. This piece has some mystery. How did he do that?!

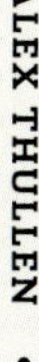

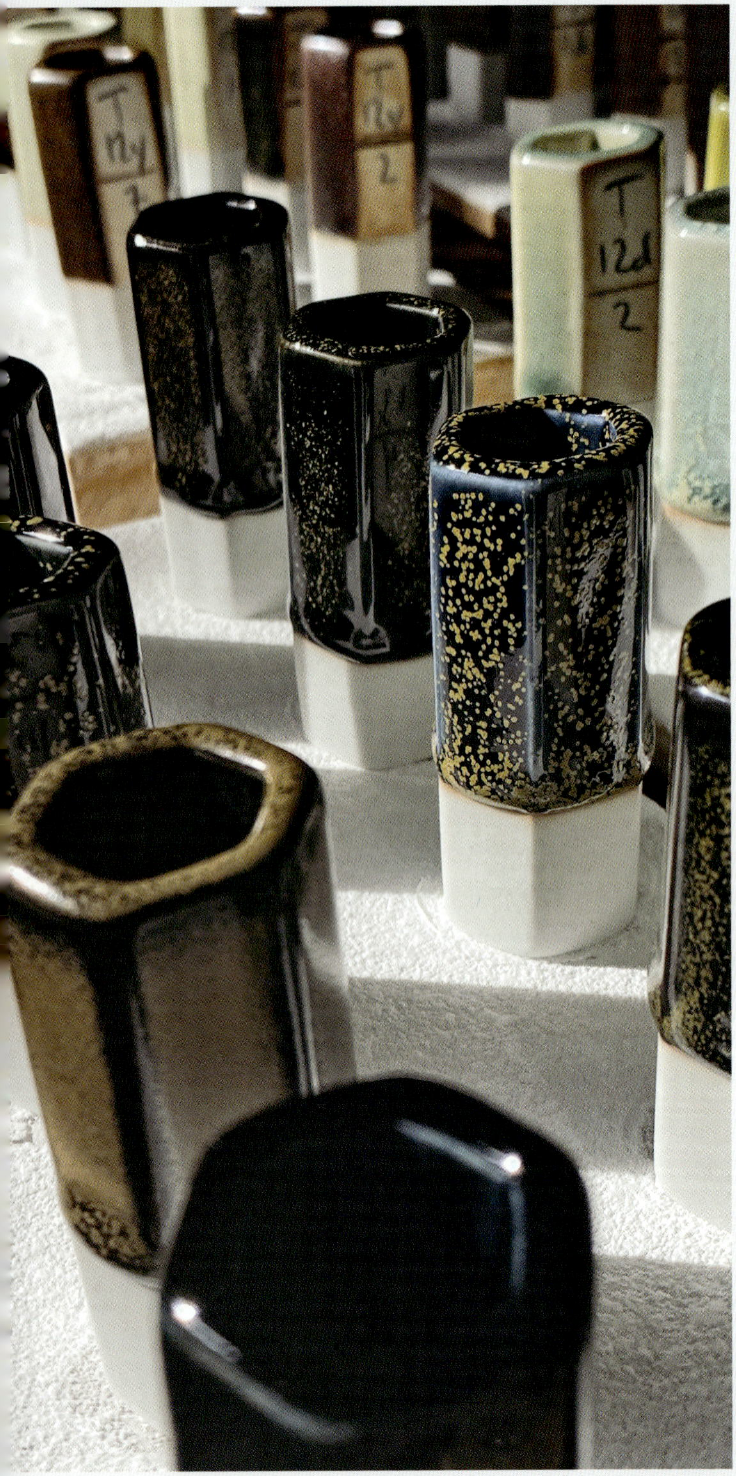

GALLERY

Teadust Tests. Alex Thullen.
These hexagonal test tiles, reminiscent of Giant's Causeway in Northern Ireland, are artworks unto themselves.

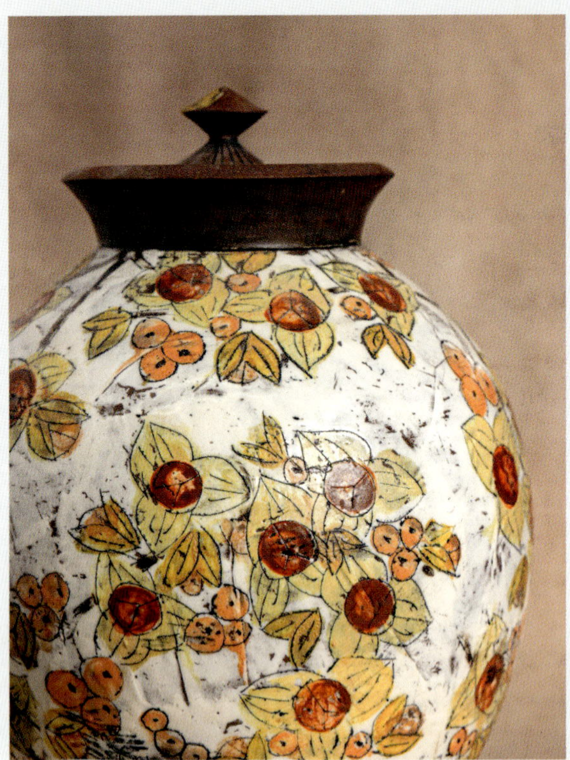

Covered Jar. Marian Draper.
Gabriel loves cookies. This jar provides a sacred space to store them.

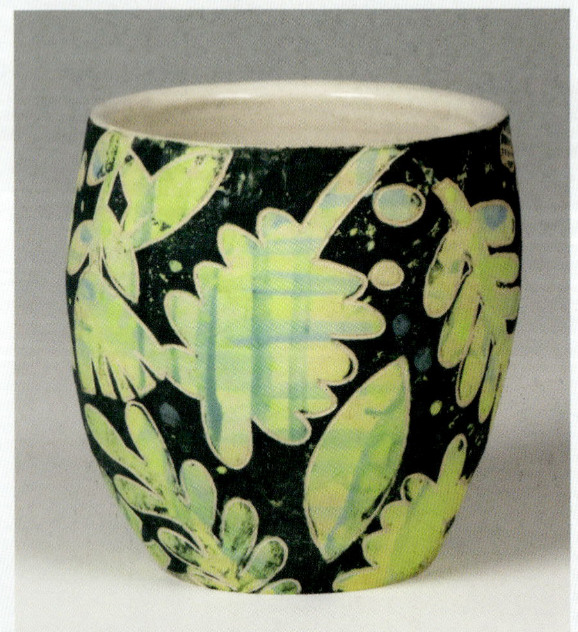

Wine Cup. Jennifer Rosseter.
You want a white interior when drinking wine so you can admire the color of your Syrah.

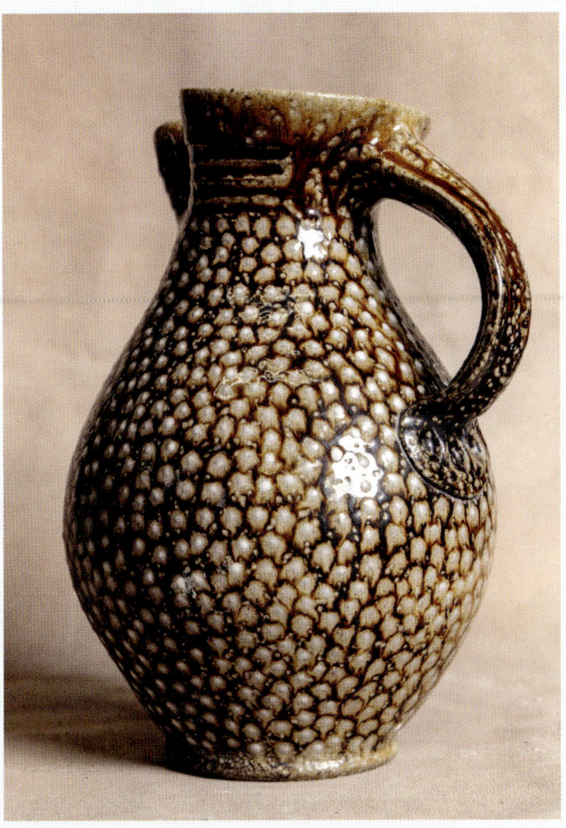

Pitcher. Daniel Johnston.
Ash glazed and wood fired, this pitcher encapsulates the tradition and evolution of pottery making in North Carolina. Collection of the author.

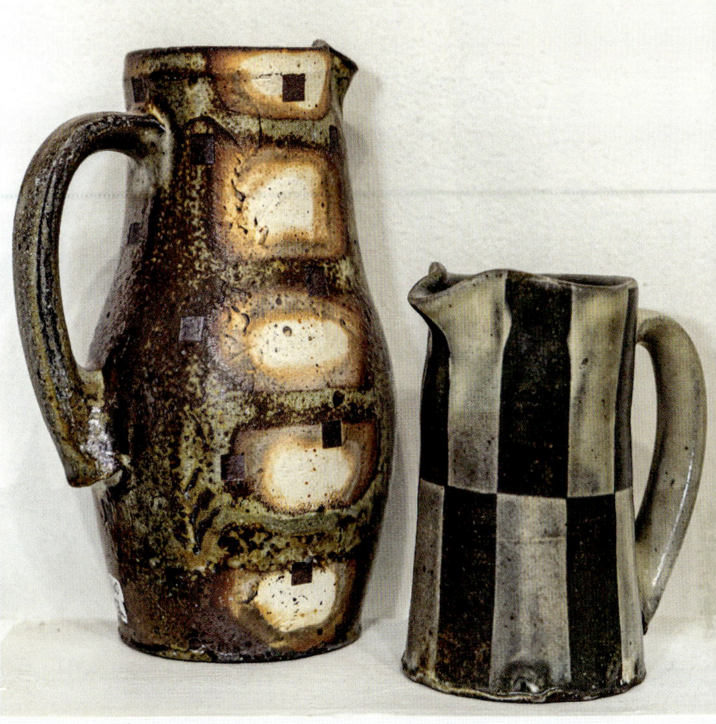

Pitcher Grouping at Odyssey ClayWorks. Gillan Doty.
Slips, liner glaze, and kiln atmosphere all come together seamlessly in these charming pitchers.

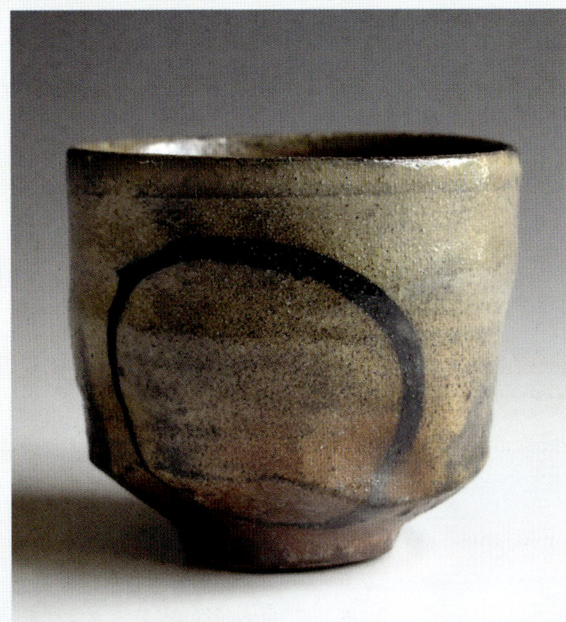

Teabowl. Micah Thanhauser.
Wood ash contains many components of a glaze, and an unglazed piece placed in the wood kiln emerges with a finished look.

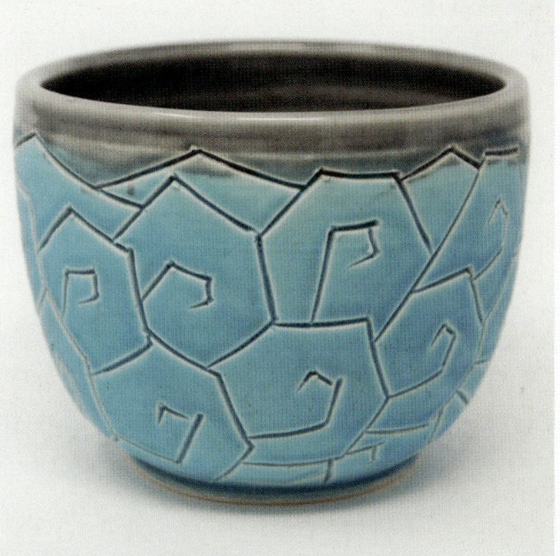

Wavy Gravy Bowl. Trish Cutler.
This matte blue glaze breaks wonderfully over the carved waves. Surf's up!

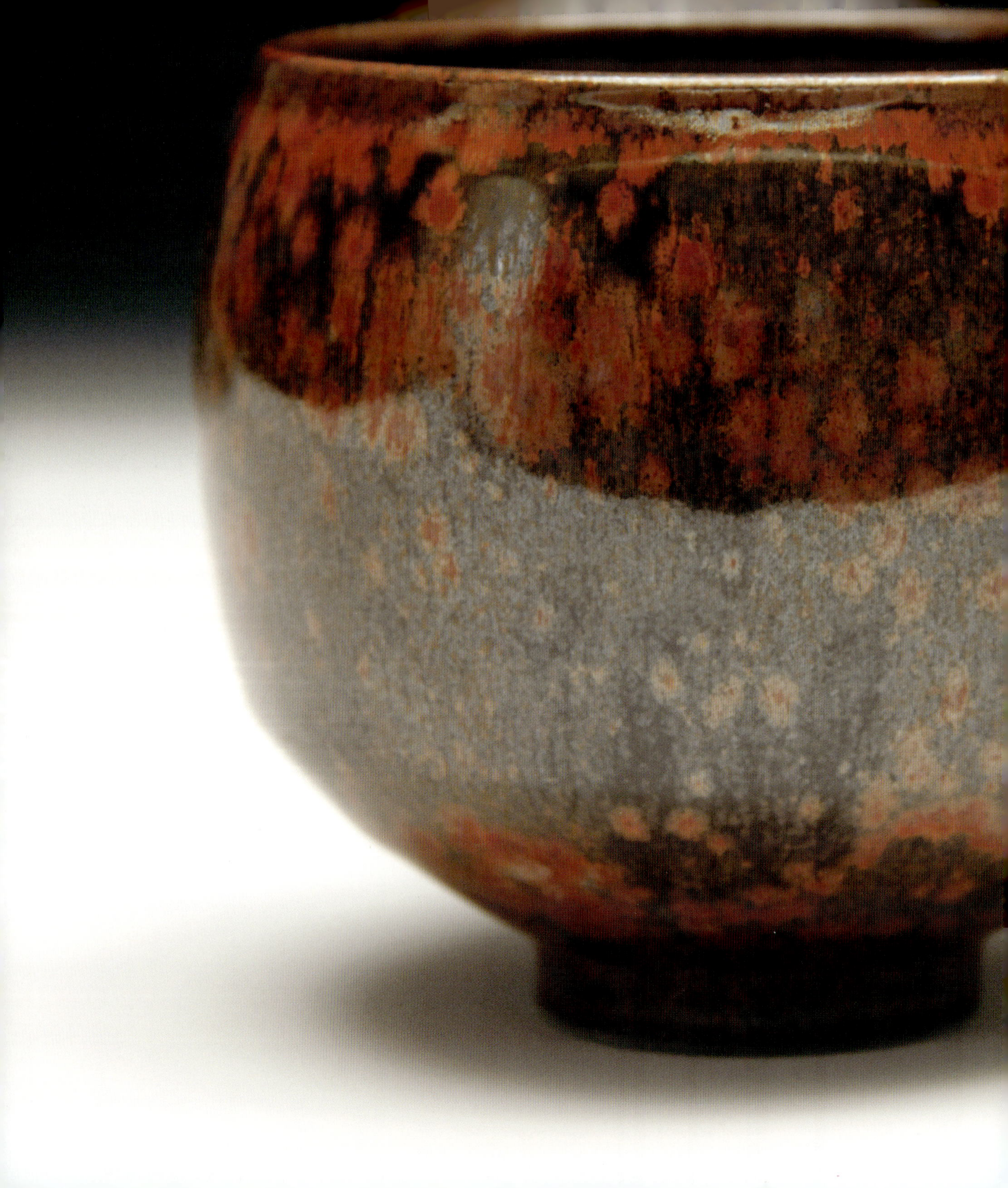

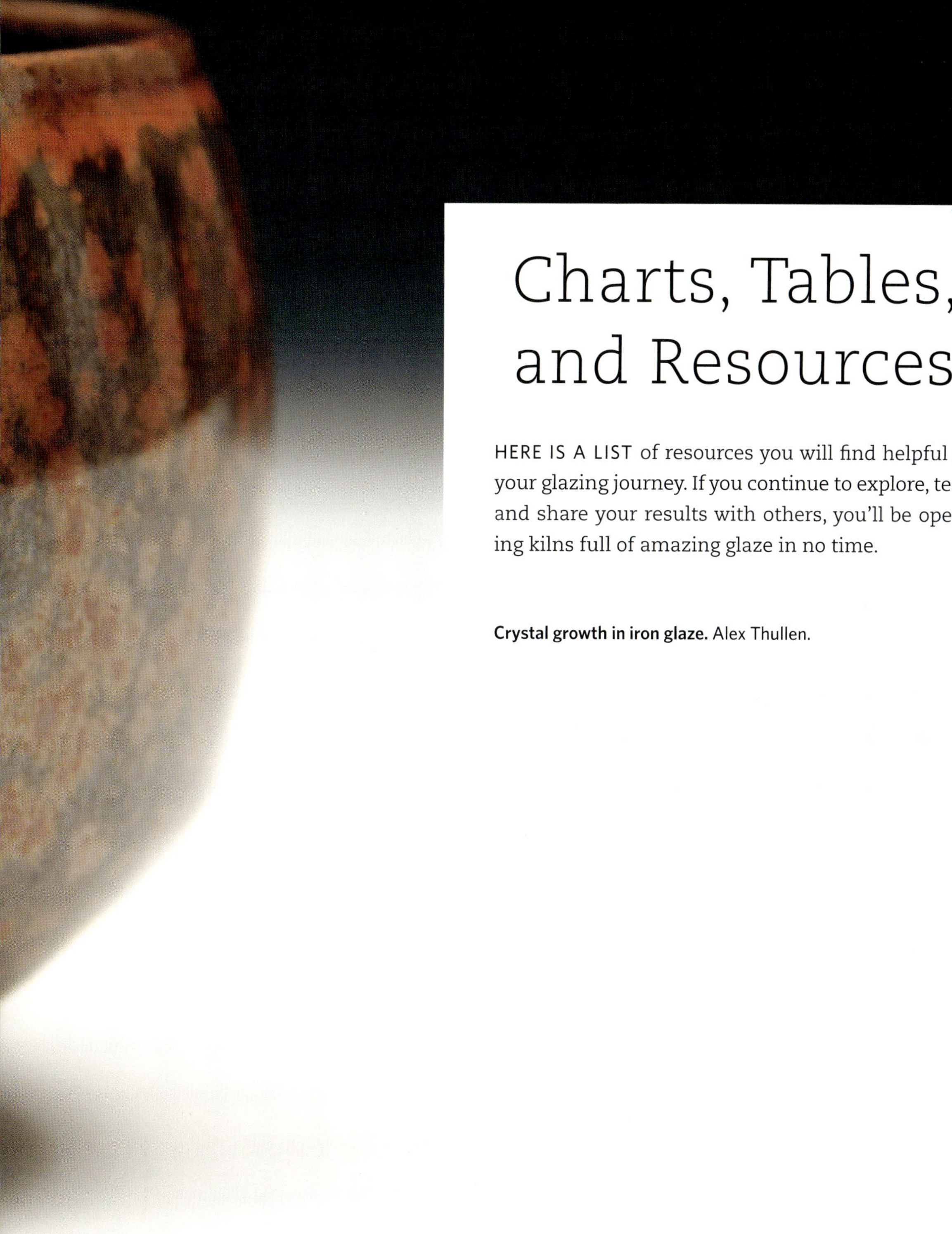

Charts, Tables, and Resources

HERE IS A LIST of resources you will find helpful in your glazing journey. If you continue to explore, test, and share your results with others, you'll be opening kilns full of amazing glaze in no time.

Crystal growth in iron glaze. Alex Thullen.

APPENDIX A: OTHER GLAZES WE TESTED

For this book, we wanted to come up with as many new combinations as we could. But, out of curiosity, we did also test a couple of the most popular glazes from *Amazing Glaze Recipes and Combinations*. Here are the results.

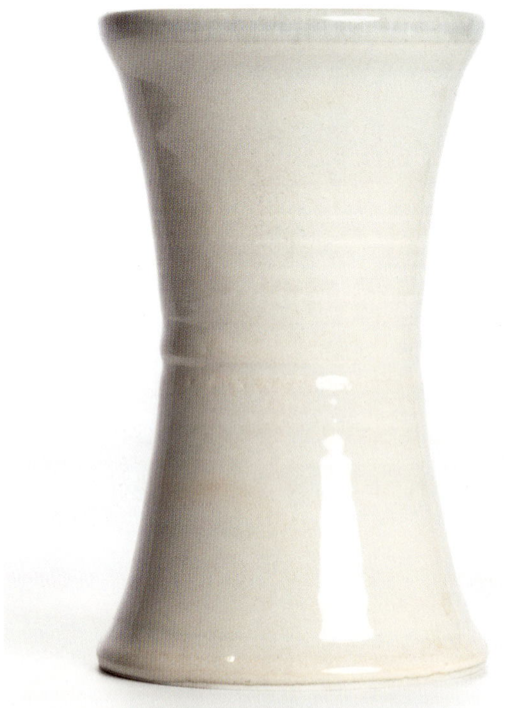

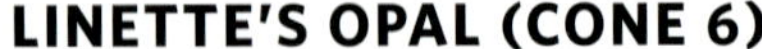

LINETTE'S OPAL (CONE 6)

INGREDIENTS	AMOUNTS
Nepheline Syenite	38.00
Silica	25.00
Gillespie Borate	10.00
EPK	8.00
Whiting	7.00
Talc	5.00
Zinc Oxide	5.00
Wollastonite	2.00
Total	**100.00**

Also Add:

Light Rutile	8.00
Bentonite	2.00

NOTES:
Chemical Analysis:
Zinc: 0.07 ppm (max 0.5 ppm)

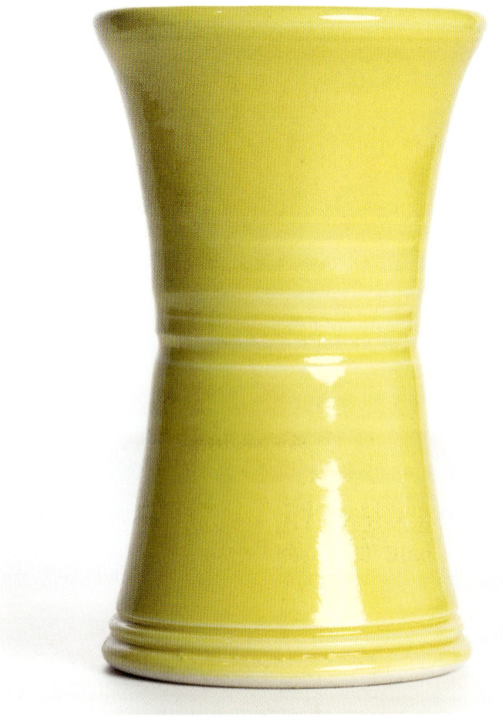

SUNSHINE YELLOW (CONE 6)

INGREDIENTS	AMOUNTS
G-200 Feldspar	45.40
Silica	24.70
Whiting	14.40
EPK	6.20
Zinc Oxide	5.20
Lithium Carbonate	4.10
Total	**100.00**

Also Add:

Mason Stain 6479 Sunshine	12.00
Bentonite	2.00

NOTES:
Chemical Analysis:
Cadmium: 0.001 (max 0.003 ppm)
Lithium: 0.04 ppm (max 0.06 ppm)
Zinc: 0.04 ppm (max 0.5 ppm)

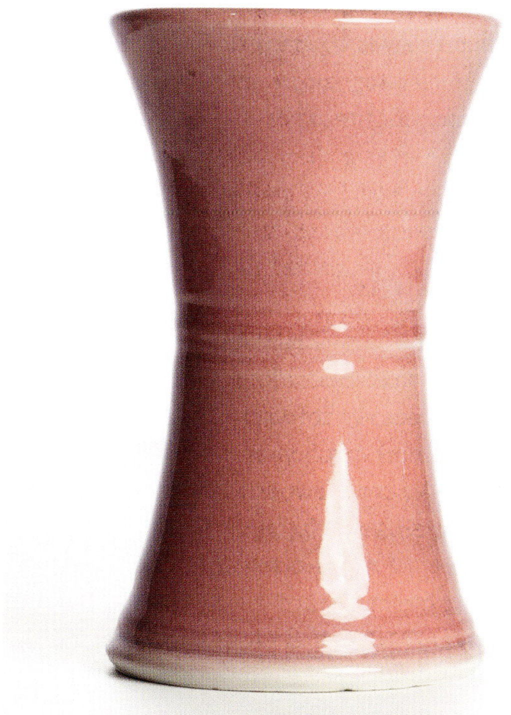

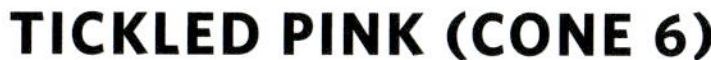

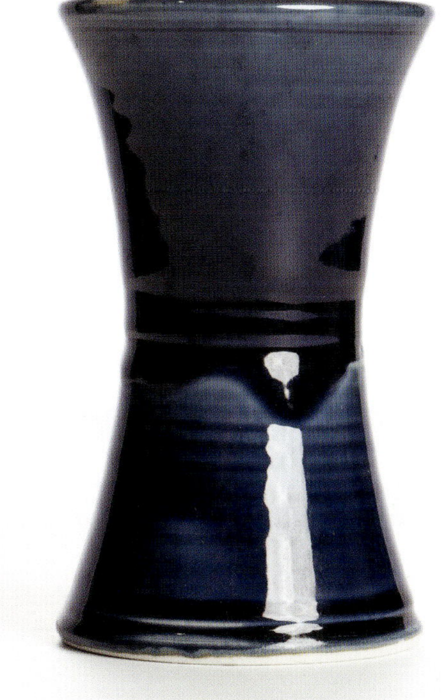

TICKLED PINK (CONE 6)

INGREDIENTS	AMOUNTS
Wollastonite	25.00
EPK	20.00
Ferro Frit 3134	20.00
Silica	20.00
G-200 Feldspar	15.00
Total	**100.00**

Also Add:

Tin Oxide	5.00
Chrome Oxide	0.02

NOTES:
Chemical Analysis:
Chromium: 0.00 ppm (max 0.05 ppm)

OL' BLUE (CONE 6)

INGREDIENTS	AMOUNTS
EPK	30.00
Wollastonite	29.00
Ferro Frit 3195	20.00
Silica	17.00
Nepheline Syenite	4.00
Total	**100.00**

Also Add:

Copper Carbonate	3.00
Light Rutile	3.00
Cobalt Carbonate	1.50

NOTES:
Chemical Analysis:
Cobalt: 0.06 ppm (max 0.5 ppm)
Copper: 0.35 ppm (max 1.3 ppm)

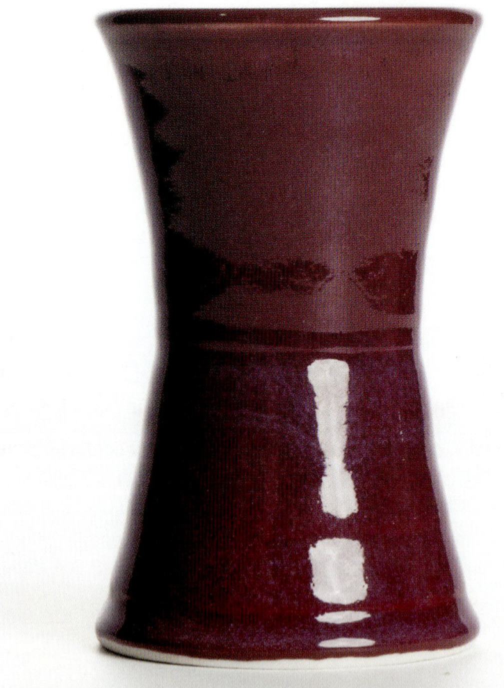
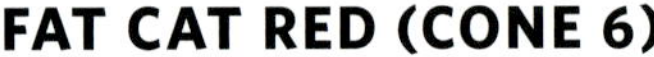
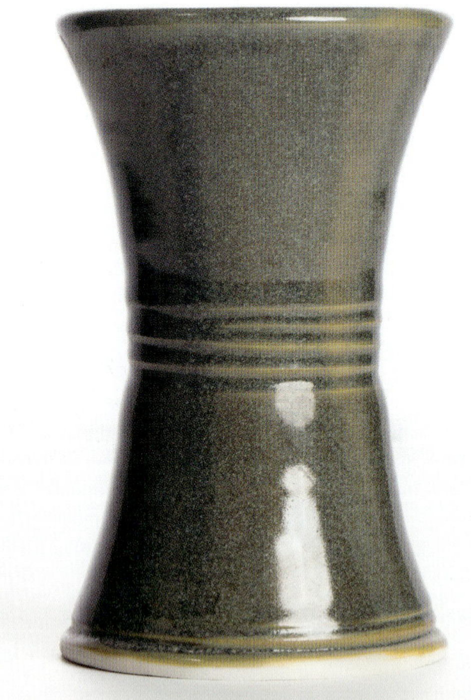

FAT CAT RED (CONE 6)

INGREDIENTS	AMOUNTS
G-200 Feldspar	31.00
Whiting	21.00
Silica	18.00
EPK	9.00
Ferro Frit 3134	9.00
Gillespie Borate	8.00
Talc	4.00
Total	**100.00**

Also Add:

Tin Oxide	5.00
Chrome Oxide	0.20

NOTES:
Chemical Analysis:
Chromium: 0.00 ppm (max 0.05 ppm)

JADE GREEN (CONE 6)

INGREDIENTS	AMOUNTS
G-200 Feldspar	22.00
Silica	21.00
EPK	20.00
Ferro Frit 3134	16.00
Whiting	12.00
Talc	9.00
Total	**100.00**

Also Add:

Rutile	5.00
Black Copper Oxide	3.00

NOTES:
Chemical Analysis:
Copper: 1.3 ppm (max 1.3 ppm)

APPENDIX B: COMBINATION TEST RESULTS

HAMADA RUST OVER FRAISER CELADON

NOTES:
Chemical Analysis:
Iron: 0.13 ppm

TIN PURPLE OVER WINOKUR YELLOW

NOTES:
Chemical Analysis:
Copper: 0.1 ppm
Cobalt: 0.07 ppm
Iron: 0.00 ppm
Zinc: 0.01 ppm

TIN PURPLE OVER WATRAL PURPLE

NOTES:
Chemical Analysis:
Copper: 0.07 ppm
Cobalt: 0.09 ppm
Manganese: 0.05 ppm
Zinc: 0.01 ppm

GAVIN'S PURPLE OVER FRAISER CELADON

NOTES:
Chemical Analysis:
Iron: 0.03 ppm
Zinc: 0.04 ppm

MCPHERSON BLUE OVER FRAISER CELADON

NOTES:
Chemical Analysis:
Iron: 0 ppm
Cobalt: 0.09 ppm
Manganese: 0.03 ppm

WINOKUR YELLOW OVER HAMADA RUST

NOTES:
Chemical Analysis:
Iron: 0.02 ppm

FRAISER CELADON OVER MCPHERSON BLUE

NOTES:
Chemical Analysis:
Iron: 0.02 ppm
Cobalt: 0.08 ppm
Manganese: 0.04 ppm

WATRAL PURPLE OVER TIN PURPLE

NOTES:
Chemical Analysis:
Copper: 0.39 ppm
Cobalt: 0.14 ppm
Manganese: 0.1 ppm
Zinc: 0.03 ppm

WATRAL PURPLE OVER CMW WHITEOUT

NOTES:
Chemical Analysis:
Cobalt: 0.06 ppm
Manganese: 0.01 ppm

APRICOT OVER GAVIN'S PURPLE

NOTES:
Chemical Analysis:
Iron: 0.00 ppm
Zinc: 0.00 ppm

APRICOT OVER MCPHERSON BLUE

NOTES:
Chemical Analysis:
Cobalt: 0.12 ppm
Manganese: 0.1 ppm

APRICOT OVER FRAISER CELADON

NOTES:
Chemical Analysis:
Iron: 0.00 ppm

SMOOTH MATTE WHITE OVER HAMADA RUST

NOTES:
Chemical Analysis:
Iron: 0.04 ppm

SMOOTH MATTE WHITE OVER TIN PURPLE

NOTES:
Chemical Analysis:
Copper: 0.06 ppm
Cobalt: 0.06 ppm
Zinc: 0.00 ppm

SMOOTH MATTE WHITE OVER WATRAL PURPLE

NOTES:
Chemical Analysis:
Manganese: 0.01 ppm
Cobalt: 0.06 ppm

CMW WHITEOUT OVER BLEU DE RUTILE

NOTES:
Chemical Analysis:
There are no elements of concern.

APPENDIX C: OXIDES AND STAINS

GLAZY.ORG MASON STAIN GUIDE

glazy.org

Note: Items in **bold** are archived stains. This chart does not include all available stains.

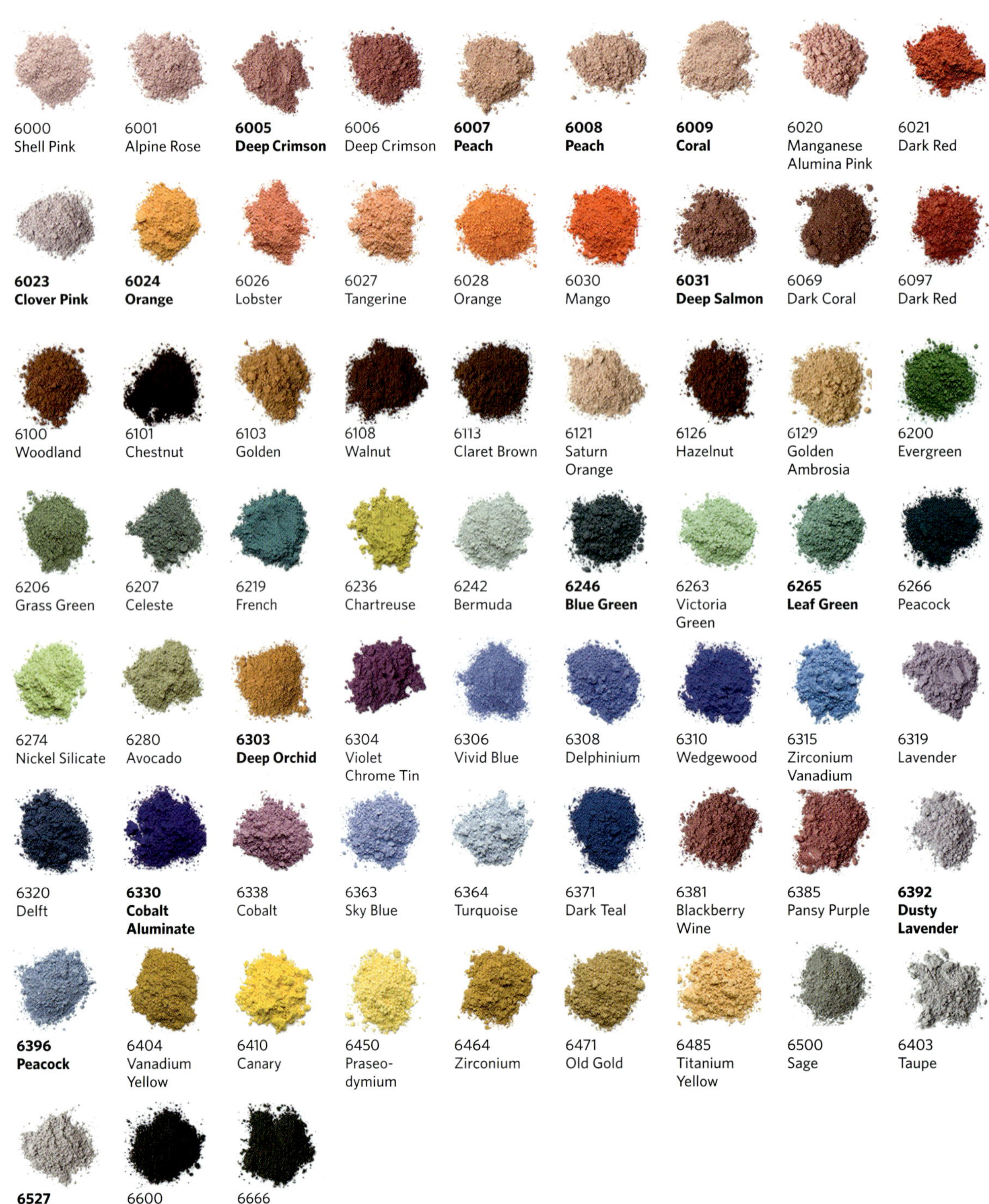

APPENDIX D: CONE CHART/TEMPCHEK CHART

TEMPERATURE EQUIVALENTS

Cone	°F	°C	Color Fire	Clay Reaction	Glazes
10 9 8 7 6 5	2345 2300 2280 2262 2232 2167	1285 1260 1249 1239 1222 1186	White	Stoneware & porcelain clays Mid-range stoneware &	High-fire glazes Salt glazes Mid-range glazes
4	2124	1162		porcelain clays	
3	2106	1152			
2	2088	1142			
1	2079	1137	Yellow		
01	2046	1119			
02	2016	1102			
03	1987	1086			
04 05 06	1945 1888 1828	1063 1031 998		Low-fire red & white clays	Low-fire glazes
07	1789	976			
08	1728	942			
09	1688	920	Orange		
010	1657	903			
011	1607	875		Sintering occurs	
012	1582	861	Cherry red		
013	1539	837			
Glass Techniques* (from)	1500	816			
014	1485	807			
015	1456	791		Organic matter burns out	
016	1422	772			
017	1360	738	Dull red		
018	1319	715			Overglazes/ china paints
019	1252	678			
Glass Techniques* (to)	1200	649			
020	1159	626			Enamels
021	1112	600			
022	1087	586		Dehydration begins	

Temperatures listed above are accurate only when the kiln is fired at 108°F (42°C)/hour during the last 200°F (93°C) of the firing.

*Glass Techniques: Slumping, Fusing, and Tacking. For more specific information on these techniques, visit skutt.com.

APPENDIX E: LIST OF LABS

Alfred Analytical Laboratory
alfred.edu/cact/analytical-testing-capabilities.cfm

ALS Global
alsglobal.com

The **Brandywine Science Center** specializes in testing metal leaching for potters. The lab is certified by the Pennsylvania Department of Environmental Protection (DEP) for drinking water and pottery glaze leaching analyses.
bsclab.com/home-page

APPENDIX F: ONLINE RESOURCES

GREAT PODCASTS

For Flux Sake
thebrickyardnetwork.org/forfluxsake

Tales of a Red Clay Rambler
talesofaredclayrambler.com

The Mud Peddlers
lindseymdillon.com

Clay In Color
brickyardnetwork.org/clayincolor

The Potter's Cast
thepotterscast.com

Trade Secret
brickyardnetwork.org/tradesecret

UNITED STATES REGULATIONS

Cadmium Regulations:
fda.gov/food/environmental-contaminants-food/cadmium-food-and-foodwares

CFR Regulations: Code of Federal regulations (title 21, part 175) that pertains to indirect food additives and required display of leaded ceramics: ecfr.gov/current/title-21/chapter-I/subchapter-B/part-175

Lead Regulations: fda.gov/media/71764/download

Lithium Regulation: usgs.gov/news/lithium-us-groundwater

Contaminant	Maximum Contaminant Level Goal (mg/L)	Maximum Contaminant Level (mg/L)
Antimony	0.006	0.006
Arsenic	0*	0.010 (as of 01/23/06
Asbestos (fiber > 10 micrometers	7 million fibers per liter	7 million fibers per liter
Barium	2	2
Beryllium	0.004	0.004
Cadmium	0.005	0.005
Chromium (total)	0.1	0.1
Copper	1.3	Action level = 1.3**
Cyanide (as free cyanide)	0.2	0.2
Fluoride	4.0	4.0
Lead	Zero	Action level = 0.015**
Mercury (inorganic)	0.002	0.002
Nitrate (measured as Nitrogen)	10	10
Nitrite (measured as Nitrogen)	1	1
Selenium	0.05	0.05
Thallium	0.0005	0.0002

*MCLGs were not established before the 1986 Amendments to the Safe Drinking Water Act. Therefore, there is no MCLG for this contaminant.

**Lead and copper are regulated by a treatment technique that requires systems to control the corrosiveness of their water. If more than 10% of tap water samples exceed the action level, water systems must take additional steps. For copper, the action level is 1.3 mg/L, and for lead is 0.015 mg/L.

CDC Cobalt Recommendations: cdc.gov/TSP/ToxProfiles/ToxProfiles.aspx?id=373&tid=64

National Primary Drinking Water Regulations (Inorganic Chemicals): epa.gov/ground-water-and-drinking-water/national-primary-drinking-water-regulations#Inorganic

MCL Levels: There is a several step process to determining MCL levels. First, a risk assessment is conducted to evaluate the potential health risks associated with exposure to a particular contaminant. This involves reviewing available scientific literature, toxicological studies, and epidemiological data. Second, a reference dose (RfD) or Cancer Slope Factor (CSF) is determined. The RfD is an estimate of the daily exposure to a contaminant that is likely to be without an appreciable risk of adverse health effects. CSF is used for contaminants with carcinogenic effects. Next, uncertainty factors are applied to these RfDs to account for potential variability in sensitivity among the population and data uncertainties. Often, this results in MCLs over a factor of 10 lower than the RfD. After evaluation by the National Drinking Water Advisory Committee (NDWAC), an economic and feasibility analysis, and public comment period, the EPA issues a final rule that establishes the MCLs for specific contaminants. These values are enforceable standards for drinking water.

Reference: epa.gov/sdwa/sdwa-evaluation-and-rulemaking-process

ASTM Method: We use an ASTM method to determine how much certain elements leach out of ceramic glazes.astm.org/c0738-94r20.html

The European Drinking Water Directive (DWD) is a piece of legislation adopted by the European Union (EU) to establish standards for the quality of drinking water across member states. The directive sets out parameters and limits for heavy metals in the European Union. environment.ec.europa.eu/topics/water/drinking-water_en

EU DWD Standards: The EU DWD standards can be found here: lenntech.com/applications/drinking/standards/eu-s-drinking-water-standards.htm

FDA Guidelines: 2022 Food Code 4-101.11 fda.gov/food/fda-food-code/food-code-2022

Many state webpages have this info relating to the FDA legal terms. For example:
codes.ohio.gov/ohio-administrative-code/rule-3717-1-04
touchngo.com/lglcntr/akstats/aac/title18/chapter031/section400.htm

ASTM Absorption Test: ASTM C373-18
astm.org/standards/c373

ISO Absorption Test: ISO 10545iso.org/obp/ui/en/#iso:std:iso:10545:-3:ed-2:v1:en

ACKNOWLEDGMENTS

A portion of this book was written in the aftermath of Hurricane Helene, which destroyed 80 percent of Asheville's River Arts District, where Gabriel works. Thankfully, the kilns and our research for this book were spared. Gabriel would like to thank the thousands of first responders, volunteers, and community members who gave their time, energy, and money to help us rebuild after the storm.

Bill would like to acknowledge his colleagues, Dr. Callie Cole, Dr. Israel Lamb, and Dr. Nathan Werner, who helped him with maintaining and operating the instrumentation needed for this book. He would also like to thank the many student researchers in his lab over the years for their infectious enthusiasm for research and discovery. Finally, he would like to thank the love of his life, Gretchen.

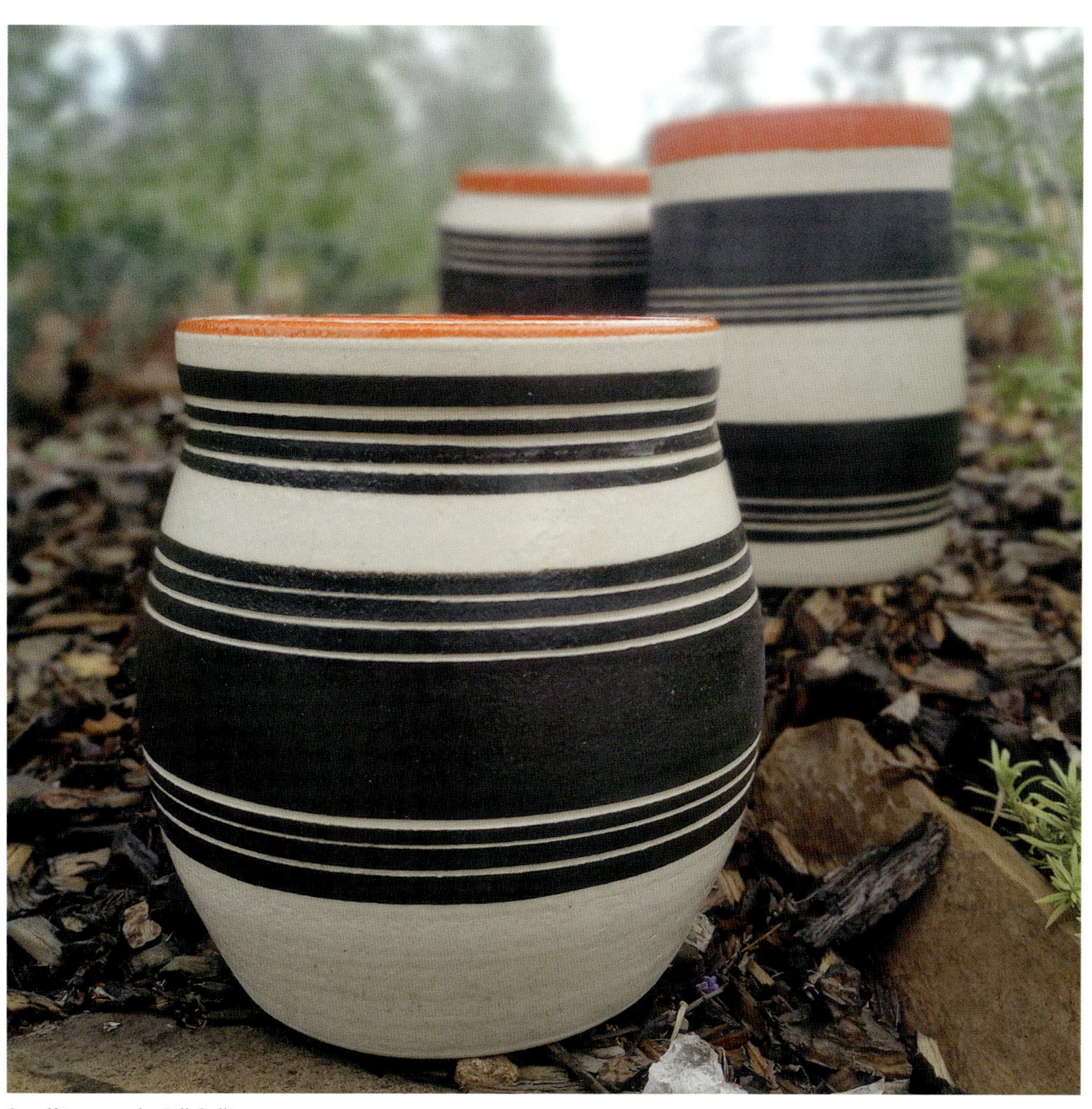

Sgraffito vases by Bill Collins.

ABOUT THE AUTHORS

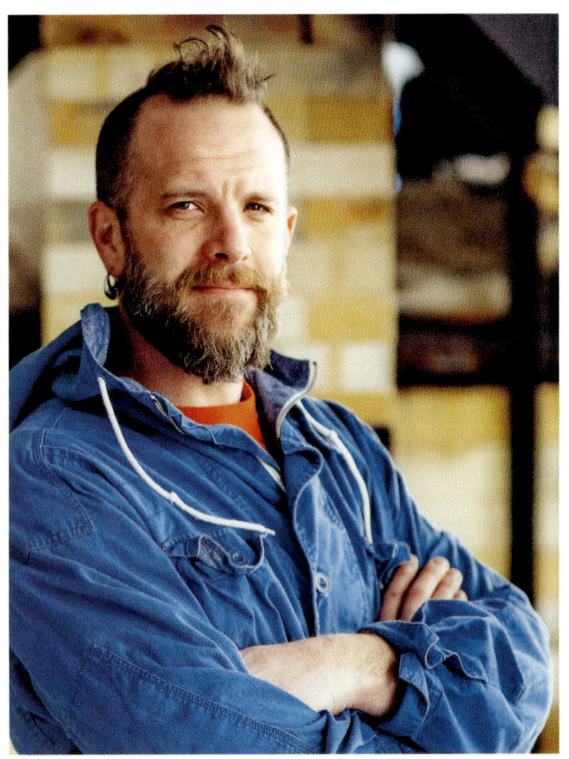

Gabriel Kline is a professional potter who has taught ceramics classes for nearly two decades. He is the founder and director of Odyssey ClayWorks. Gabriel serves as the resident artist program director, fostering connections with university programs and up-and-coming artists from around the world. He also directs Odyssey's community volunteer and nonprofit work, including partnerships with various substance abuse and recovery programs as well as Creative Forces, a collaboration between the Departments of Defense and Veterans Affairs, the National Endowment for the Arts, and state arts agencies. He is the author of *Amazing Glaze* and *Amazing Glaze Recipes and Combinations* and is the co-author of *Amazing Glaze Food-Safe Recipes*. His work has been featured in numerous publications, including *The Complete Guide to Mid-Range Glazes* and the 500 series. He lives in Asheville, North Carolina.

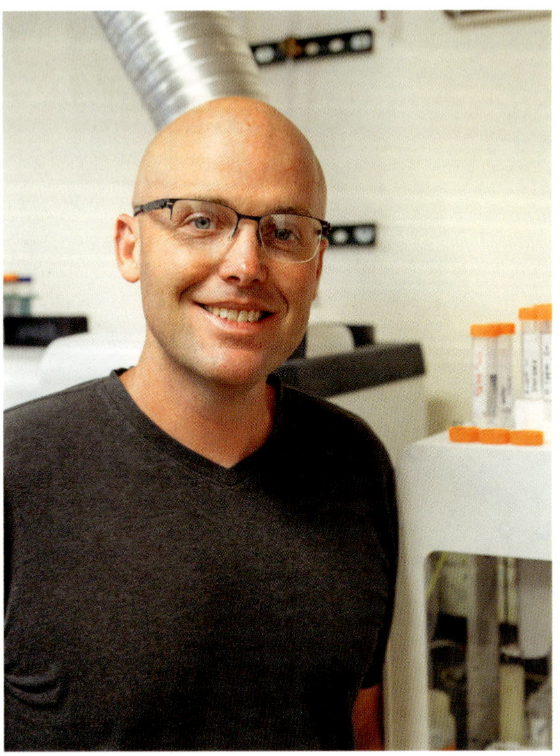

The co-author of *Amazing Glaze Food-Safe Recipes*, **Bill Collins, PhD**, is a professor of chemistry at Fort Lewis College in Colorado. He joined the college in 2011. With a background in synthetic organic and materials chemistry, his research focuses on developing and analyzing chemically durable glasses for ceramic applications, bringing a rigorous scientific approach to the testing and formulation of food-safe glazes. Before joining Fort Lewis, Dr. Collins was a postdoctoral fellow at MIT, studying graphene and carbon nanotube chemistry. He lives in Durango, Colorado.

Skyscraper vase by Gabriel Kline.

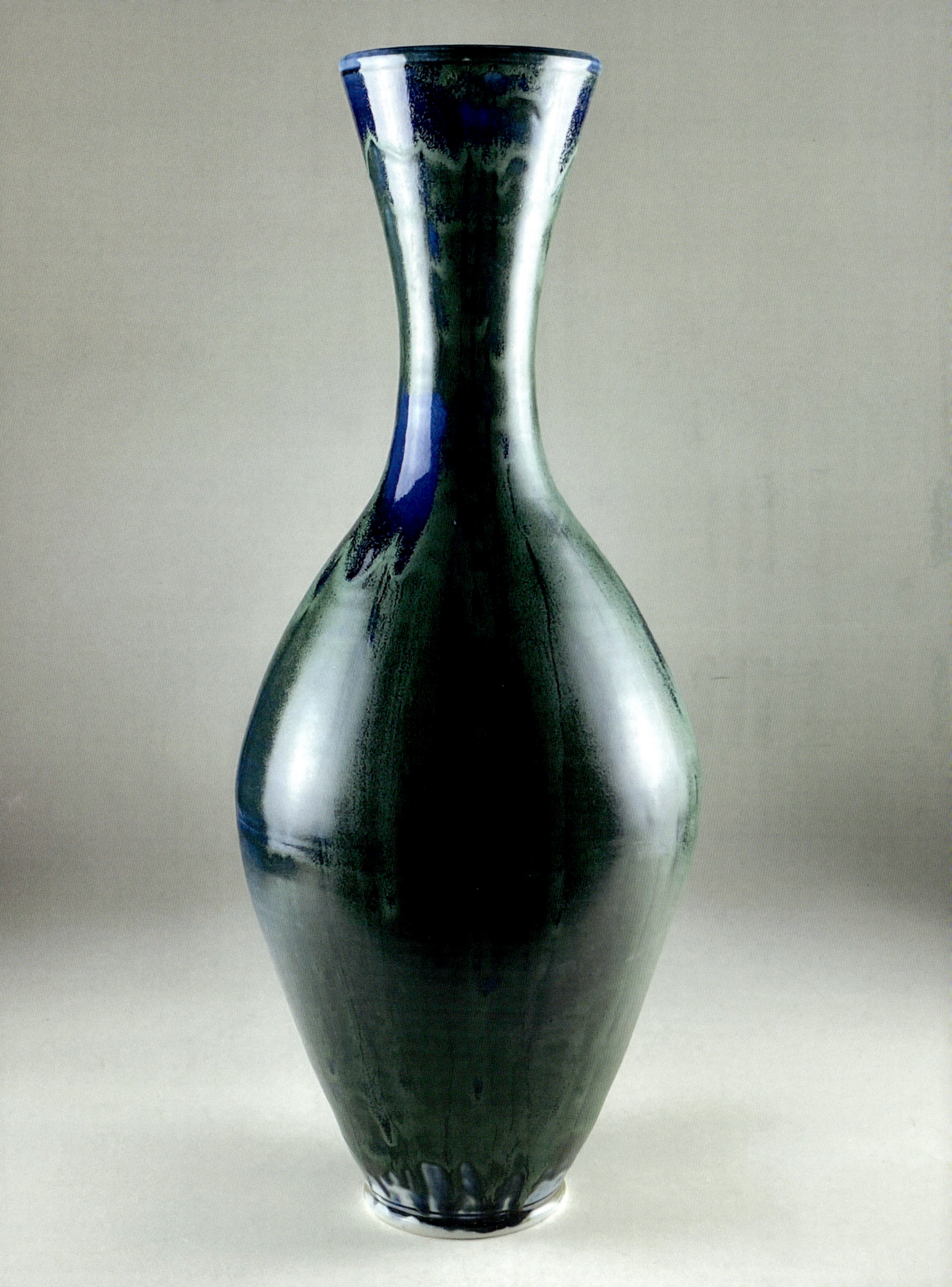

INDEX

H

I

J

K

L

M

N

O

P

R

S

T

ALSO AVAILABLE

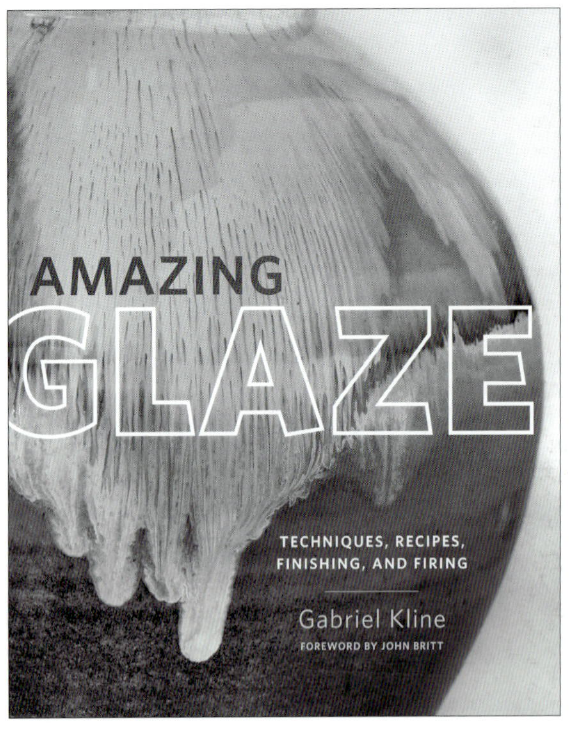

Amazing Glaze
978-0-7603-6103-0

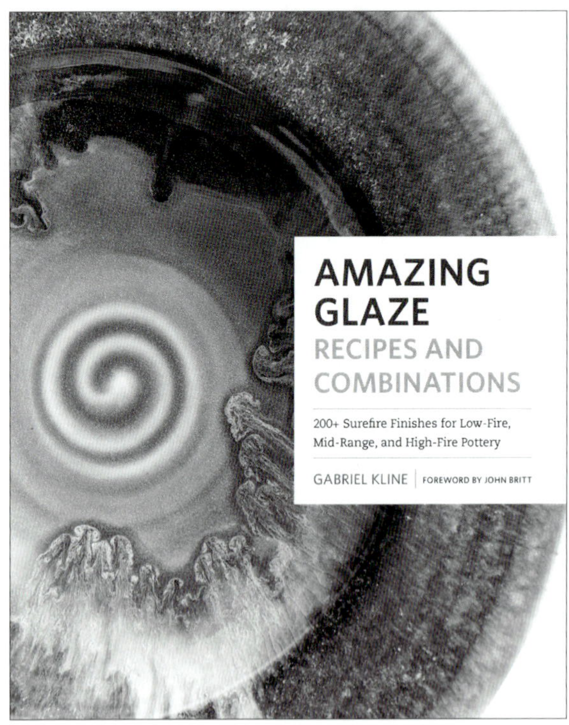

Amazing Glaze Recipes and Combinations
978-1-58923-980-7